Also translated by David Magarshack

The Storm and Other Russian Plays
Stanislavsky on the Art of the Stage
Platonov

By David Magarshack

Chekhov the Dramatist

1970

ANTON CHEK

Anton Chekhov

FOUR PLAYS

Translated by
DAVID MAGARSHACK

A MERMAID DRAMABOOK
HILL AND WANG · NEW YORK

Standard book number (clothbound edition): 8090-3409-3
Standard book number (paperback edition): 8090-0743-6
Library of Congress catalog card number: 69-16833

First Edition May 1969

Manufactured in the United States of America
by The Colonial Press Inc., Clinton, Mass.

CONTENTS

INTRODUCTION

The most remarkable thing about the four great Chekhov plays in this volume is the amazing consistency with which their themes and ideas are developed. These themes deal with the meaning of life, man's duty toward his fellow men, work and leisure, the desire for a "new life," improved social conditions, justice and fair play, and the great complexity of the relationships between men and women. All through his plays Chekhov insists that work is the only remedy for the evils that lead to the disintegration of moral values.

Chekhov wrote *The Seagull* in October, 1895. The play was published in March, 1896. It was a failure when produced in St. Petersburg in the same year, but a resounding success when produced by Konstantin Stanislavsky in Moscow in December, 1898, at the end of the first season of the Moscow Art Theatre. The central theme in the play deals with the hard and slogging path of true talent as exemplified by Nina and, in the case of Konstantin, with the vulnerability and ultimate defeat of the *avant garde* writer who does not possess enough genius to sustain his extravagant claims. Dr. Dorn expresses Chekhov's own views on the *avant garde* movement in Russia toward the end of the nineteenth century, which gave rise to the symbolist movement. Dorn criticizes Konstantin's play not so much because its subject is taken from the realm of abstract ideas but because the idea it expresses is not "clear and definite." The dramatist, or indeed any other creative artist, Chekhov insists, must know why he is writing his play or novel. If he does not, he is bound "to lose his way, and his talent will be his ruin." That is exactly what happens to Konstantin and leads to his suicide. Indeed, toward the very end of the play Konstantin himself comes to the conclusion that "it isn't old or new forms that matter. What matters is that . . . whatever one has to say should come straight from the heart." What is not generally realized is that in *The Seagull* Chekhov went even further in his condemnation of the *avant garde*. For in the play within a play he has written a biting satire on the symbolist writers of his time, who had been greatly influenced by Vladimir Solovyov, the Russian poet, mystic, and philosopher. Konstantin, like the rest of the symbolists, is, in fact, a faithful follower of Solovyov's ideas. In his play he paraphrases Solovyov's description of the World Soul, which, according to Solovyov, "is a living entity, the first of all living entities, *materia prima*, and the substratum of the created world . . . It is the future potential mother of the world, existing outside God, corresponding as an ideal addition to the eternally actual Father of the Three-in-One God" (*The Spiritual Foundations of Life*). To Solovyov, the World Soul was not just a metaphysical concept; he and his disciples, the symbolists, believed in its actual existence. Tolstoy dismissed Solovyov's beliefs as "the ravings of a lunatic." Chekhov, who was always very careful not to be violent in his literary judgments, preferred the more subtle way of putting the reincarnated World Soul on the stage, followed by the fiery eyes of the devil and the smell of sulphur, and letting Arkadina express the widely held view on the so-called decadents.

Chekhov subtitled *The Seagull* "A Comedy in Four Acts" because its characters, like the characters in *The Cherry Orchard*, do not possess any of the heroic attributes of tragedy. They are merely figures in "the human comedy."

Chekhov completed *Uncle Vanya* before the end of 1896, and it was first published in 1897. When performed by the Moscow Art Theatre in October, 1899, it was only moderately successful. Although a free adaption of *The Wood Demon*, which Chekhov wrote during his short-lived Tolstoyan period, Chekhov always insisted that *Uncle Vanya* was quite a new play. Both structurally and psychologically it is not only compact but highly expressive dramatically. Chekhov described the play as "old-fashioned." What he meant was that as a revived version of *The Wood Demon* it did not possess the consummate technical skill of his three other great indirect-action plays. It was for that reason that he subtitled it "Country Scenes in Four Acts."

Chekhov completed *The Three Sisters* in October, 1900. It was first performed by the Moscow Art Theatre on January 31, 1901. It was published in the same year in the February number of the monthly *Russian Thought*. He subtitled it "A Drama in Four Acts" to distinguish it from *The Sea-*

gull and *The Cherry Orchard*, which he described as "comedies." In this play, as well as in *Uncle Vanya*, Chekhov gives the lie to the critics who assert that he is the creator of "forlorn and ineffectual women." Nothing, in fact, has been more distorted by the critics than the Moscow theme in *The Three Sisters*, which is generally taken to be an expression of the ineffectual yearning for the unobtainable. Not that there is anything remotely ineffectual about the longing of the three sisters to go back to a place that is full of happy memories for them or about their desire to get out of a small provincial town where they had lived for eleven years. From the very first scene of the play, however, Chekhov makes it quite clear that the sisters' desire to go back to Moscow, that is, to a life that can never return, is not only impossible but also extremely foolish. When the world of illusion, personified by Moscow, crashes about their ears, when Masha's only love affair ends unhappily with Colonel Vershinin's departure with his regiment, when Irina's future with a man she respects but does not love ends in disaster with Tusenbach's death in a senseless duel with a jealous bully of an army officer, when Olga's hopes of finding happiness in marriage and children fade away, when the three sisters lose everything they possess and are driven out of their own home —the accumulation of disasters does not break their spirit. "They're going away from us," Masha says before the fall of the final curtain, "and we shall be left alone to start our life anew." "We must live," Irina says. "We must work . . ." "Our lives are not finished yet," Olga declares. "Let us live!" They are ready to begin "a new life." Death itself is but a harbinger of new life. "Time will pass," Olga says, "and we shall be gone forever. We shall be forgotten . . . But our sufferings will pass into joy for those who live after us."

The theme of "a new life" and hope in a better future assumes almost a joyous note in *The Cherry Orchard*, Chekhov's last play. "A new life is beginning, Mother!" Anya cries in the last act, and earlier, heartbroken at the sale of the cherry orchard, she tells her mother: "We shall plant a new orchard, an orchard more splendid than this one." The play was first performed by the Moscow Art Theatre on January 17, 1904, Chekhov's forty-fourth birthday, or rather nameday, and less than six months before his death. The play is in the real sense of the word "a comedy" and its misinterpretation as a tragedy is mainly due to a misunderstanding of the nature of high comedy. Perhaps its most misinterpreted character is that of Lopakhin, the peasant who becomes a successful businessman, whom Chekhov described in a letter to Stanislavsky as "a decent fellow . . . who must behave with the utmost courtesy and decorum." This becomes particularly clear when contrasted with the "liberal" aristocrat Gayev, who does not miss any opportunity of expressing his contempt for his sister's valet, Yasha, while Lopakhin shakes hands with him and with the clerk Yepikhodov, whom every other character in the play treats with the utmost contempt.

Writing to his wife while working on *The Cherry Orchard*, Chekhov could not conceal his feeling of relief and satisfaction that there is not a single shot in the whole play. In all his other full-length plays the pistol shot rounds off the dramatic climax. Another distinguishing feature of the play is that, unlike his other three full-length plays, there are no complicated love triangles in it.

Chekhov's attitude toward the characters in his plays is one of profound understanding without any false sentimentality. It is this that explains best of all the marvelous blend of the tragic and the comic that is so characteristic of them.

The reader will find a thorough analysis of all Chekhov's plays in my book *Chekhov the Dramatist*.

D. M.

THE SEAGULL

A Comedy in Four Acts

CHARACTERS

IRINA NIKOLAEVNA ARKADINA, *married name Treplyov, an actress*

KONSTANTIN GAVRILOVICH TREPLYOV, *her son, a young man*

PETER (PYOTR) NIKOLAEVICH SORIN, *her brother*

NINA MIKHAILOVNA ZARECHNAYA, *a young girl, daughter of a rich landowner*

ILYA AFANASYEVICH SHAMRAYEV, *a retired army lieutenant, Sorin's estate agent*

PAULINE (POLINA) ANDREYEVNA, *his wife*

MASHA, *his daughter*

BORIS ALEXANDROVICH TRIGORIN, *a novelist*

EUGENE (YEVGENY) SERGEYEVICH DORN, *a doctor*

SIMON (SEMYON SEMYONOVICH) MEDVEDENKO, *a schoolmaster*

YAKOV, *a workman*

A COOK

A MAID

The action takes place on SORIN'S *country estate. Between Acts Three and Four there is an interval of two years.*

THE SEAGULL

ACT ONE

Part of the park on Sorin*'s estate. A hastily erected stage for private theatricals stands across a broad avenue leading into the park toward the lake. The view of the lake is completely concealed by the stage. To the right and the left of the stage—bushes. A few chairs, a little table.*

The sun has just set. Yakov *and other workmen are busy on the stage behind the lowered curtain. Sounds of hammering and coughing.* Masha *and* Medvedenko *come in from left, returning from a stroll.*

Medvedenko. Why do you always wear black?

Masha. Because I'm in mourning for my life. I'm unhappy.

Medvedenko. Why? [*Wonderingly.*] I don't understand. . . . I mean, there's nothing wrong with your health, and though your father is not rich, he's not badly off. My life is much harder than yours. I only earn twenty-three rubles a month and my insurance is deducted from that. But I don't wear mourning.

Masha. Money is not everything. Even a poor man can be happy.

Medvedenko. That may be all right in theory, but in practice it is quite different. I have to provide for my mother, my two sisters, my little brother, and myself, and all on twenty-three rubles. We must eat and drink, mustn't we? And what with the price of tea and sugar and tobacco . . . What a life!

Masha [*glancing at the stage*]. The play will be starting soon.

Medvedenko. Yes. Nina will be acting, and the play was written by Konstantin. They are in love. Tonight their souls will unite in an endeavor to give expression to one and the same artistic idea. But your soul and mine have no points of contact. I'm in love with you. I long for you so much that I find it impossible to stay at home. Every day I walk four miles here and four miles back, but all

I get from you is indifference. I can't say I'm surprised at it. I haven't any private means, and I have a large family to support. What's the use of marrying a man who can't even provide for himself?

MASHA. That's not important. [*Takes snuff.*] I'm touched by your love and sorry I can't return it—that's all. [*Offers her snuffbox to him.*] Help yourself.

MEDVEDENKO. No, thank you. I don't feel like it. [*Pause.*]

MASHA. It's awfully close. I expect there'll be a thunderstorm. You're always holding forth or talking about money. According to you, there's no greater misfortune than poverty. But I'd a hundred times rather walk about in rags and beg than . . . But you wouldn't understand that.

SORIN *and* KONSTANTIN *enter on right.*

SORIN [*leaning on his cane*]. I don't know, my boy, but somehow or other the country never agrees with me, and I think it's clear that I shall never get used to it now. Last night I went to bed at ten. This morning I woke up at nine, feeling as though my brains were glued to my skull from too much sleep, and all that. [*Laughs.*] But after lunch I dropped off again, and now every bone in my body is aching. I feel wretched; I mean, after all . . .

KONSTANTIN. I suppose you really ought to live in town, Uncle. [*Seeing* MASHA *and* MEDVEDENKO.] You two shouldn't be here. I'll let you know when we're ready to start. Please, go.

SORIN [*to* MASHA]. Will you ask your father to tell them to let the dog off the chain. It howls. It kept my sister awake again last night.

MASHA. I'd rather you spoke to my father yourself. I'm not going to say anything to him. Please don't ask me. [*To* MEDVEDENKO.] Come along.

MEDVEDENKO [*to* KONSTANTIN]. You won't forget to call us before it begins, will you? [*Both go out.*]

SORIN. Well, I suppose that means the damned dog will be howling all night again. It's a funny thing, but I've never managed to live as I liked in the country. I used to get leave for twenty-eight days to come down here for a rest and so on; but the moment I arrived, they worried me with all sorts of trifles, so that on the very first day I wished I'd never come. [*Laughs.*] I've always been glad to get away from here. But now I've retired, I've nowhere to go, and I've got to live here whether I like it or not.

YAKOV [*to* KONSTANTIN]. May we go for a dip in the lake, sir?

KONSTANTIN. All right, go. But see that you're in your places in ten minutes. [*Looks at his watch.*] We shall be starting soon.

YAKOV. Very good, sir.

KONSTANTIN [*examining the stage*]. Now here's a theatre for you, Uncle. The curtain, the first wing, the second, and beyond that—open space. No scenery. You look straight across toward the lake and the horizon. The curtain goes up at exactly half past eight, just when the moon rises.

SORIN. Splendid!

KONSTANTIN. If Nina's late, then of course the whole effect will be ruined. It's time she was here. Her father and stepmother don't let her out of their sight. She finds it as hard to get out of her house as to break out of prison. [*Puts his uncle's cravat straight.*] You do look an awful mess, Uncle. Hair and beard disheveled. You should have had a trim or something.

SORIN [*combing out his beard*]. Ah, it's the tragedy of my life. I used to look just the same when I was young. As though I were always drunk. Women never cared for me. [*Sitting down.*] Why's your mother in such a bad temper?

KONSTANTIN. Why? Bored, I suppose. [*Sitting down beside* SORIN.] Jealous. Already she's against me, against the performance, and against my play because Nina is acting in it and not she. She doesn't know my play, but that doesn't stop her hating it.

SORIN [*laughs*]. Good Lord, you get strange ideas, don't you?

KONSTANTIN. Oh, no. I tell you she can't bear to think that on this little stage it will be Nina and not she who'll shine. [*Glances at his watch.*] Mother's a psychological case. An amusing case, if you like. She's undoubtedly talented, she's clever, she's capable of crying over a book, she'll recite you the whole of the poet Nekrasov by heart, she'll nurse you when you're sick like an angel—but just try praising Duse in her presence! Dear me, no! Only she must be praised, only she must be written about, only she must be acclaimed! You have to be in raptures over her marvelous acting in *La dame aux camélias* or in *Life's Dizzy Whirl*. But in the country she doesn't find this constant adulation, so she feels bored, she's in a temper: we're all her enemies, it's all our fault! And then she's terribly superstitious—afraid of three candles, of the number thirteen. She's mean. She has seventy thousand rubles in a bank in Odessa. I know that for a fact. But ask her to lend you some money and she'll burst into tears.

SORIN. You've got it into your head that your mother does not like your play and you're getting upset about it, and so on. Calm down, my boy. Your mother adores you.

KONSTANTIN [*plucking the petals of a flower*]. She loves me, she loves me not. Loves me, loves me not. Loves me, loves me not. [*Laughs.*] You see, Mother doesn't love me. And no wonder! She wants to live, to love, to wear gay clothes, and here am I, a man of twenty-five, constantly reminding her that she's no longer young. When I'm away, she's only thirty-two, but when I'm with her, she's forty-three. That's why she hates me. Besides, she knows that I do not recognize the theatre. She loves the theatre; she thinks she's serving humanity and the sacred cause of art. But to me the modern theatre is nothing but a mass of prejudice and dead convention. When the curtain goes up and—by artificial light, in a room with three walls—these great actors and actresses, priests and priestesses of sacred art, show how people eat, drink, and make love, move about and wear their clothes, when they try to draw some moral from those dreary scenes and phrases, some cheap, smug, cosy little moral, some moral useful in the home, when in thousands of different ways they go on shoving the same old thing over and over again under our noses, then I run like hell, run like Maupassant ran from the Eiffel Tower, which drove him to distraction by its vulgarity.

SORIN. But you can't do without the theatre, my boy.

KONSTANTIN. What we want is new forms, Uncle. We must have new forms. If we can't get them, I'd rather have nothing at all. [*Looks at his watch.*] I love my mother. I love her very much. But she leads a silly sort of life. Always running about with that novelist fellow. Her name is always bandied about in the newspapers. Oh, I'm so tired of it all. But I don't mind admitting that sometimes I'm influenced by the egoism of an ordinary mortal. You see, I resent the fact that my mother is a famous actress, and I can't help thinking that if she were an ordinary woman, I'd have been much happier. Now, please tell me, Uncle, could there be anything more dreadful or more idiotic than, for instance, this sort of situation. Often she has visitors who are all without exception celebrities of one sort or another: actors, writers. And among them all only I am a nobody, and the only reason they tolerate me is because I am her son. And, really, who am I? What am I? I left the university in my third year "owing to circumstances beyond our control," as they say in the papers. I have no particular talents. I have no money—not a penny. And so far as my social position is concerned, I'm still described on my passport as a Kiev artisan. My father, you know, was a native of Kiev and of humble birth, though that did not prevent him from becoming a famous actor. So, as I was saying, when all those great actors and writers in her drawing room are gracious enough to take notice of me, I cannot help feeling from the way they look at me that they are just weighing my insignificance. I know what they are thinking, and I don't mind telling you I feel pretty small.

SORIN. By the way, tell me, what kind of a man is this novelist? I can't make him out. He never says a word.

KONSTANTIN. Oh, he's an intelligent man, unaffected, a bit on the melancholy side. A very decent fellow. He won't be forty for some time yet, but he is famous and has everything he wants. As for his writings—well, what shall I say? Charming, able, but—er—after Tolstoy and Zola you'd hardly want to read Trigorin.

SORIN. Well, you know, my boy, I can't help liking literary men. A long time ago I wanted to do two things passionately: I wanted to marry, and I wanted to be a writer, but I failed in both ambitions. Ah, well, I suppose it must be nice to be even a second-rate writer. I mean, after all . . .

KONSTANTIN [*listens*]. I think I hear footsteps. [*Embraces his uncle.*] Oh, I can't live without her! Even the sound of her footsteps is beautiful. Oh, I'm so happy, so deliriously happy! [*Goes quickly to meet* NINA, *who enters.*] My darling, my dearest!

NINA [*excitedly*]. I hope I'm not late. I'm not late, am I?

KONSTANTIN [*kissing her hand*]. No, no, of course not!

NINA. All day I've been worried. I was so frightened! I was terrified that my father wouldn't let me come. But he's just gone out with my stepmother. The sky's red, the moon's just rising, and . . . and I've been driving so fast—fast! [*Laughs.*] Oh, I'm so thrilled! [*Presses* SORIN's *hand warmly.*]

SORIN [*laughs*]. I do believe I can see tears in those pretty eyes of yours. Ha ha! That's bad.

NINA. I'm afraid I did cry a little. Oh, I was in such a hurry! You can see how out of breath I am. I shall have to leave in half an hour. I mustn't be late. No, no, I can't stay. I can't. Please, please, don't try to keep me. Father doesn't know I'm here.

KONSTANTIN. Anyway, it's time we started. I'd better go and tell them.

SORIN. No, no, don't you bother, my boy. I'll go. Right away. [*Goes to the right, singing.*] "Into France two grenadiers . . ." [*Looks round.*] Once, you know, I started singing like that and an assistant public prosecutor said to me, "You've got a very powerful voice, sir." Then he thought a little and added: "But it's rather unpleasant." [*Laughs and goes out.*]

NINA. My father and his wife have forbidden me to come here. They say you're bohemians. They're afraid I might go on the stage. But I feel drawn here, to the lake, like a seagull. Oh, my heart is so full of you! [*Looks round.*]

KONSTANTIN. We're quite alone.

NINA. I thought there was someone there.

KONSTANTIN. There's no one there. [*A kiss.*]

NINA. What tree is this?

KONSTANTIN. An elm.

NINA. Why is it so dark?

KONSTANTIN. Well, it's evening. Everything's getting dark. Don't rush away after the play, please don't.

NINA. I must.

KONSTANTIN. And what if I went to your place, Nina? I'd spend a whole night in your garden looking at your window.

NINA. You'd better not. The watchman would see you. Besides, our dog isn't used to you yet. He'll bark.

KONSTANTIN. I love you.

NINA. Sh-sh . . .

KONSTANTIN [*hearing footsteps*]. Who's there? Is that you, Yakov?

YAKOV [*offstage*]. Yes, sir.

KONSTANTIN. In your places everybody! Time to begin. Is the moon rising?

YAKOV. Yes, sir.

KONSTANTIN. Got the methylated spirit? The sulphur? When the red eyes appear, there must be a smell of sulphur. [*To* NINA.] You'd better go now. Everything's ready. Nervous?

NINA. I'm afraid I am. But it isn't your mother. I don't mind her a bit. But there's Trigorin, and I shall feel frightened and self-conscious acting in front of him. He's such a famous writer. Is he young?

KONSTANTIN. Yes.

NINA. His stories are wonderful!

KONSTANTIN [*coldly*]. I don't know. I haven't read them.

NINA. It's so difficult to act in your play. There are no living people in it.

KONSTANTIN. Living people! Life should be shown not as it is, nor as it ought to be, but as we see it in our dreams.

NINA. But there's so little action in your play. Just talk. And I think there ought to be love in a play. [*Both walk off behind the stage.*]

Enter PAULINE *and* DORN.

PAULINE. It's getting damp. Do go back and put on your galoshes.

DORN. I'm hot.

PAULINE. You don't look after yourself properly. It's sheer stubbornness. You're a doctor and you know perfectly well that damp is bad for you, but you just want to make me miserable. Yesterday you deliberately spent the whole evening on the veranda.

DORN [*sings softly*]. "Don't tell me my youth was my ruin . . ."

PAULINE. You were so carried away by your conversation with Irina that you didn't notice how chilly it was. You like her, don't you?

DORN. My dear, I'm fifty-five.

PAULINE. That doesn't mean anything. A man isn't old at fifty-five. You're well preserved and still attractive to women.

DORN. All right, so what do you want me to do?

PAULINE. You're all ready to prostrate yourselves before an actress. All of you!

DORN [*sings*]. "Once more before thee . . ." If actors are liked in society and treated differently from—shall I say?—tradespeople, it's as it should be. That's idealism.

PAULINE. Women have always fallen for you. They've always thrown themselves on your neck. Is that idealism too?

DORN [*shrugging his shoulders*]. Why not? There was a lot that was good in women's attitude toward me. What they liked most about me was that I was a good doctor. Ten or fifteen years ago, you remember, I was the only decent obstetrician in the county. Then again I've always been an honest man.

PAULINE [*grasps him by the hand*]. Oh, my dearest!

DORN. Not so loud. They're coming.

Enter ARKADINA, *arm in arm with* SORIN, TRIGORIN, SHAMRAYEV, MEDVEDENKO, *and* MASHA.

SHAMRAYEV. She was an extraordinarily fine actress. She acted marvelously at the Poltava Fair in 1873. Phenomenal acting. Phenomenal. I don't suppose you happen to know, madam, where Chadin is now? Paul Chadin, the comic actor. He was inimitable as Rasplyuyev. Much better than Sadovsky, I assure you, dear lady. I wonder where he is now.

ARKADINA. You keep asking me about antediluvian actors. How should I know? [*Sits down.*]

SHAMRAYEV. Paul Chadin! There are no such actors now. The stage is no longer what it was, madam. In the old days we had mighty oaks. All we have now are tree stumps.

DORN. It's true there aren't many geniuses left on our stage, but I should say the general standard of acting is much higher than it used to be.

SHAMRAYEV. I don't agree with you, sir. However, I suppose it's all a matter of taste. *De gustibus aut bene aut nihil.*

KONSTANTIN *comes out from behind the stage.*

ARKADINA [*to her son*]. When are you going to begin, dear?

KONSTANTIN. In a minute, Mother. Please be patient.

ARKADINA [*recites from* Hamlet].

"O Hamlet, speak no more;
Thou turn'st mine eyes into my very soul;
And there I see such black and grained spots
As will not leave their tinct."

KONSTANTIN [*from* Hamlet].

"Nay, but to live
In the rank sweat of an enseamed bed,
Stewed in corruption, honeying and making love
Over the nasty sty—"

[*A horn is sounded offstage.*] Ladies and gentlemen, the play is about to begin. Quiet, please, quiet! I begin. [*Taps with a stick and speaks in a loud voice.*] O ye venerable old shades that hover over this lake at nighttime, send us to sleep and let us dream of what will be in two hundred thousand years.

SORIN. There'll be nothing in two hundred thousand years.

KONSTANTIN. Very well, let them show us that nothing.

ARKADINA. Let them. We are asleep.

The curtain goes up; the view of the lake is revealed; the moon above the horizon is reflected in the water; NINA, *all in white, is sitting on a big stone.*

NINA. Men, lions, eagles and peacocks,* horned stags, geese,

* In the Russian, *kuropatki*, "partridges," which introduces certain aural and semantic elements in English that are not in the Russian [D.M.].

spiders, silent fish that inhabit the water, starfish, and creatures no eye can see—all living things, all living things, all living things, having completed their round of sorrow, are extinct. . . . For thousands and thousands of years the earth has borne no living creature upon it, and this poor moon lights its lamp in vain. No longer do the cranes waken in the meadow with a cry, and in the lime groves the drone of the May beetles is heard no more. It is cold, cold, cold. Empty, empty, empty. Horror, horror, horror. [*Pause.*] The bodies of living creatures have dissolved into dust, and eternal matter has transformed them into stones, into water, into clouds, and their souls have all merged into one soul. That world soul am I—I. . . . In me is the soul of Alexander the Great, of Caesar, of Shakespeare, of Napoleon, and the soul of the last leech. In me man's mind is merged with the instincts of animals, and I remember all, all, all. . . . And every life I relive anew in myself.

Will-o'-the-wisps appear on the stage.

ARKADINA [*softly*]. This is something decadent.

KONSTANTIN [*imploringly, and in a reproachful voice*]. Please, Mother!

NINA. I am lonely, lonely. Once in a hundred years I open my lips to speak, and my voice re-echoes forlornly in this desert, and no one hears. And you, too, pale lights, do not hear me. The stagnant marsh gives birth to you before daybreak and you wander until dawn—without thought, without will, without a flutter of life. Fearing lest life be born within you, Satan, the father of eternal matter, every moment produces a change of atoms within you, as in the stones and in the water, and you go on changing and changing. In the universe only the spirit abides, constant and unchangeable. [*Pause.*] Like a prisoner cast into a deep, empty well, I know not where I am, nor what awaits me. One thing only is not hidden from me: I know that in the hard and cruel struggle with Satan, the origin of all the forces of matter, I am destined to conquer, and that after that, matter and spirit will blend harmoniously and become one, and the glory of eternal beauty will be achieved, and the Kingdom of Universal Will will come. But that will only come to pass when—little by little and after thousands of years—the moon and the bright dog-star and the earth have all turned to dust. Till then—horror, horror. [*Pause. Against the background of the lake two red spots appear.*] Here comes Satan, my mighty adversary. I can see his terrible blood-red eyes——

ARKADINA. There's a smell of sulphur. Is that really necessary?

KONSTANTIN. Yes.

ARKADINA [*laughs*]. It's certainly very effective!

KONSTANTIN. Mother!

NINA. He feels lost without man——

PAULINE [*to* DORN]. You've taken your hat off. Please put it on, or you'll catch cold.

ARKADINA. Why, the doctor's only taken his hat off to the devil, the father of eternal matter!

KONSTANTIN [*flaring up, aloud*]. The play's finished! Enough! Curtain!

ARKADINA. What are you so cross about?

KONSTANTIN. Enough! Curtain! Lower the curtain! [*Stamps.*] Curtain! [*The curtain drops.*] Sorry, I forgot it's only a few chosen ones who can act and write plays. I've infringed the monopoly. I—I— [*Tries to say something more, but waves his hand instead and goes out on left.*]

ARKADINA. What's the matter with him?

SORIN. Irina, you really shouldn't wound a young man's pride like that.

ARKADINA. But what did I say to him?

SORIN. You hurt his feelings.

ARKADINA. But he told me himself that it was all a joke, so I treated his play as a joke.

SORIN. All the same——

ARKADINA. Now it seems he has written a masterpiece. Well, well . . . So he has put on this play of his and nearly suffocated us with sulphur not for a joke but as a demonstration. He wanted to show us how to write and what to act. Oh dear, this really is getting too much. These constant sallies against me, these pinpricks—say what you like—would try anyone's patience. What a conceited, headstrong boy!

SORIN. He only wanted to please you.

ARKADINA. So that's what he wanted, was it? Then why didn't he choose some ordinary play? Why did he make us listen to that decadent drivel? Not that I mind listening even to drivel for the sake of a joke, but here we have all these pretensions to new forms, to a new era in art. Well, I didn't notice any new forms but simply bad temper.

TRIGORIN. Everyone writes as he likes and as he can.

ARKADINA. Well, in that case let him write as he likes and as he can, only let him leave me in peace.

DORN. Jupiter, thou'rt angry.

ARKADINA. I'm not Jupiter, I'm a woman. [*Lights a cigarette.*] And I'm not angry. I just can't help feeling annoyed that a young man should waste his time so stupidly. I didn't mean to hurt him.

MEDVEDENKO. There's no justification for separating spirit from matter, for may not spirit itself be only an agglomeration of material atoms? [*Brightly, to* TRIGORIN.] Why not write a play about a schoolmaster, sir? Someone ought to write a play to show how we teachers live. Oh, it's a hard life, sir, a very hard life.

ARKADINA. You're quite right, but don't let us talk of plays or atoms. It's such a lovely evening. Do you hear? People are singing. [*Listening.*] How nice!

PAULINE. It's coming from the other side of the lake.

Pause.

ARKADINA [*to* TRIGORIN]. Sit down beside me, please. Ten or fifteen years ago there would be music and singing on the lake almost every night. It would never stop. There are six country houses on the shore of the lake. Oh, I remember it all so well! Laughter, noise, shooting, and, of course, love affairs. Oh, those never-ending love affairs! The *jeune premier* and general favorite of the ladies in those days was our dear doctor there. [*Motions with her head toward* DORN.] Eugene Dorn. He's a very handsome man still, but then he was irresistible. Oh, my conscience is beginning to trouble me. Why did I hurt my poor boy's feelings? I'm worried. [*Calls.*] Konstantin! Darling! Konstantin!

MASHA. I'll go and look for him.

ARKADINA. Please do, my dear.

MASHA [*goes to the left*]. Konstantin! Coo-ee! Konstantin! [*Goes out.*]

NINA [*coming out from behind the stage*]. It doesn't look as if we shall go on with the play, so I suppose I can come out. How do you do? [*Exchanges kisses with* ARKADINA *and* PAULINE.]

SORIN. Bravo! Bravo!

ARKADINA. Bravo! . . . Bravo! We were charmed, my dear, charmed. With your figure and your lovely voice it's a shame to bury yourself in the country. I'm sure you have talent. Why, of course, you have. You must go on the stage, my dear.

NINA. Oh, it's one of my dreams! [*Sighing.*] But I'm afraid it will never come true.

ARKADINA. You can never tell, my dear. Let me introduce—Boris Trigorin.

NINA. I'm so glad to meet you. [*Covered with confusion.*] I'm always reading your books.

ARKADINA [*making* NINA *sit down beside her*]. Don't be so shy, my dear. He may be a famous man, but he isn't at all conceited. Are you, dear? You see, he's shy himself.

DORN. I suppose we may raise the curtain now, mayn't we? It's giving me the creeps.

SHAMRAYEV [*loudly*]. Yakov, raise the curtain; there's a good lad!

The curtain goes up.

NINA [*to* TRIGORIN]. Don't you think it's rather a strange play?

TRIGORIN. I couldn't make head or tail of it. Still, I enjoyed watching it. You played so sincerely. And the scenery was lovely. [*Pause.*] I expect there must be lots of fish in that lake.

NINA. Yes. . . .

TRIGORIN. I love fishing. Nothing gives me more pleasure than to sit on the bank of a stream in the evening, watching the float.

NINA. But, surely, anyone who has experienced the joys of creation can't possibly enjoy anything else!

ARKADINA [*laughing*]. Don't talk like that, dear. When people say nice things to him, he feels terribly embarrassed.

SHAMRAYEV. I remember in Moscow once, at the opera, the famous Silva took the lower C. As it happened, the bass of our cathedral choir was in the gallery at the time, and imagine our utter astonishment when we suddenly heard from the gallery: "Bravo, Silva!" a whole octave lower. [*In a low bass.*] Bravo, Silva! The audience was entranced.

Pause.

DORN. Dead silence.

NINA. I'm afraid I must go. Good-bye.

ARKADINA. Why? Where are you off to so early? We shan't let you go.

NINA. Father's expecting me.

ARKADINA. Oh, what an awful man he is! [*They exchange kisses.*] Well, I suppose it can't be helped. I'm very sorry to let you go.

NINA. If you knew how I hate to have to go.

ARKADINA. Don't you think someone ought to see you home, my pet?

NINA [*frightened*]. Oh, no, no!

SORIN [*to* NINA, *in an imploring voice*]. Do stay!

NINA. I'm awfully sorry, but I can't.

SORIN. Please, stay for just one hour. Really, I mean to say . . .

NINA [*after thinking it over, tearfully*]. I can't. [*Shakes hands and hurries off.*]

ARKADINA. Poor child, I'm sorry for her. I understand her mother left the whole of her huge fortune to her father, and now this young girl hasn't a farthing in the world, for her father has made a will leaving everything to his second wife. Isn't it dreadful?

DORN. Yes, to do him justice, her father is a mean old rascal.

SORIN [*rubbing his cold hands*]. Let us go, too, ladies and gentlemen. It's getting damp. My legs ache.

ARKADINA. Poor darling, they're like wooden legs. You can

hardly drag them along. Well, come along, hapless old man! [*Takes his arm.*]

SHAMRAYEV [*offering his arm to his wife*]. Madam?

SORIN. There's that damned dog howling again! [*To* SHAMRAYEV.] Will you kindly tell them to let that dog off the chain, sir!

SHAMRAYEV. Sorry, it can't be done. You see, I'm afraid of thieves breaking into the barn. I've got millet there. [*To* MEDVEDENKO, *who is walking beside him.*] Yes, my dear fellow, a whole octave lower: "Bravo, Silva!" Not that he was a professional singer, mind you. Good Lord, no! Just a plain church chorister.

MEDVEDENKO. And what salary does a church chorister get?

All go out, except DORN.

DORN [*alone*]. I don't know; perhaps I don't understand anything or have gone off my head, but I liked the play. There's something in it. When the girl talked about loneliness, and later on when the devil's red eyes appeared, my hands shook with excitement. Fresh, naïve . . . Here he comes, I think. I must say something nice to him, congratulate him.

KONSTANTIN [*enters*]. All gone.

DORN. I'm here.

KONSTANTIN. Masha's looking for me all over the park. What a nuisance she is!

DORN. I liked your play very much, Konstantin. It's rather unusual, and I haven't heard the end, but I couldn't help being gripped by it. You've talent, young man. You must persevere. [KONSTANTIN *presses his hand warmly and embraces him impulsively.*] Dear me, how overwrought you are! Tears in your eyes. Now, what did I want to say? What I mean is that you've taken a subject from the realm of abstract ideas. That's as it should be. A work of art ought to express some great idea. It's only the serious that is beautiful. How pale you are!

KONSTANTIN. So you think I ought to go on?

DORN. Of course! But remember, deal only with what is important and eternal. You know, I have had an interesting and varied life. I've nothing to grumble about. But if I had experienced the ecstasy artists experience while creating, I should, I believe, have despised this material husk of mine and everything that goes with it. I should have soared away from the earth, higher and ever higher.

KONSTANTIN. Doctor, I'm awfully sorry, but where's Nina?

DORN. And one more thing. There must be a clear and definite idea in every work of art. You ought to know why you're writing. If you don't, if you walk along this picturesque road without any definite aim, you'll lose your way, and your talent will be your ruin.

KONSTANTIN [*impatiently*]. Where's Nina?

DORN. She's gone home.

KONSTANTIN [*in despair*]. But what am I to do? I want to see her. I must see her! I'm going——

MASHA *comes in.*

DORN [*to* KONSTANTIN]. Compose yourself, my friend.

KONSTANTIN. I'm going after her all the same. I must go.

MASHA. You'd better go indoors, Konstantin. Your mother's waiting for you. She's worried about you.

KONSTANTIN. Tell her I've gone away. And please leave me alone, all of you! Leave me alone! Don't follow me about!

DORN. Come, come, you mustn't carry on like that! You really shouldn't, you know.

KONSTANTIN [*in a voice choked with tears*]. Good-bye, Doctor. Thank you. [*Goes out.*]

DORN [*sighs*]. Youth! Youth!

MASHA. When people have nothing better to say, they say, "Youth! Youth!" [*Takes snuff.*]

DORN [*takes the snuffbox away from her and throws it into the bushes*]. Disgusting habit! [*Pause.*] They're playing the piano indoors. We'd better go in.

MASHA. Please wait a moment!

DORN. Why? What is it?

MASHA. I'd like to tell you—I—I wanted to before. I must talk to someone. [*Agitatedly.*] I dislike my father, but I—I am very fond of you. I don't know why, but I feel you're very close to me. So please help me. Help me or I shall do something silly; I shall make a mess of my life; I shall ruin it. I can't go on!

DORN. What's the matter? How can I help you?

MASHA. Oh, I'm so miserable! No one, no one, knows how wretched I am! [*Puts her head on his chest. Softly.*] I love Konstantin!

DORN. How overwrought they all are! How overwrought! And so much love, too. . . . Oh, that spellbinding lake! [*Gently.*] But what can I do, my child? What? . . . What? . . .

Curtain.

ACT TWO

A croquet lawn. The house, with a large terrace in front of it, is on the right; the lake, in which the blazing sun is reflected, can be seen on the left. Flower beds.

Midday. ARKADINA, MASHA, *and* DORN *are sitting on a garden seat in the shade of an old lime tree on one side of the lawn.* DORN *has an open book on his knees.*

ARKADINA [*to* MASHA]. Come on, let's stand up. [*Both get up.*] Let's stand side by side. You're twenty-two, aren't you? Well, I'm almost twice your age. Which would you say was the younger of us, Dr. Dorn?

DORN. Why, you, of course.

ARKADINA. There you are. . . . And why? Because I work, because I'm wide awake, because I'm always active, while you just sit about in the same old place and do nothing! You're not alive at all! And another thing: I make it a strict rule never to look into the future, never to worry about old age or death. What will be, will be.

MASHA. I always feel as though I had been born ages ago. I drag my life like an endless train behind me. And very often I don't want to go on living at all. [*Sitting down.*] Of course, that's all nonsense. I must pull myself together. Shake it all off.

DORN [*sings softly*]. "Tell her, oh, tell her, my flowers sweet. . . ."

ARKADINA. Besides, I'm always well turned out, just like the English. My dress and my hair are always *comme il faut*. Do I ever go out of the house even for a stroll in the garden in an old blouse or with untidy hair? Never! Shall I tell you why I look so young? It's because I've never neglected my appearance, never let myself go like some women. [*Struts about the lawn with arms akimbo.*] There—look at me—fresh as paint. I could play a girl of fifteen.

DORN. Admirable, but if you don't mind, I'd like to go on

SHAMRAYEV. Hm . . . I see. It's an excellent idea of course, but, pray, madam, how do you propose to get to town? I can't spare anyone to drive you there. We're bringing in the rye today, and everybody is busy in the fields. Besides, what horses are you going to have?

ARKADINA. What horses? What do I care what horses?

SORIN. We've got carriage horses, haven't we?

SHAMRAYEV [*growing agitated*]. Carriage horses? And where am I to get the harness for them? Where am I to get the harness? I must say this is really incredible. It's phenomenal! No, madam, I'm sorry, but I can't let you have horses. I'm full of admiration for you as an actress; I'd gladly sacrifice ten years of my life for you, but I can't let you have any horses!

ARKADINA. But what if I have to go? Well, really!

SHAMRAYEV. My dear lady, you've no idea what it means to run an estate!

ARKADINA [*flaring up*]. That's an old story! If that's the case, I'm leaving for Moscow today. Tell them to hire horses for me in the village, or I shall walk to the station!

SHAMRAYEV [*flaring up*]. In that case, I throw up my job! Find yourself another agent! [*Goes out.*]

ARKADINA. Every summer it's the same thing! Every summer I'm insulted here! I shall never come here again! Never!

Goes out on left, where the bathing hut is supposed to be. In another minute she can be seen entering the house; TRIGORIN *follows her with rod and pail.*

SORIN [*flaring up*]. The nerve of the man! What cheek! Damned if I'm going to put up with it any longer! I mean, after all! Get me all my horses here this very minute!

NINA [*to* PAULINE]. Refuse a famous actress like Arkadina! Isn't her slightest wish, her slightest whim, more important than the whole of the estate? It's unbelievable!

PAULINE [*in despair*]. But what can I do? Put yourself in my place, my dear. What can I do?

SORIN [*to* NINA]. Let's go to my sister. Let's plead with her not to leave. Shall we, my dear? [*Looking in the direction*

reading. [*Takes up the book.*] We got up to the corn merchant and the rats.

ARKADINA. And the rats. Please, go on. [*Sits down.*] Or shall I? Yes, I think I will. Give me the book. It's my turn. [*Takes the book and scans the page.*] And the rats—here we are. [*Reads.*] "And of course for society people to spoil novelists and try to draw them into their company is as dangerous as for a corn-dealer to breed rats in his barns. And yet they are undoubtedly sought after. So much so that when a society woman picks out an author she wishes to capture, she overwhelms him with compliments, she tries to meet his slightest wish, she does her best to please him. . . ." Well, I suppose that may be the French way, but nothing like that happens here. We have no set rules. With us, if a woman tries to capture a writer, she is usually head over heels in love with him first. We have no need to look far; take me and Trigorin, for instance.

Enter SORIN, *leaning on his cane, and* NINA *with him;* MEDVEDENKO *pushes an empty wheel chair behind them.*

SORIN [*in the fond voice with which one speaks to children*]. So we're happy, aren't we? Very happy? We're gay today, eh? After all? [*To his sister.*] We're happy! Father and stepmother have gone off to Tver, and we're free for three whole days.

NINA [*sits down beside* ARKADINA *and embraces her*]. Yes, I'm awfully happy. Now I belong to you.

SORIN [*sits down in his wheel chair*]. She looks very sweet today, doesn't she?

ARKADINA. Elegant and charming. . . . I never dreamt you could dress like that! [*Kisses* NINA.] But we mustn't praise you too much, must we? It may bring you bad luck. Where's Mr. Trigorin?

NINA. He's by the bathing hut, fishing.

ARKADINA. I can't understand why he doesn't get sick of it! [*Is about to continue reading.*]

NINA. What are you reading?

ARKADINA. Maupassant's "On the Water," my dear. [*Reads a few lines to herself.*] Well, the rest isn't interesting or true. [*Closes the book.*] I'm awfully worried. Tell me, what's the matter with my son? Why is he so moody and bad-tempered? He spends days on the lake, and I hardly ever see him.

MASHA. He's not feeling very happy. [*To* NINA, *shyly.*] Won't you read us something out of his play, please?

NINA [*shrugging*]. Do you really want me to? It's so dull!

MASHA [*restraining her eagerness*]. When he reads something himself, his eyes blaze and his face goes pale. He has such a beautiful, sad voice and the look of a poet.

SORIN *can be heard snoring.*

DORN. Pleasant dreams!

ARKADINA. Peter! Dear!

SORIN. Eh?

ARKADINA. Are you asleep?

SORIN. Me? Not a bit.

Pause.

ARKADINA. You don't look after yourself, Peter. I wish you would.

SORIN. I'd be glad to, my dear. It's the doctor who won't do anything for me.

DORN. Do something for a man of sixty!

SORIN. Why not? Doesn't a man of sixty want to live?

DORN [*annoyed*]. Oh, very well, take some valerian drops!

ARKADINA. I think he ought to go to a spa, don't you? I'm sure it would do him good.

DORN. Well, why not? Let him by all means. On the other hand, he needn't if he doesn't want to.

ARKADINA. You're a great help, aren't you?

DORN. Yes, aren't I? Well, everything is really quite simple.

Pause.

MEDVEDENKO. I think Mr. Sorin ought to give up smoking.

SORIN. Rubbish!

DORN. No. It isn't rubbish. Wine and tobacco rob a man of his personality. After a cigar or a glass of vodka you're no longer Mr. Sorin, but Mr. Sorin plus someone else. Your personality has become blurred, and you even think of yourself in the third person—as *he.*

SORIN [*laughs*]. You're a fine one to talk! You've had a life, haven't you? But what about me? I served i law courts for twenty-eight years, but I never really I don't know what real life is, so it isn't surpris want to get all I can from life. You have had al could offer you, and that's why you're so philosop But I want to live, and that's why I like to have a of sherry at dinner, a cigar, and so on. That's all th to it.

DORN. A man should take life seriously. To worry a your health at the age of sixty, to regret you haven' joyed yourself enough in your youth, that, if you'll pa my saying so, is sheer folly!

MASHA [*gets up*]. I suppose it's almost lunch time. [*W off lazily, limply.*] My leg's gone to sleep. [*Goes ou*

DORN. Gone to have a couple of drinks before lunch.

SORIN. The poor girl's so unhappy.

DORN. Nonsense, sir!

SORIN. You talk like a man who's had all he wanted f life.

ARKADINA. Oh, what can be more boring than this deli ful country boredom! Quiet, hot, nobody does anyth everybody's airing his views. . . . How nice it is to with you, my friends, how pleasant to listen to you, how much nicer to be alone in a hotel room studyi part!

NINA [*ecstatically*]. Oh, it must be! I quite understand!

SORIN. Of course, life is much nicer in town. You sit in study, your butler admits no one you don't want to there's the telephone, cabmen in the street, and so c

DORN [*sings softly*]. "Tell her, oh, tell her, my flc sweet. . . ."

Enter SHAMRAYEV, *followed by* PAULINE.

SHAMRAYEV. Here they all are! Good afternoon, ladies gentlemen. [*Kisses* ARKADINA*'s hand, then* NINA*'s* glad to see you looking so well. [*To* ARKADINA.] My tells me that you're thinking of driving to town wit today. Is that right?

ARKADINA. Yes, we were thinking of it.

in which Shamrayev *has gone.*] What a brute! A real despot!

Nina [*preventing him from getting up*]. Sit still, please. We'll wheel you there. [*She and* Medvedenko *wheel the chair.*] Oh, it's dreadful!

Sorin. Yes, it is dreadful. Still, don't you worry, my dear, he won't go. I'll talk to him at once.

They go out; only Dorn *and* Pauline *remain.*

Dorn. People are tiresome. Your husband ought to have been kicked out of here long ago, but I suppose it'll end in that old woman Sorin and his sister apologizing to him. You'll see.

Pauline. He's sent the carriage horses into the fields too. Every day the same rows! If you only knew how it upsets me! It makes me ill. Look, I'm shaking all over. I can't bear his coarseness. [*Imploringly.*] Eugene, my dearest, take me away from here! Our time is passing. We're no longer young. Don't let's pretend and lie any more now that we have so few years left to us.

Pause.

Dorn. I'm fifty-five, my dear. It's too late for me to change my life.

Pauline. That's not why you refuse. You've other women who mean as much to you as I do, haven't you? You can't have them all, can you? I understand. I'm sorry; you must find me an awful nuisance.

Nina *appears near the house; she is picking flowers.*

Dorn. You know I don't.

Pauline. I can't help being jealous. I don't suppose you can avoid women, being a doctor, can you?

Dorn [*to* Nina, *who walks up to them*]. What's happening in there?

Nina. Irina is crying, and Mr. Sorin has had an attack of asthma.

Dorn [*getting up*]. I suppose I'd better go and give them both some valerian drops.

Nina [*gives him the flowers*]. They're for you, Doctor.

Dorn. *Merci bien.* [*Walks off in the direction of the house.*]

PAULINE [*going with him*]. What lovely flowers! [*Near the house, in a strangled voice.*] Give me those flowers! Give me those flowers! [*Getting the flowers, she tears them up and throws them away; they both go into the house.*]

NINA [*alone*]. How strange to see a famous actress crying about some silly trifle! And isn't it even stranger that so popular and famous a writer should spend all day fishing and be so pleased because he has caught two chub? A writer, too, whose name is always in the papers, whose photographs are sold in the shops, whose works are translated into foreign languages! I thought famous people would be proud and unapproachable! I thought they despised the mob and used their fame and popularity only to revenge themselves on it for worshiping rank and wealth. But here they cry, fish, play cards, laugh, and lose their tempers just like anybody else!

KONSTANTIN [*enters hatless with a gun and a dead seagull*]. Are you alone?

NINA. Yes. [KONSTANTIN *lays the seagull at her feet.*] What does that mean?

KONSTANTIN. I did a vile thing today: I killed this seagull. Let me lay it at your feet.

NINA. What's the matter with you? [*Picks up the seagull and gazes at it.*]

KONSTANTIN [*after a pause*]. I shall kill myself in the same way soon.

NINA. You look strange. I hardly know you.

KONSTANTIN. That's not surprising. I hardly know you. You've changed toward me. You look so coldly. I seem to make you feel uncomfortable.

NINA. You've been so irritable lately. It's so hard to understand you, almost as though you were talking in symbols. I expect this seagull is some kind of a symbol too. I'm sorry, but I don't understand it. [*Puts the seagull down on bench.*] I'm afraid I'm too unsophisticated to understand you.

KONSTANTIN. It goes back to the evening when my play was such a failure, doesn't it? Women never forgive a failure. I have burnt my play, every page of it. Oh, if only you knew how unhappy I am! Your sudden indifference is so awful, so incredible! It is as if I woke up and found the lake had suddenly run dry or vanished under the ground. You said just now that you were not sophisticated enough to understand me. Oh, what is there to understand? My play was a failure. You despise my work. You think I'm worthless, commonplace, like hundreds of others. [*Stamping.*] How well I understand it, how well! Oh, my head, my head! My brain feels as though it had been pierced with a red-hot nail. To hell with it, and with my pride, which is sucking my lifeblood, sucking it like a serpent. [*Seeing* TRIGORIN, *who is walking toward them, reading a book.*] Here comes real genius! Walks like Hamlet, and with a book too! [*Mimicking.*] "Words, words, words . . ." That sun is still miles away from you and already you're smiling. Your gaze has melted in its rays. Good-bye; I won't be in your way. [*Walks away quickly.*]

TRIGORIN [*writing in his notebook*]. Takes snuff and drinks vodka. Always wears black. The schoolmaster is in love with her.

NINA. Good afternoon, Mr. Trigorin.

TRIGORIN. Good afternoon. I'm afraid we shall probably be leaving today. Events, you know, have taken rather an unexpected turn. So I don't think we're likely to meet again. A pity. I don't often meet charming young girls now. I hardly know what a girl of eighteen or nineteen is feeling or thinking about. That's why the girls in my stories and novels are usually so unconvincing. I wish I could put myself in your place just for an hour to find out what you're thinking about and what you're really like.

NINA. And I wish I could be in your place.

TRIGORIN. Why?

NINA. To find out what it is like to be a famous and gifted writer. What does it feel like to be famous? How does the fact you're so popular affect you?

TRIGORIN. How does it affect me? I don't believe it affects me at all. I—I've never thought of it. [*Thinking it over.*] If you really want to know, it's one of two things: Either you are exaggerating my fame, or it's something I'm hardly aware of.

NINA. But when you read about yourself in the papers?

TRIGORIN. When I'm praised, I like it, and when I'm abused, I'm upset for a day or two.

NINA. How wonderful the world is! If only you knew how I envy you. People's fates are so different. Some live dreary, miserable, inconspicuous lives, everyone just like everyone else, and all terribly unhappy. But others, you, for instance, you—one in a million—are fated to have such interesting, bright, happy lives, lives worthwhile, full of significance. You must be very happy.

TRIGORIN. Me? [*Shrugging.*] I wonder. . . . You talk about fame, happiness, some bright, interesting life, but—I hope you won't mind my saying so—to me all these fine words are just like Turkish delight, which I hate. I'm afraid you're very kind and very young!

NINA. Your life must be wonderful!

TRIGORIN. Must it? What is there particularly good about it? [*Looks at his watch.*] I must go in now. Have to do some writing. Sorry, but I'm busy. [*Laughs.*] I'm afraid you've touched me on a raw spot, and I'm beginning to get worked up and a little cross. However, let's talk. Let's talk about my bright and beautiful life. Where shall we begin? [*After a little thought.*] There are certain ideas which take possession of a man's mind so completely that he can't shake them off. For instance, a man may be obsessed day and night by the thought of the moon. Well, I have my own moon. Day and night one persistent thought takes possession of me: I must write, I must write! I must! I must! No sooner do I finish one story than I must start on another, then on a third, a fourth, and so on. I go on writing incessantly, without a break, and there seems to be no other way for it. What is there so bright and beautiful about that? Oh, it's a crazy sort of life! Even now, while talking to you, I can't forget for a single moment that there is an unfinished story waiting in my room. Do you see that cloud? Looks remarkably like a grand piano, doesn't it? The moment I saw it, I thought, I mustn't forget to mention somewhere in my story that a cloud looking like a grand piano sailed across the sky. I catch a whiff of heliotrope. Aha, I say to myself, quick, make a mental note: a sickly smell, the widow's color—must mention that in a description of a summer evening. I snap up every word, every sentence, you or I utter, just for the sake of locking them away in my literary lumber-room. They may come in handy one day!

When my work's done, I rush off to the theatre or go away to do a bit of fishing. There, at least, one would have thought, I could take a rest and forget my work. But not a bit of it! A heavy iron cannon-ball is already turning round and round in my head—an idea for a new story! It drags me back to my desk, and off I go again: writing, writing, writing! And so it goes on and on, and I find no rest from myself. I feel I am consuming my own life, that for the honey I give away to someone I don't know, I gather up the pollen from my best flowers, tear the flowers themselves, and crush them under my feet. Don't you think I'm just stark staring mad? Do my friends and those near and dear to me treat me like a normal human being? "Ah, what are you writing now, old man? What masterpiece are you going to give us next?" And so it goes on and on. Always the same thing, over and over again. And I cannot help feeling that all the attention of my acquaintances, all their praises and cries of delight—all that is nothing but a piece of the most elaborate deception. They deceive me as a doctor deceives a patient, and sometimes I'm really afraid that they may steal up behind me, seize me, and drag me off to a lunatic asylum, like Gogol's madman, Poprishchin. Even when I was starting on my literary career, in those best days of my youth, life was one long drawn-out agony. A minor writer, especially when he is unlucky, can't help feeling awkward, clumsy, unwanted. His nerves are frayed; they're always at the breaking point. He feels drawn irresistibly to people who have some connection with literature and art—unrecognized, ignored by everybody, too shy to look people straight in the face, like an incurable gambler without money. I had never met any of my readers, but for some reason I always imagined them skeptical and hostile. I was afraid of a theatre audience. It terrified me. And every time I put on a new play, I had the feeling that the dark people in the audience were my enemies and the fair ones coldly indifferent. Oh, it was awful! It was simply torture.

NINA. But, surely, inspiration and the very act of creation must give you moments of ecstasy and happiness.

TRIGORIN. Well, yes, in a way. When I'm writing, I feel happy. And I enjoy reading the proofs. But the moment my book is published, I'm in despair. I realize that it isn't what I wanted, that the whole thing is a mistake, that I shouldn't have written it at all. And I feel worried and rotten—rotten. [*Laughing*.] Well, the public reads it: "Yes, yes, very charming stuff, clever! Very charming, but it's a long way from Tolstoy!" or "Excellent, but Turgenev's *Fathers and Sons* is better!" And so to my dying day everything will be charming and clever, nothing more. And when I'm dead, my friends, as they walk past my grave, will say, "Here lies Trigorin. He was a good writer, but not as good as Turgenev."

Nina. I'm sorry, but I don't agree with you. You're just spoilt by success.

Trigorin. What success? I've never liked my own stuff. No, I don't like myself as a writer. The worst of it is that I am in a kind of daze and often scarcely know what I am writing. Now, I like this stretch of water. I like the trees, the sky. I appreciate nature. It arouses passion in me, an irresistible urge to write. But after all, I am not just a descriptive writer. I'm also a citizen. I love my country, my people. And I feel that if I am a writer, I must speak of the people, of their sufferings, of their future. I must speak of science, of the rights of man, and so on. So I talk about everything. I'm always in a hurry, being pushed on all sides. People prod me on, they're angry with me. I rush about—here, there, everywhere. Like a fox with the hounds in full cry after it. And I can see that life and knowledge are getting further and further away from me, that I'm lagging behind more and more, like the peasant who tried to overtake a train. So that in the end I'm beginning to feel that all I'm good for is descriptive stuff, and in everything else I'm false, false, false to the marrow of my bones.

Nina. You've been working too hard, and I don't suppose you have the time or the wish to realize your own importance. What does it matter that you are dissatisfied with yourself? Everybody thinks you're great and wonderful. If I were a writer like you, I'd dedicate my whole life to the people, but I'd realize at the same time that they could only be happy by raising themselves to my level, and I'm sure they would draw me along in a chariot.

TRIGORIN. A chariot! I'm not Agamemnon, am I? [*Both smile.*]

NINA. For the happiness of being a writer or an actress, I'd put up with the disapproval of my relations and friends, endure poverty and disappointment, live in an attic, eat nothing but dry bread. I'd suffer agonies from the realization of my own shortcomings, but I'd also demand fame—real, resounding fame! [*Buries her face in her hands.*] Oh, my head's spinning. . . .

ARKADINA [*from within the house*]. Boris!

TRIGORIN. They're calling me. I suppose I shall have to go in and pack. Lord, how I wish I could stay! [*Looks round at the lake.*] How glorious it is! What a lovely spot!

NINA. Do you see the house and garden on the other side of the lake?

TRIGORIN. Yes.

NINA. That was my mother's house. I was born there. I've spent all my life on the banks of this lake, and I know every little island on it.

TRIGORIN. You've a nice place here. [*Seeing the seagull.*] And what's this?

NINA. A seagull. Konstantin shot it.

TRIGORIN. A beautiful bird. No, I don't want to leave, not really. I wonder if you could persuade Irina to stay? [*Writes something down in his notebook.*]

NINA. What are you writing?

TRIGORIN. Oh, nothing. Just making a note. Got an idea. [*Putting away his notebook.*] An idea for a short story: A young girl has lived in a house on the shore of a lake since her childhood, a young girl like you; she loves the lake like a seagull, and she's as free and happy as a seagull. But a man comes along, sees her, and just for the fun of it destroys her like that seagull there.

NINA [*shudders*]. Don't please, don't! Not like that!

Pause.

ARKADINA *appears at the window.*

ARKADINA. Boris, where are you?

TRIGORIN. Coming! [*As he walks toward the house, he*

turns round a few times to look at NINA. *Stops by the window. To* ARKADINA.] Well?

ARKADINA. We're staying.

TRIGORIN *goes into the house.*

NINA [*goes up to the footlights; after a moment's reflection*]. A dream!

Curtain.

ACT THREE

Dining room in SORIN'S *country house. On the right and left, doors. A sideboard. A medicine chest. A table in the middle of the room. A suitcase and hatboxes. Signs of preparations for a journey.* TRIGORIN *is having lunch.* MASHA *stands by the table.*

MASHA. I'm telling you all this because you're a writer. You can use it if you like. I'll be quite frank with you; if he had hurt himself badly, I wouldn't have gone on living another minute. But that doesn't mean that I haven't any courage. As a matter of fact, I've made up my mind to tear this love out of my heart, tear it out by the roots.

TRIGORIN. How are you going to do that?

MASHA. By getting married. I'm marrying Simon Medvedenko.

TRIGORIN. The schoolmaster?

MASHA. Yes.

TRIGORIN. I don't see why you should.

MASHA. To love without hope, to wait for years and years for something to happen—no, thank you. Once I get married, I shan't have time to think of love. New worries will make me forget my past. Anyway, it will be a change. Shall we have another?

TRIGORIN. Don't you think you've had enough?

MASHA. Good Lord, no! [*Fills a glass for each of them.*] Don't look at me like that! Women drink more often than you think. A few, like me, drink openly, but most drink in secret. Yes, and it's always vodka or brandy. [*Clinks glasses.*] Your health! You're a nice man. Easy to get on with. I'm sorry you're going.

They drink.

TRIGORIN. So am I.

MASHA. Why don't you ask her to stay?

TRIGORIN. No, she won't stay now. Her son's behaving

rather tactlessly. First he tries to shoot himself, and now, I'm told, he wants to challenge me to a duel. And what for? He sulks, snorts, preaches new forms of art. Isn't there room in the world for everybody? For the new as well as the old? Why get in each other's way?

MASHA. Well, I suppose it's jealousy, too. However, it's none of my business. [*Pause.* YAKOV *crosses the room from left to right with a suitcase;* NINA *comes in and stands by the window.*] My schoolmaster isn't very clever, but he is a good sort, and as poor as a church-mouse. He's very much in love with me. I'm sorry for him. And I'm sorry for his old mother, too. Well, let me wish you the best of luck. Don't think too badly of me. [*Shakes him warmly by the hand.*] Thank you for your kindness and your sympathy. Send me your books, and don't forget to autograph them. Only please don't inscribe them "To my dear ——" etc., but simply "To Masha, the world-forgetting, and by the world forgot." Good-bye! [*Goes out.*]

NINA [*holding out her clenched fist to* TRIGORIN]. Odd or even?

TRIGORIN. Even.

NINA [*sighing*]. Wrong. I've only one pea in my hand. I was trying to find out whether to go on the stage or not. I wish someone would tell me what to do.

TRIGORIN. I'm afraid it's something you'll have to decide for yourself.

Pause.

NINA. You're going away and . . . I don't suppose we shall ever see each other again. I'd like you to have this little medallion as a keepsake. I had your initials engraved on it—and on the other side, the title of your book: *Days and Nights.*

TRIGORIN. How nice! [*Kisses the medallion.*] What a lovely present!

NINA. I hope you'll think of me sometimes.

TRIGORIN. I will. I shall think of you as you were on that lovely day—remember?—a week ago, when you wore that summer dress. We had a long talk, and there was a white seagull lying on the seat.

NINA [*thoughtfully*]. Yes, a seagull. [*Pause.*] We can't talk any more. Someone's coming. Let me have two minutes before you go. Please.

NINA *goes out on left; at the same time* ARKADINA, SORIN, *in a frock coat with a star on it, followed by* YAKOV, *busy with the luggage, enter on the right.*

ARKADINA. I wish you'd stay at home, Peter. With your rheumatism and at your age you oughtn't to go gallivanting about. [*To* TRIGORIN.] Who left the room just now? Nina?

TRIGORIN. Yes.

ARKADINA. Sorry we disturbed you. [*Sits down.*] I think I have packed everything. My goodness, I'm worn out.

TRIGORIN [*reads the inscription on the medallion*]. "*Days and Nights,* page one hundred and twenty-one, lines eleven and twelve."

YAKOV [*clearing the table*]. Am I to pack your fishing rods too, sir?

TRIGORIN. Yes, I may need them again. The books you can give away to anyone you like.

YAKOV. Very good, sir.

TRIGORIN [*to himself*]. Page one hundred and twenty-one, lines eleven and twelve. I wonder what there is in those lines. [*To* ARKADINA.] Have you my books in the house?

ARKADINA. Yes, you'll find them in my brother's study, in the corner bookcase.

TRIGORIN. Page one hundred and twenty-one . . . [*Goes out.*]

ARKADINA. Really, Peter, dear, I do wish you'd stay at home.

SORIN. You're going away and I shall find it awfully dull here without you.

ARKADINA. And what about the town? There's nothing in particular happening there.

SORIN. No, perhaps not, but it'll make a change. [*Laughs.*] They're going to lay the foundation stone of the rural council building, and all that sort of thing. I'm fed up with this silly sort of life. Want to liven up a bit, if only for an hour or two. Been on the shelf too long, like an old pipe. I've ordered the carriage for one o'clock. We'll leave together.

ARKADINA [*after a pause*]. Very well, but don't fret too much when you come back. Don't catch cold. Look after my son. Take care of him. Get some sense into his head. [*Pause.*] Here I'm going away, and I shall never know why he tried to shoot himself. I believe the main reason was jealousy, and the sooner I take Trigorin away from here, the better.

SORIN. Well, I don't know. I daresay there were other reasons, too. And no wonder. He's young and intelligent, living in the country in some Godforsaken hole, with no money, no position, and no future. Nothing to do. Ashamed of doing nothing and afraid of it. I'm very fond of him, and I think he's fond of me, too, but all the same—I mean, after all, he can't help feeling that he isn't any use here, that he is a poor relation, a dependent. It's—I mean, it's pretty obvious, isn't it? His vanity——

ARKADINA. Oh, what a trial that boy is to me! [*Reflectively.*] I wish he'd get himself a job. In the Civil Service or something.

SORIN [*whistles, then diffidently*]. I think it wouldn't be a bad idea if you—er—if you let him have a little money. You see, he should really—I mean, he really does want some decent clothes, and so on. He's been wearing the same old coat for the last three years. Walks about without an overcoat. [*Laughs.*] And it wouldn't be a bad thing for the young man to . . . go abroad for a while. It wouldn't cost a lot, would it?

ARKADINA. Well, I don't know. I suppose I might manage a new suit, but as for going abroad—no, that's out of the question. I don't think I can even afford a suit just now. [*Firmly.*] I haven't any money! [SORIN *laughs.*] I've no money!

SORIN [*whistles*]. I see. I'm sorry, my dear. Don't be angry with me. I—I believe you. You're such a warmhearted, generous woman.

ARKADINA [*crying*]. I have no money!

SORIN. Of course, if I had any money, I'd give him some myself, but I haven't anything—not a penny! [*Laughs.*] My agent grabs all my pension and spends it on the estate. He rears cattle, keeps bees, and all my money just goes down the drain. The damned bees die, the damned cows die, and when I ask for a carriage, the horses are wanted for something else.

ARKADINA. Of course, I have some money, but you must realize that I'm an actress. My dresses alone are enough to ruin me.

SORIN. You're very kind, my dear. I—I respect you. Indeed I do. Oh dear, I—I'm afraid—I—I'm not feeling well again. [*Swaying.*] My head's going round. [*Holding on to the table.*] I—I'm going to—faint—and—so on.

ARKADINA [*frightened*]. Peter! My dear! [*Trying to support him.*] Peter, darling! [*Shouts.*] Help! Help! [*Enter* KONSTANTIN *with a bandage on his head, followed by* MEDVEDENKO.] He's going to faint!

SORIN. Oh, it's nothing—nothing. [*Smiles and has a drink of water.*] It's passed off—and—so on.

KONSTANTIN [*to his mother*]. Don't be alarmed, Mother. It's not serious. Uncle often has these attacks now. [*To his uncle.*] You ought to go and lie down, Uncle.

SORIN. Yes, for a bit. But I'm going to town all the same. I'll lie down for a bit, and then I'll go. I mean, it's obvious, isn't it? [*Walks to the door, leaning on his cane.*]

MEDVEDENKO [*taking his arm*]. Have you heard this riddle, sir? In the morning on all fours, in the afternoon on two, in the evening on three——

SORIN [*laughs*]. That's right. And at night on the back. Thank you, I can manage by myself now.

MEDVEDENKO. Good Lord, sir, this is no time to stand on ceremony!

SORIN *and* MEDVEDENKO *go out.*

ARKADINA. Oh, he gave me such a fright!

KONSTANTIN. It isn't good for him, living in the country. He frets too much. I wish you'd feel generous for once, Mother, and lend him fifteen hundred or two thousand rubles. Then he could manage a whole year in town.

ARKADINA. I have no money. I'm an actress, not a banker.

Pause.

KONSTANTIN. Please change the bandage for me, Mother. You do it so well.

ARKADINA [*takes some iodine and a box of bandages from the medicine chest*]. The doctor is late today.

KONSTANTIN. Yes. Promised to be here at ten, and it's twelve already.

ARKADINA. Sit down, dear. [*Takes the bandage off his head.*] You look as if you were wearing a turban. Yesterday a stranger in the kitchen asked what nationality you were. The wound has almost healed. Just a little scar left. [*Kisses his head.*] You won't do anything so stupid again while I'm away, will you?

KONSTANTIN. No, Mother. I did it in a moment of insane despair, when I lost control of myself. It won't happen again. [*Kisses her hand.*] You've clever fingers, Mother. I remember long ago when you were still acting on the Imperial stage—I was a little boy then—there was a fight in our yard, and a washerwoman who lived in our house was badly hurt. Remember? She was unconscious when they picked her up. You looked after her, gave her her medicine, bathed her children in a tub. Don't you remember?

ARKADINA. No. [*Puts on a fresh bandage.*]

KONSTANTIN. Two ballet dancers lived in our house at the time. They used to come and have coffee with you.

ARKADINA. Oh, I remember that.

KONSTANTIN. They were such pious women, weren't they? [*Pause.*] Lately, I mean these last few days, Mother, I've loved you as I used to love you when I was a little boy: so dearly and tenderly. I've no one left in the whole world now except you, Mother. Only why, oh why, are you so much under the influence of that man?

ARKADINA. You don't understand him, Konstantin. He's one of the most honorable men I've ever known.

KONSTANTIN. Yet when he was told that I was going to challenge him to a duel, his honor did not prevent him from playing the coward, did it? He's running away. What an ignominious flight!

ARKADINA. What nonsense! It was I who asked him to leave.

KONSTANTIN. A most honorable man! Here we are almost quarreling over him, and he's probably somewhere in the drawing room or the garden laughing at us, broadening Nina's mind, doing his best to convince her that he is a genius.

ARKADINA. You seem to enjoy saying all sorts of disagreeable things to me. I tell you, I think very highly of him, and I'd thank you not to speak badly of him in my presence.

KONSTANTIN. I don't think highly of him. You want me to think of him as a genius. Well, I'm sorry, Mother, but the truth is, his books make me sick.

ARKADINA. You're jealous. Mediocrities who have grand ideas about themselves naturally turn up their noses at men of real genius. Much good does it do them, I must say!

KONSTANTIN [*ironically*]. Men of real genius! [*Angrily.*] I've got more genius than any of you, if it comes to that! [*Tears the bandage off his head.*] You, with your hackneyed ideas, have scrambled to the top in the world of art and, according to you, only what you do is legitimate and genuine. You stifle and persecute everything else. I don't acknowledge your authority! I don't care a damn for you or him!

ARKADINA. You decadent, you!

KONSTANTIN. Go to your precious theatre and act in your miserable third-rate plays!

ARKADINA. Never in my life have I acted in third-rate plays! Leave me alone, will you? You couldn't even write the words for a cheap revue. You Kiev artisan! You parasite!

KONSTANTIN. Miser!

ARKADINA. Tramp! [KONSTANTIN *sinks into a chair and weeps quietly.*] Nonentity! [*After pacing the room in agitation.*] Don't cry, please. You mustn't cry. [*Crying.*] Please, don't. [*Kisses his forehead, cheeks, and head.*] Oh, my darling, forgive me. Forgive your silly mother. I'm so unhappy. Please, please forgive me.

KONSTANTIN [*embracing her*]. Oh, Mother, if only you knew! I've lost everything. She doesn't love me, and now I can't write. All my hopes are shattered.

ARKADINA. Don't give up, my darling. Everything will come right. He'll be gone soon, and she'll love you again.

[*Wiping his tears.*] There, there, stop crying. We've made it up now, haven't we?

KONSTANTIN [*kissing her hands*]. Yes, Mother.

ARKADINA [*gently*]. Won't you make it up with him too? You don't really want a duel, do you? The whole thing's so silly, darling!

KONSTANTIN. All right, only don't ask me to meet him, Mother. It would be too painful. I couldn't stand it. [*Enter* TRIGORIN, *carrying a book.*] Here he comes. I'll go. [*Replaces the bandages, etc., quickly in the medicine chest.*] The doctor will do the bandage.

TRIGORIN [*turning over the pages of the book*]. Page one hundred and twenty-one, lines eleven and twelve. Here it is. [*Reads.*] "If my life should ever be of any use to you, come and take it."

KONSTANTIN *picks up the bandage from the floor and goes out.*

ARKADINA [*glancing at the clock*]. The carriage will be here soon.

TRIGORIN [*to himself*]. "If my life should ever be of any use to you, come and take it."

ARKADINA. You've finished packing, I hope?

TRIGORIN [*impatiently*]. Yes, yes. [*Musing.*] Why does that appeal from so pure a heart fill my soul with sadness? Why does my heart contract with pain? "If my life should ever be of any use to you, come and take it." [*To* ARKADINA.] Let's stay for one more day. [ARKADINA *shakes her head.*] Let's stay.

ARKADINA. My dear, I know what's keeping you here. But please take yourself in hand. You're a little infatuated. Do be reasonable.

TRIGORIN. You, too, be reasonable, sensible, wise. I entreat you, look on this as a true friend. [*Presses her hand.*] You're capable of sacrifice. Be my friend; set me free.

ARKADINA [*in great agitation*]. Are you so much in love with her?

TRIGORIN. I feel drawn to her. Perhaps this is just what I need.

ARKADINA. The love of a provincial girl! Oh, how little you know yourself!

TRIGORIN. Sometimes people walk in their sleep. I feel like that now. Here I am talking to you, and yet I seem to be asleep and dreaming of her. Sweet dreams, such wonderful dreams, have taken possession of me! Set me free, please!

ARKADINA [*trembling*]. No, no! I'm an ordinary woman. You mustn't talk like that to me. Don't torment me, Boris. I'm frightened.

TRIGORIN. If you really don't want to, you needn't be ordinary. The love of a young girl—delightful, poetic, carrying me away into a world of dreams—can there be any greater happiness on earth? I have never known a love like that. As a young man, I never had time; I was too busy running from one editorial office to another, trying to earn a living. But it is here, this love, it has come at last! It beckons me. I'd be a fool to run away from it!

ARKADINA [*angrily*]. You're out of your mind!

TRIGORIN. Well, what if I am?

ARKADINA. All of you seem to have conspired to torment me today. [*Bursts out crying.*]

TRIGORIN [*clutches at his head*]. She doesn't understand! She doesn't want to understand!

ARKADINA. Am I so old and ugly that you can talk to me about other women without embarrassment? [*Embracing and kissing him.*] Oh, you're mad! Oh, my darling, my dear, my beautiful one! You—you're the last page of my life! [*Goes down on her knees.*] Oh, my joy, my pride, my happiness! [*Embracing his knees.*] If you forsake me now, if you leave me for only one hour, I shall not survive it! I shall go mad! Oh, my darling, my dear, my master!

TRIGORIN. Someone may come in! [*Helps her to get up.*]

ARKADINA. Let them come in. I'm not ashamed of my love for you! [*Kisses his hands.*] My treasure, why do such a desperate thing? You want to behave like a madman, but I don't want you to. I won't let you. [*Laughs.*] You're mine—mine! This forehead is mine, these eyes are mine, this lovely silky hair is mine! You're all mine! You're so talented, so clever. You're the greatest of our modern writers. You're Russia's only hope. You have so much sincerity, simplicity, freshness, healthy humor. With one stroke of the pen you can express what is most significant and typical of any person and place. Your characters are so wonderfully alive. One can't read you without delight. You think I'm exaggerating? Flattering you? Look into my eyes! Please, please! Do I look as if I were lying? You see! I alone know how to appreciate you; I alone am telling you the truth! Oh, my darling, my precious darling! You will come with me, won't you? You won't leave me, will you?

TRIGORIN. I have no will of my own. I never had. Listless, flabby, always submissive. No! No woman can possibly care for a man like me. Take me with you, carry me off, only for heaven's sake don't let me out of your sight for a single moment!

ARKADINA [*to herself*]. Now he's mine! [*Cheerfully, as though nothing had happened.*] But, of course, if you like, you can stay. I'll go by myself and you can join me later. In a week perhaps. Why should you be in such a hurry?

TRIGORIN. No, we'd better go together.

ARKADINA. As you wish. If you really want to, then let's go together. [*Pause.* TRIGORIN *jots something down in his notebook.*] What are you writing?

TRIGORIN. A phrase I heard this morning. I liked it very much. "A glitter of girls." It may come in handy. [*Stretching.*] So we are going. More railway carriages, stations, refreshment bars, mutton chops, talk——

SHAMRAYEV [*enters*]. I have the honor to announce with the utmost regret, dear lady, that the carriage is at the door. Time you left for the station. The train is due at five past two. So you won't forget to let me know where the actor Suzdaltsev is now, will you? Is he alive? Is he well? There was a time when we used to go out drinking together, he and I. He was inimitable in *The Mail Robbery*. Inimitable! The tragedian Izmaylov used to appear with him at Yelisavetgrad. He was a remarkable man, too, quite remarkable. No need to hurry, dear lady. You've got another five minutes. Once they acted two conspirators in a melodrama, and when they were suddenly discovered, Izmaylov had to say, "We've been caught in a trap!" But instead he said, "We've been trapped in a caught!" [*Roars with laughter.*] Trapped in a caught!

While SHAMRAYEV *is speaking,* YAKOV *busies himself with the suitcases, and the* MAID *brings* ARKADINA *her hat, coat, umbrella, and gloves; they all assist her in putting on her things. The* COOK *peeps through the door on the left and, after a little while, comes in diffidently. Enter* PAULINE, *followed by* MEDVEDENKO *and later by* SORIN.

PAULINE [*with a little basket*]. I brought you some plums for the journey. They're delicious. You might like to have some on the train.

ARKADINA. Thank you. It's very kind of you, my dear.

PAULINE. Good-bye, my dear. I'm sorry if everything wasn't quite all right. [*Bursts into tears.*]

ARKADINA [*embracing her*]. Everything was perfect, everything! But please don't cry. That certainly isn't right.

PAULINE. We're growing old!

ARKADINA. Well, we can't help that, can we, my dear?

SORIN, *in overcoat with cape, with his hat on and a cane in his hand, comes in through door on left and crosses the room.*

SORIN. We'd better hurry, sister, or we shall miss our train. I mean, after all, I'm going to get into the carriage. [*Goes out.*]

MEDVEDENKO. I think I'll walk to the station to see you off. If I walk fast enough, I can get there in time. [*Goes out.*]

ARKADINA. Good-bye, my dears. If we are alive and well, we shall meet again next summer. [*The* MAID, YAKOV, *and the* COOK *kiss her hands.*] Thank you for everything. [*Gives the* COOK *a ruble.*] Here's a ruble for the three of you.

COOK. Thank you kindly, madam. A happy journey to you. You've been very good to us.

YAKOV. May the Lord bless you, madam. Good luck, madam.

SHAMRAYEV. Don't forget to drop us a line, dear lady. Good-bye, Mr. Trigorin.

ARKADINA. Where's Konstantin? Tell him I'm going. I want to say good-bye to him. Well, good-bye to you all.

Good-bye. [*To* YAKOV.] I've given Cook a ruble. It's for the three of you.

All go out on right. The stage is empty. Behind the scenes the usual farewell noises. The MAID *comes back, takes the basket of plums from the table, and goes out again.*

TRIGORIN [*coming back*]. I've forgotten my stick. Must have left it on the veranda. [*Goes toward door on left, where he meets* NINA, *who is coming in.*] Is that you? We're leaving——

NINA. I knew we'd meet again. [*Excitedly.*] Mr. Trigorin, I've made up my mind once and for all: I'm taking the plunge. I'm going on the stage. I shan't be here tomorrow. I'm running away, I'm leaving everything, starting a new life. I'm leaving for Moscow, like you. We shall meet there.

TRIGORIN [*looking round*]. Stop at the Slav Bazaar. And let me know at once. Molchanovka, Grokholsky's House. Sorry, I must run.

Pause.

NINA. One moment, please!

TRIGORIN [*in an undertone*]. You're so lovely! I'm so happy that we shall meet again soon! [*She lays her head on his chest.*] I shall see your wonderful eyes again, your sweet tender smile, your dear face, your look of angelic purity. Oh, my dear!

A lingering kiss.

Curtain.

ACT FOUR

There is an interval of two years between the third and fourth acts.

One of the drawing rooms in Sorin's *country house, converted into a study by* Konstantin. *To the right and left, doors leading into the inner rooms. Upstage center, a French window leading onto the veranda. In addition to the usual furniture of a drawing room, a writing desk in corner on right, a Turkish divan by the door on the left, a bookcase, and books on window sills and chairs.*

Evening. One lamp is burning under a lampshade. The room is only dimly lit. The trees rustle outside, and the wind is howling in the chimney. The night watchman knocks.

Medvedenko *and* Masha *enter.*

Masha [*calling*]. Konstantin! Konstantin! [*Looking round.*] There's no one here. The old man keeps asking, "Where's Konstantin? Where's Konstantin?" He can't live without him.

Medvedenko. He's afraid of being left alone. [*Listening.*] What awful weather! It's been like this for two days.

Masha [*turning up the lamp*]. There are waves on the lake. Great big ones.

Medvedenko. It's dark in the garden. I wish to goodness they'd tell someone to knock down that stage in the park. There it stands, bare and hideous, like a skeleton, with the curtain flapping in the wind. As I passed it yesterday evening, I thought I could hear someone crying there.

Masha. You do imagine things, don't you?

Pause.

Medvedenko. Let's go home, Masha.

Masha [*shakes her head*]. I'm staying here for the night.

MEDVEDENKO [*imploringly*]. Please let's go, Masha. The baby must be starving.

MASHA. Don't be silly, Simon. Nurse won't let him starve.

Pause.

MEDVEDENKO. It's such a shame. Three nights now he's been without his mother.

MASHA. You're getting to be an awful bore, Simon. At least before we were married you used to hold forth on every imaginable subject, but now all one hears from you is, "baby," "come home," "baby," "come home."

MEDVEDENKO. Let's go, Masha.

MASHA. You go yourself.

MEDVEDENKO. Your father won't let me have a horse.

MASHA. He will. You ask him and see if he won't.

MEDVEDENKO. Well, I suppose I might as well ask him. But you'll come home tomorrow, won't you?

MASHA [*takes snuff*]. All right. I'll come tomorrow. [*Enter* KONSTANTIN *and* PAULINE, KONSTANTIN *carrying pillows and blankets, and* PAULINE, *sheets. They lay them on the Turkish divan. Then* KONSTANTIN *goes to his desk and sits down.*] Who is it for, Mother?

PAULINE. Mr. Sorin wants his bed made up in Konstantin's study.

MASHA. Let me do it. [*Making the bed.*]

PAULINE [*sighs*]. The old man is getting more and more like a baby every day. [*Goes up to writing desk and, leaning on her elbow, looks at the manuscript.*]

Pause.

MEDVEDENKO. I'd better be going. Good-bye, Masha. [*Kisses his wife's hand.*] Good-bye, Mother. [*Tries to kiss his mother-in-law's hand.*]

PAULINE. Oh, for goodness' sake go!

MEDVEDENKO. Good-bye, Konstantin.

KONSTANTIN *offers him his hand in silence.* MEDVEDENKO *goes out.*

PAULINE [*looking at the manuscript*]. No one ever thought you'd be a real writer one day, Konstantin. Now, thank God, you're even getting money from the magazines.

[*Smooths his hair.*] And you've grown so handsome, too. Dear, dear Konstantin, please try to be kinder to Masha.

MASHA [*making the bed*]. Leave him alone, Mother.

PAULINE [*to* KONSTANTIN]. She's such a nice girl. [*Pause.*] All a woman wants, Konstantin, is that a man should look kindly at her. Don't I know that?

KONSTANTIN *gets up from his desk and leaves the room without a word.*

MASHA. You've made him angry. Why do you pester him, Mother?

PAULINE. I'm sorry for you, my child.

MASHA. A lot of good that does.

PAULINE. My heart's been bleeding for you, dear. Do you think I don't know what's going on? I see everything and I understand everything.

MASHA. It's just nonsense, Mother. It's only in novels you read about unhappy love. It's nothing. The only sensible thing is not to brood over it, not to sit about waiting for something to happen. If you're silly enough to fall in love with a man who doesn't care for you, then you must get over it. They've promised to transfer Simon to another district. As soon as we have moved, I shall forget all about this. I shall tear it out of my heart by the roots.

In the next room but one someone is playing a melancholy waltz.

PAULINE. That's Konstantin playing. That means he's unhappy.

MASHA [*dances a few waltz steps noiselessly*]. The chief thing, Mother, is not to see him. I wish they'd give Simon his transfer. I'd forget Konstantin in a month. All this is so damn silly!

The door on left opens. DORN *and* MEDVEDENKO *bring in* SORIN *in his wheel chair.*

MEDVEDENKO. I've six people to provide for now, and flour is two kopecks a pound.

DORN. What a life, eh?

MEDVEDENKO. It's all very well for you to laugh. You're rolling in money.

DORN. Rolling in money, am I? My dear fellow, I've been in medical practice for thirty years—damned troublesome practice, too, for there was not a moment either day or night when I could call my soul my own. Do you know how much money I saved up in all those years? Two thousand rubles. And that I spent during my recent trip abroad. No, I've nothing.

MASHA [*to her husband*]. Haven't you gone yet?

MEDVEDENKO [*guiltily*]. Well, how can I when your father won't let me have a horse?

MASHA [*with bitter annoyance, in an undertone*]. I wish I'd never set eyes on you!

The wheel chair comes to a stop in the left half of the room; PAULINE, MASHA, *and* DORN *sit down beside it;* MEDVEDENKO, *with a hangdog expression, walks off to the other side of the room.*

DORN. I see you've made a lot of changes here. You've turned this drawing room into a study.

MASHA. Konstantin finds it much more convenient to work here. He can walk out into the garden whenever he likes and do his thinking there.

The night watchman knocks.

SORIN. Where's my sister?

DORN. Gone to the station to meet Trigorin. She'll be back soon.

SORIN. I suppose if you thought it necessary to send for my sister, I must be pretty bad. [*After a moment's silence.*] How do you like that? Here I'm seriously ill and they won't give me any medicine.

DORN. Well, what would you like? Valerian drops? Bicarbonate of soda? Quinine?

SORIN. There he goes again! Bless my soul, what a trial that man is! [*Motioning with his head toward the sofa.*] Has that bed been made up for me?

PAULINE. Yes, Mr. Sorin. It's for you.

SORIN. Thank you.

DORN [*sings softly*]. "The moon is sailing across the sky at night. . . ."

SORIN. I've thought of a damned good idea for a short story for Konstantin. Now, let me see. Yes. It will be called, "The Man Who Wanted To." *L'homme qui a voulu.* When I was young, I wanted to become a writer—and I didn't. I wanted to speak well—and I spoke abominably. [*Mimicking himself.*] I mean—I mean to say—I—er—this and—er—that. Sometimes I'd go on like that for hours, till I was in a regular sweat. I wanted to marry—and I didn't. I always wanted to live in town, and here I am ending my days in the country. And so on.

DORN. You wanted to become a state councilor—and you did.

SORIN [*laughs*]. I didn't want to become that. It just happened.

DORN. You must admit that to express dissatisfaction with life at sixty-two is a bit ungenerous.

SORIN. What a damned obstinate fellow you are! Can't you understand? I don't want to die.

DORN. That's folly. According to the laws of nature, every life must come to an end.

SORIN. You talk like a man who's had his fill. You've had all you wanted and so you can be philosophic about life. It makes no difference to you. But even you will be frightened when your time comes.

DORN. The fear of death, sir, is an animal fear. We must overcome it. Only those who believe in life everlasting are consciously afraid to die, but what they are really afraid of is their sins. But you, sir, are, in the first place, an unbeliever, and in the second, what sort of sins could you have committed? Served in the Ministry of Justice for twenty-five years? That's all, isn't it?

SORIN [*laughs*]. Twenty-eight, my dear sir, twenty-eight.

Enter KONSTANTIN, *who sits down at* SORIN'S *feet.* MASHA *never takes her eyes off him.*

DORN. I'm afraid we must be interfering with Konstantin's work.

KONSTANTIN. No, not at all.

Pause.

MEDVEDENKO. May I ask you, Doctor, which city you liked best abroad?

DORN. Genoa.

KONSTANTIN. Why Genoa?

DORN. The crowds in the streets of Genoa are so wonderful. When you leave your hotel in the evening, the streets are swarming with people. You move about aimlessly in the crowd, swept along this way and that, up and down the street; you live with it, you acquire, as it were, a collective personality, and you begin to believe that there really is such a thing as a world soul, like the one Nina acted in your play. By the way, where is Nina now? Where is she and how is she getting on?

KONSTANTIN. I believe she is quite well.

DORN. I was told she was leading a rather peculiar sort of life. What's happened?

KONSTANTIN. Oh, it's a long story, Doctor.

DORN. Well, make it short then.

Pause.

KONSTANTIN. She ran away from home and went to live with Trigorin. You know that, don't you?

DORN. Yes, I know.

KONSTANTIN. She had a child. The child died. Trigorin got tired of her and went back to his old love, as might have been expected. Not that he had ever really broken with her, but being such a spineless character, he managed to make the best of both worlds. As far as I can gather, Nina's private life was a complete failure.

DORN. And her stage career?

KONSTANTIN. Her stage career was even worse, I believe. Her first appearance on the stage was at a holiday resort near Moscow. Then she went on tour in the provinces. At that time I never lost sight of her, and for some months I used to follow her about wherever she went. She always took big parts, but her acting was crude and with no taste. She'd tear a passion to tatters, and her gestures were grotesquely melodramatic. Now and then she would utter a cry in a way that showed some talent or do a death scene really well, but those were only moments.

DORN. So she has some talent after all?

KONSTANTIN. I don't know. It's hard to say. I suppose she must have. I saw her, of course, but she would not see me. I was never admitted to her hotel room. I realized how she felt, and I did not insist on meeting. [*Pause.*] Well, what more do you want to know? Later, after I got home, I had some letters from her. Warm, sensible, interesting letters. She never complained, but I could feel she was terribly unhappy. Every line showed how strained her nerves were. She seemed a little unhinged, too. Always signed herself: "The Seagull." In Pushkin's "Water Nymph," the miller calls himself a raven, and so she kept repeating in her letters that she was a seagull. She's here now.

DORN. How do you mean, here?

KONSTANTIN. She's staying at an inn in town. She's been there for five days. I nearly went to see her, but Masha has been there, and she won't see anyone. Medvedenko assured me that he saw her yesterday afternoon walking across a field a mile and a half from here.

MEDVEDENKO. Yes, that's right. She was walking toward the town. I spoke to her and asked her why she had not been to see us. She said she'd come.

KONSTANTIN. She'll never come. [*Pause.*] Her father and stepmother will have nothing to do with her. They've put men everywhere on their estate to make sure she doesn't get near the house. [*Walks away with* DORN *to the writing desk.*] How awfully easy it is to be a philosopher on paper, Doctor, and how damned difficult to be one in life.

SORIN. She was such a sweet girl!

DORN. I beg your pardon?

SORIN. I said, she was a very sweet girl. State Councilor Sorin, sir, was even in love with her for a time.

DORN. You old rake!

SHAMRAYEV *is heard laughing.*

PAULINE. They're back from the station.

KONSTANTIN. Yes, I can hear Mother.

Enter ARKADINA *and* TRIGORIN, *followed by* SHAMRAYEV.

SHAMRAYEV [*as he comes in*]. We're growing older and older, madam, falling, as they say, into the sere and yellow; but you're as young as ever. Gay clothes, vivacious, exquisite!

ARKADINA. You want to bring me bad luck, you awful man!

TRIGORIN [*to* SORIN]. How do you do, sir? Why are you always ill? That's very naughty. [*Seeing* MASHA, *joyfully.*] Masha!

MASHA. So you recognized me? [*Presses his hand.*]

TRIGORIN. Married?

MASHA. Ages ago.

TRIGORIN. Happy? [*Exchanges bow with* DORN *and* MEDVEDENKO, *then approaches* KONSTANTIN *diffidently.*] Your mother has told me that you've forgotten the past and are no longer angry with me.

KONSTANTIN *holds out his hand to him.*

ARKADINA [*to her son*]. Boris has brought you the magazine with your new story.

KONSTANTIN [*accepting the magazine, to* TRIGORIN]. Thank you. It's very kind of you.

They sit down.

TRIGORIN. Your admirers want to be remembered to you. You'd be surprised how interested they are in you in Petersburg and Moscow. They're always asking all sorts of questions about you. What you are like, how old you are, whether you are dark or fair. For some reason they all assume you can't be young. And no one knows your real name, as you write under a pseudonym. You're as mysterious as the Man in the Iron Mask.

KONSTANTIN. Will you be staying long?

TRIGORIN. I'm afraid not. I'm thinking of leaving for Moscow tomorrow. I want to finish my novel and I've promised something for a collection of short stories. As you see, it's the old, old story. [*While they are talking,* ARKADINA *and* PAULINE *place a card table in the middle of the room and open it out;* SHAMRAYEV *lights candles and sets chairs. A game of lotto is brought out.*] I'm afraid the weather hasn't been very kind to me. The wind is terrible. If it drops by morning, I'll do a bit of fishing in the lake. And I might take a walk round the park. I'd like to have a look at the place where—you remember?—your play was acted.

I've got a very good plot for a story. All I need is to refresh my memory a little: get the local color right.

MASHA [*to her father*]. Please, Father, let Simon have a horse. He's got to go home.

SHAMRAYEV [*mimicking her*]. Horse—home! [*Sternly.*] Don't you realize the horses have just been to the station? You don't want me to send them out again in this weather, do you?

MASHA. But there are other horses. [*Seeing that her father makes no reply, she just dismisses it with a wave of the hand.*] What's the use? . . .

MEDVEDENKO. I don't mind walking home, Masha. Really, I don't.

PAULINE [*sighs*]. Walk in this weather? [*Sitting down at the card table.*] Shall we start, ladies and gentlemen?

MEDVEDENKO. It's only four miles. Good-bye, dear. [*Kisses his wife's hand.*] Good-bye, Mother. [*His mother-in-law holds out her hand reluctantly for him to kiss.*] I wouldn't trouble anyone if it were not for the baby. [*Bows to the company.*] Good-bye. [*Slinks out guiltily.*]

SHAMRAYEV. He'll get there all right. He's not a general, is he?

PAULINE [*raps on the table*]. Please, ladies and gentlemen, don't let's waste time. Dinner will be served soon.

SHAMRAYEV, MASHA, *and* DORN *sit down at the card table.*

ARKADINA [*to* TRIGORIN]. During the long autumn evenings we always play lotto here. Look, it's the same old lotto Mother used to play with us when we were children. Won't you join us in a game before dinner? [*Sits down with* TRIGORIN *at the card table.*] It's not a very exciting game, but it's not bad once you get into it. [*Deals out three cards to each.*]

KONSTANTIN [*turning over the pages of the magazine*]. He's read his own story, but he hasn't even cut the pages of mine. [*Puts the magazine down on the desk, then goes to the door on left; as he passes his mother, he kisses her on the head.*]

ARKADINA. And what about you, darling?

KONSTANTIN. No, thank you, Mother. I don't feel like it, somehow. I'll go out for a stroll. [*Goes out.*]

ARKADINA. The stake is ten kopecks. Put it down for me, Doctor, will you?

DORN. Certainly, madam.

MASHA. Have you all put down your stakes? I begin. Twenty-two.

ARKADINA. Got it.

MASHA. Three.

DORN. Right.

MASHA. Have you put three down? Eight. Eighty-one. Ten.

SHAMRAYEV. Don't be in such a hurry.

ARKADINA. What a wonderful reception I had in Kharkov! My goodness, my head's still swimming!

MASHA. Thirty-four.

A melancholy waltz is played offstage.

ARKADINA. The students gave me an ovation. Three baskets of flowers, two bouquets, and look at this! [*Takes a brooch off her dress and throws it on the table.*]

SHAMRAYEV. Ah, now that is something!

MASHA. Fifty.

DORN. Did you say fifty?

ARKADINA. I wore a lovely dress. Say what you like, but I do know how to dress.

PAULINE. Konstantin's playing again. Poor boy, he's unhappy.

SHAMRAYEV. They've been going for him in the papers, I see.

MASHA. Seventy-seven.

ARKADINA. Why worry about it?

TRIGORIN. He's unlucky, poor fellow. Quite unable to find his own individual style. He writes such queer stuff, so vague. At times it almost reminds me of the ravings of a lunatic. Not one living character!

MASHA. Eleven.

ARKADINA [*looking round at* SORIN]. Are you bored, Peter, dear? [*Pause.*] He's asleep.

DORIN. State Councilor Sorin is peacefully asleep.

MASHA. Seven. Ninety.

TRIGORIN. Do you think I'd ever have written anything if I

lived in a country house like this by a lake? I'd have conquered this mania and spent all day fishing.

MASHA. Twenty-eight.

TRIGORIN. To catch a roach or a perch—that's my idea of heaven.

DORN. Well, I believe in Konstantin. There's something in him. He thinks in images; his stories are vivid, brilliant. They affect me strongly. A great pity, though, he hasn't any definite aim. He produces an impression and that's all. But you can't go far by just producing an impression. Are you glad your son's a writer, Irina?

ARKADINA. I'm ashamed to confess it, Doctor, but I haven't read any of his things. I can never find the time.

MASHA. Twenty-six.

KONSTANTIN *comes in quietly and goes to his desk.*

SHAMRAYEV [*to* TRIGORIN]. I forgot to tell you, Mr. Trigorin. We've still got something here of yours.

TRIGORIN. Oh? What?

SHAMRAYEV. You remember the seagull Konstantin shot down? You asked me to have it stuffed for you.

TRIGORIN. Did I? I don't remember. [*Thinking.*] I don't remember.

MASHA. Sixty-six. One.

KONSTANTIN [*flings open the window and listens*]. How dark it is! I wonder why I feel so restless.

ARKADINA. Konstantin, dear, shut the window. There's an awful draught.

KONSTANTIN *closes the window.*

MASHA. Eighty-eight.

TRIGORIN. My game, ladies and gentlemen.

ARKADINA [*gaily*]. Bravo, bravo!

SHAMRAYEV. Bravo!

ARKADINA. What marvelous luck that man has! He always wins. [*Gets up.*] Now let's go and have something to eat. Our great man hasn't had his lunch today. We'll carry on with the game after dinner. [*To her son.*] Leave your manuscripts, dear. Let's go in to dinner.

KONSTANTIN. I don't want to, Mother. I'm not hungry.

ARKADINA. As you wish, dear. [*Wakes* SORIN.] Dinner, Peter, dear. [*Takes* SHAMRAYEV'*s arm.*] Let me tell you about the marvelous reception I had in Kharkov.

PAULINE *puts out the candles on the table; then she and* DORN *wheel the chair. All go out by door on left;* KONSTANTIN *alone remains on the stage, sitting at his desk.*

KONSTANTIN [*preparing to write; runs through what he has written already*]. I've talked so much about new forms, but I can't help feeling that little by little I'm lapsing into clichés myself. [*Reads.*] "The poster on the wooden fence announced . . ." "A pale face framed by dark hair." Announced, framed—it's so trite! [*Crosses it out.*] I'd better begin where the hero is awakened by the patter of rain and cross out the rest. The description of the moonlight evening is too long and too precious. Trigorin has his methods all worked out. He finds it easy. The neck of a broken bottle gleaming on the milldam, the black shadow of the water wheel—and there's your moonlight night all ready for you. But I have to bring in the tremulous light, the gently twinkling stars, and the distant strains of the piano dying away in the still, scented air. Oh, it's dreadful! [*Pause.*] New forms! No! I'm coming more and more to believe that it isn't old or new forms that matter. What matters is that one should write without thinking about forms at all. Whatever one has to say should come straight from the heart. [*There is a knock at the window nearest to the desk.*] What's that? [*Looks out of the window.*] Can't see a thing. [*Opens French window and looks out into the garden.*] Someone ran down the steps. [*Calls.*] Who's there? [*Goes out into the garden; he can be heard walking rapidly on the veranda; presently he comes back with* NINA.] Nina! Nina! [*She lays her head on his breast and sobs quietly.* KONSTANTIN *is moved.*] Nina, oh, my darling, it's you—you! I had a feeling you'd come. All day I've been so restless. [*Takes off her hat and cloak.*] Oh, my darling, my precious darling, so you've come! Don't let's cry, don't!

NINA. There's someone here.

KONSTANTIN. There's no one, no one.

NINA. Lock the doors. Someone may come in.

KONSTANTIN. No one will come in.

NINA. I know your mother's here. Please, lock the doors.

KONSTANTIN [*locks the door on right; going to the door on left*]. There's no lock on this door. I'll put a chair against it. [*Puts an armchair against the door.*] Don't be afraid. No one will come in.

NINA [*scanning his face intently*]. Come, let me look at you. [*Looking round the room.*] It's warm here, nice. This used to be a drawing room. Am I very much changed?

KONSTANTIN. Yes, you are thinner and your eyes are larger. Nina, it's strange to be seeing you. Why wouldn't you let me see you? Why haven't you come all this time? I know you've been here almost a week. I've been to your hotel several times a day. I stood under your window like a beggar.

NINA. I was afraid you might hate me. Every night I dream that you look and look at me and don't recognize me. If only you knew! Ever since I got back I've been coming here to walk by the lake. I've been near the house many times, but I couldn't bring myself to go in. Let's sit down. [*They sit.*] Let's sit down and talk and talk. Oh, it's so nice here, cosy, warm. Listen to the wind! There's a passage in Turgenev: "Happy is he who on a night like this has a roof over his head, a warm corner." I'm a sea-gull—no, that's not what I was going to say. [*Rubs her forehead.*] I'm sorry. What was I saying? Oh, yes. Turgenev: "And may the Lord help all homeless wanderers." Never mind. [*Sobs.*]

KONSTANTIN. Nina, again? Nina, Nina!

NINA. It's nothing. I feel much better now. I haven't cried for two years. Late last night I went to see if our stage was still in the park. Well, it was still there. It was then that I cried for the first time in two years, and I felt much better, I felt more at ease in my mind. See? I'm not crying any more. [*Takes his hand.*] And so you're a writer now. You . . . a writer, and I . . . an actress. We're right in it now, the two of us. I used to be so happy. I'd wake up like a child, bright and early, as merry as a lark. I loved you. I dreamed of fame. And now? Early tomorrow morning I shall have to leave for Yelets. Travel third class, with peasants. And in Yelets the educated business-men will pester me with their attentions. Life is sordid.

KONSTANTIN. Why are you going to Yelets?

NINA. I've an engagement there for the whole winter. I shall have to go tomorrow.

KONSTANTIN. Oh, Nina, I cursed you, hated you, tore up your letters and photographs, but every minute I knew that I belonged to you, that my heart was yours forever. Nina, I can't stop loving you. Ever since I lost you and my stories began to appear in print, life has been unbearable. I suffered agonies, agonies. It was as if my youth were suddenly snatched away. I felt as though I were an old man of ninety. I prayed for you to come back; I kissed the ground you had walked on. Wherever I looked, I saw your face, your sweet smile, which brought sunshine into the best years of my life.

NINA [*bewildered*]. Why does he talk like this? Why does he talk like this?

KONSTANTIN. I am alone in the world, Nina. I have no one whose affection can warm me. I'm cold, cold, as though I lived in some dungeon, and everything I write is dry, harsh, gloomy. Please stay, Nina. I implore you. Or let me go with you. [NINA *quickly puts on her hat and cloak.*] Nina, why? For God's sake! [*Looks at her while she puts her things on; pause.*]

NINA. My cab is waiting for me at the gate. Don't see me out, please. I'll find my way alone. [*Bursts into tears.*] Could you give me some water, please?

KONSTANTIN [*gives* NINA *a glass of water*]. Where are you going now?

NINA. Back to town. Is your mother here?

KONSTANTIN. Yes. Uncle was taken ill on Thursday, so we wired her to come.

NINA. Why did you say that you kissed the ground on which I'd walked? I ought to be killed. [*Leans over the table.*] Oh, I'm so tired. I want to rest, rest. [*Raises her head.*] I'm a seagull. No, that's not it. I'm an actress. Yes! [*Hearing* ARKADINA *and* TRIGORIN *laughing, she listens for a minute, then runs to the door on left and looks through the keyhole.*] He is here too. [*Returning to* KONSTANTIN.] Oh, well, it doesn't matter. No, he didn't believe in the theatre. He was always laughing at my dreams, and little by little I stopped believing in them myself and lost heart. Besides, I had the worries of love to cope with; jealousy, constant anxiety for my little one. I grew trivial, cheap. I acted badly. Didn't know what to do with my hands, how to stand on the stage, how to control my voice. You've no idea what it feels like to know that you're acting badly. I'm a seagull. No, that's not it. Remember you shot a seagull? A man came along, saw it, and just for fun destroyed it. An idea for a short story. No, I don't mean that. [*Rubs her forehead.*] What was I saying? I was talking about the stage. I'm different now. I'm a real actress. I enjoy my acting. I revel in it. The stage intoxicates me. I feel that I am peerless. But now, while I've been here, I've been walking about a lot and thinking, thinking and feeling that the powers of my mind and soul are growing stronger every day. Now I know, now I understand, that in our calling, whether we act on stage or write, what matters is not fame, nor glory, nor the things I used to dream of. No. What matters is knowing how to endure, knowing how to bear your cross and have faith. I have faith, and it doesn't hurt so much now. And when I think of my calling, I'm no longer afraid of life.

KONSTANTIN [*sadly*]. You have found your path; you know which way you are going. But I'm still whirled about in a maze of dreams and images, not knowing what it is all about and who wants it. I have no faith, and I do not know what my calling is.

NINA [*listening*]. Sh-sh. . . . I'm going. Good-bye. When I am a famous actress, come and see me in a play. Promise? But now . . . [*Presses his hand.*] It's late. I can hardly stand. I'm worn out. Famished.

KONSTANTIN. Stay and have supper. Please do.

NINA. No, thank you. I can't. I can't. Don't see me off. I'll find my way alone. My cab isn't far from here. So she brought him with her? Oh, well, it doesn't matter really. When you see Trigorin, don't say anything to him. I love him. I love him more than ever. An idea for a short story. I love him. I love him passionately. I love him to distraction. How beautiful it all was before! Remember? What a bright, glorious, happy life! Our feelings for each other were like sweet, exquisite flowers. Remember? [*Recites.*] "Men, lions, eagles and peacocks, horned stags, geese, spiders, silent fish that inhabit the water, starfish, and creatures no eye can see—all living things, all living things, all living things, having completed their round of sorrow, are extinct. For thousands and thousands of years the earth has borne no living creature upon it, and this poor moon lights its lamp in vain. No longer do the cranes waken in the meadow with a cry, and in the lime groves the drone of May beetles is heard no more." [*Embraces* KONSTANTIN *impulsively and runs out through the French window.*]

KONSTANTIN [*after a pause*]. I hope no one sees her in the park and tells Mother about it. It would upset Mother. [*During the next two minutes* KONSTANTIN *tears up all his manuscripts and throws them under the desk; then he unlocks the door on right and goes out.*]

DORN [*trying to open the door on left*]. Extraordinary! The door seems to be locked. [*Enters and puts armchair in its place.*] An obstacle course!

Enter ARKADINA *and* PAULINE, *followed by* YAKOV, *carrying a tray with bottles, and* MASHA; *then* SHAMRAYEV *and* TRIGORIN.

ARKADINA. Put the claret and the beer for Mr. Trigorin on the table, please. We can have our drinks while we play. Come on, sit down everybody, please.

PAULINE [*to* YAKOV]. Bring the tea at once, Yakov.

PAULINE *lights the candles. They all sit down at the card table.*

SHAMRAYEV [*leading* TRIGORIN *to the bookcase*]. Here's the thing I was telling you about. [*Takes out the stuffed seagull.*] Your order, sir.

TRIGORIN [*gazing at the seagull*]. Don't remember. [*After a moment's thought.*] Don't remember.

A shot offstage on the right; they all start.

ARKADINA [*frightened*]. What was that?

DORN. It's nothing. I expect something must have gone off in my medicine bag. Please, don't be alarmed. [*Goes out at door on right and returns in half a minute.*] Just as I thought. A bottle of ether has gone off. [*Sings softly.*] "Once more before thee I stand enchanted . . ."

ARKADINA [*sitting down at the table*]. Heavens, what a

fright it gave me! It reminded me . . . [*Covers her face with her hands.*] Oh dear, for a moment everything went black before my eyes.

DORN [*turning over the pages of the magazine, to* TRIGORIN]. There was an article published here about two months ago, a letter from America, and I meant, incidentally, to ask you about it. [*Puts his arm round* TRIGORIN'*s waist and leads him to the footlights.*] I'm rather interested in this question. [*Lowering his voice, in an undertone.*] Get Arkadina away somehow. You see, Konstantin has shot himself.

Curtain.

UNCLE VANYA

Country Scenes in Four Acts

CHARACTERS

ALEXANDER VLADIMIROVICH SEREBRYAKOV, *a retired university professor*
YELENA ANDREYEVNA SEREBRYAKOV, *his wife, aged twenty-seven*
SOPHIA (SONIA) ALEXANDROVNA, *his daughter by his first marriage*
MARIA VASSILYEVNA VOYNITSKY, *the mother of the Professor's first wife*
IVAN PETROVICH VOYNITSKY, *her son*
MIKHAIL LVOVICH ASTROV, *a country doctor*
ILYA ILYICH TELEGIN, *an impoverished landowner*
MARINA, *an old nurse*
A LABORER
A WATCHMAN

The action takes place on SEREBRYAKOV'S *estate.*

UNCLE VANYA

ACT ONE

A garden. Part of the house can be seen, with the veranda. Under an old poplar, by the avenue of trees, a table set for tea. Benches, chairs; a guitar on one of the benches. Not far from the table, a swing. About three o'clock in the afternoon. An overcast sky.

MARINA, *a heavily built old woman, who moves with difficulty, sits by the samovar, knitting a sock;* ASTROV *is walking up and down near her.*

MARINA [*pours out a glass of tea*]. Have some tea, dear.

ASTROV [*accepts the glass reluctantly*]. Thank you. I don't feel like it, somehow.

MARINA. You wouldn't like a drop of vodka, would you?

ASTROV. No, thank you. I don't drink vodka every day, you know. Besides, it's so close. [*Pause.*] How long have we known each other, Nanny?

MARINA [*thinking it over*]. How long? Dear me, let me think. . . . You first came here—into these parts—when? . . . Sonia's mother was still living then. You visited us regularly for two winters before she died. Well, that makes eleven years to my way of reckoning. [*After a moment's thought.*] Perhaps even longer.

ASTROV. Have I changed much since then?

MARINA. Yes, I'm afraid you have, dear. You were young and handsome then, but now you look much older. And you aren't as handsome as you used to be. If you don't mind me mentioning it, you drink a lot, too.

ASTROV. Yes. . . . In ten years I've grown a different man. And the reason? Overwork, Nanny. Overwork. On my feet from morning till night. Don't know the meaning of rest. And at night I lie awake under the bedclothes in constant fear of being dragged out to a patient. Haven't had a single free day ever since I've known you. I couldn't help growing old, could I? And, besides, life here is dull, stupid, sordid. . . . This sort of life wears you down.

You're surrounded by cranks—cranks, all of them. Spend two or three years with them and gradually, without noticing it, you become a crank yourself. It's inevitable—sure as fate. [*Twisting his long mustache.*] Just look at this enormous mustache I've grown. An idiotic mustache. I've become a crank, Nanny. . . . Haven't grown stupid yet, thank God; there's nothing wrong with my brains, but my feelings have, I'm afraid, grown numb. I want nothing, I need nothing, there's no one I'm fond of—except, perhaps, you, Nanny. [*Kisses her on the head.*] I had a nurse like you when I was a little boy.

MARINA. You wouldn't like something to eat, would you?

ASTROV. No, thank you. In the third week of Lent I went to Malitskoye. There was an epidemic there. Spotted fever. In the cottages people were lying side by side on the floor. . . . Filth, stench, smoke . . . Calves, too, lying about on the floor, among the sick. And pigs. Spent a whole day there looking after the patients without sitting down and without a bite of food, and when I got back home, they wouldn't let me rest. Brought a signalman from the railway. I got him on the table and was about to operate on him when damned if he didn't go and die on me under the chloroform. It was then, when I didn't want them, that my feelings awakened and my conscience pricked me, as though I had killed him on purpose. . . . I sat down, closed my eyes like this, and thought to myself: Will those who will be living a hundred or two hundred years after us spare a thought for us who are now blazing a trail for them? Will they have a good word to say for us? No, Nanny, they won't, they won't!

MARINA. Men won't, but God will.

ASTROV. Thank you, Nanny. You spoke well.

VOYNITSKY *enters from the house; he has had a nap after lunch and looks rumpled. He sits down on a bench and straightens his fashionable tie.*

VOYNITSKY. Yes. [*Pause.*] Yes. . . .

ASTROV. Had a good sleep?

VOYNITSKY. Yes. Very. [*Yawns.*] Ever since the Professor and his wife have come to live with us, our life has been turned upside down. . . . I go to sleep at the wrong time, at lunch and dinner I eat all sorts of fancy concoctions, drink wine—all this can't be good for me. Before I hadn't a free minute to myself. Sonia and I worked like Trojans, but now only Sonia works, while I sleep, eat, and drink—it's too bad!

MARINA [*shaking her head*]. Shameful's what I call it! The Professor gets up at twelve o'clock, and the samovar's kept on the boil all morning waiting for him. Before they came, we used to have dinner at one o'clock, like everybody else, but now we're having it at about seven. The Professor spends the night reading and writing and all of a sudden at two in the morning he rings his bell. Why, what is it? Tea, if you please! Wake the servants for him. Put on the samovar. Shameful—that's what it is!

ASTROV. And are they going to stay here long?

VOYNITSKY [*whistles*]. A hundred years. The Professor has decided to stay here for good.

MARINA. Same thing now. The samovar has been on the table for the last two hours, and they've gone for a walk.

VOYNITSKY. They're coming, they're coming. Keep calm, Nanny.

Voices are heard; from the far end of the garden, returning from their walk, enter SEREBRYAKOV, YELENA, SONIA, *and* TELEGIN.

SEREBRYAKOV. Excellent, excellent . . . Wonderful scenery.

TELEGIN. Remarkable, sir.

SONIA. We'll go to the plantation tomorrow, Father. Would you like to?

VOYNITSKY. Let's have tea, ladies and gentlemen.

SEREBRYAKOV. My friends, be so kind as to send my tea up to my study. I've still some work to do today.

SONIA. I'm sure you'll like the plantation, Father.

YELENA, SEREBRYAKOV, *and* SONIA *go into the house;* TELEGIN *goes up to the table and sits down beside* MARINA.

VOYNITSKY. It's hot, close, and our eminent scholar walks about in an overcoat and galoshes, wearing gloves, and carrying an umbrella.

ASTROV. Which shows that he takes good care of himself.

VOYNITSKY. But how lovely she is, how lovely! I've never seen a more beautiful woman in my life.

TELEGIN [*to* MARINA]. Whether I drive through the fields or take a walk in the shade of the trees in the garden or look on this table, I experience a feeling of indescribable bliss! The weather is enchanting, the birds are singing, we all live in peace and harmony—what more do we want? [*Accepting a glass from* MARINA.] I'm infinitely obliged to you!

VOYNITSKY [*dreamily*]. Her eyes . . . A wonderful woman!

ASTROV. Tell us something.

VOYNITSKY [*phlegmatically*]. What do you want me to tell you?

ASTROV. Is there nothing new at all?

VOYNITSKY. Nothing. Everything's old. I'm the same as I was. Grown worse, I daresay, for I've grown lazy, do nothing, just grumble like an old fogy. My mother, the old crow, still goes about croaking about women's emancipation. She's got one foot in the grave, but she's still looking in her clever books for the dawn of a new life.

ASTROV. And the Professor?

VOYNITSKY. The Professor, as always, spends all his time from morning till late at night in his study—writing. "Racking his wits, with furrowed brow, odes, odes, odes we write, without one word of praise for them or us, our labor to requite." Pity the poor paper! He'd much better write his autobiography. What a wonderful subject! A retired professor, you understand, an old dry-as-dust, a learned minnow . . . Gout, rheumatism, migraine. Got himself an enlarged liver from jealousy and envy. . . . This minnow lives on the estate of his first wife. Lives there against his will, for he can't afford to live in the town. Always complaining of his hard luck, though as a matter of fact he's damned lucky. [*Nervously.*] Just think how lucky he is! The son of an ordinary sacristan, a divinity student, he obtained all sorts of degrees and was given a chair at a university. Now he is the son-in-law of a senator, and so on, and so on. All that is not important, though. What is important is this: The man has been lecturing and writing about art for exactly twenty-five years, and yet he doesn't know a thing about art. For twenty-five years he's been chewing over other men's ideas about realism, naturalism, and all sorts of other nonsense.

For twenty-five years he has been lecturing and writing on things intelligent people have known about for ages and stupid people aren't interested in, anyway. Which means that for twenty-five years he's been wasting his time. And yet the self-conceit of the man! What pretensions! He has retired, and not a living soul knows or cares about him. He's totally unknown, which means that for twenty-five years he's been doing somebody else out of a job. But look at him: struts about like a demigod!

ASTROV. You're jealous!

VOYNITSKY. Yes, I'm jealous! And the success he has with women! No Don Juan has ever known such amazing success! His first wife, my sister, a sweet, gentle creature, pure as this blue sky, noble, generous, a woman who had had more admirers than he has had students, loved him as only pure angels can love beings as pure and beautiful as themselves. My mother, his mother-in-law, dotes on him to this day, and he still inspires a feeling of reverential awe in her. His second wife, a beautiful, clever woman—you've just seen her—married him when he was already an old man. She sacrificed her youth, her beauty, her freedom, her brilliance to him. Whatever for? Why?

ASTROV. Is she faithful to the Professor?

VOYNITSKY. Unfortunately, yes.

ASTROV. Why unfortunately?

VOYNITSKY. Because that loyalty of hers is false from beginning to end. There's a lot of fine sentiment in it, but no logic. To be unfaithful to an old husband whose company is insufferable—that is immoral. But to try to stifle your unhappy youth and your natural feelings—that's not immoral.

TELEGIN [*in a tearful voice*]. Vanya, I don't like to hear you talk like that. Really, you know, anyone who betrays a wife or husband is a person you cannot trust, a person who might betray his country, too.

VOYNITSKY [*with vexation*]. Dry up, Waffles!

TELEGIN. No, listen, Vanya. My wife ran away from me with her lover the day after our wedding because of my unprepossessing appearance. I never swerved from my duty after that. I still love her and I'm still faithful to her. I do all I can to help her. I gave her all I had for the education of her children by the man she loved. My happiness may have been ruined, but I've still got my pride. And what about her? She's no longer young; under the influence of the laws of nature her beauty has faded; the man she loved is dead. . . . What has she got left?

Enter SONIA *and* YELENA; *a little later enter* MARIA VOYNITSKY *with a book. She sits down and reads, is given tea, and drinks it without raising her head.*

SONIA [*hurriedly to nurse*]. Some peasants have come, Nanny. Please go and talk to them. I'll see to the tea myself. [*Pours out the tea.*]

MARINA *goes out.* YELENA *takes her cup of tea and drinks, sitting on the swing.*

ASTROV [*to* YELENA]. I've really come to see your husband. You wrote to me that he was very ill—rheumatism and something else—but it seems there's nothing the matter with him at all.

YELENA. He felt very depressed last night. Complained of pains in his legs. But today he's quite all right.

ASTROV. And I've galloped like mad for twenty miles! Oh, well, never mind. It's not the first time. I can stay with you now till tomorrow and at least have a good night's sleep.

SONIA. Yes, do. It's not often you stay the night with us. I don't expect you've had dinner, have you?

ASTROV. No, as a matter of fact I haven't.

SONIA. Well, in that case you will have some dinner, too. We dine at about seven now. [*Drinks.*] The tea's cold!

TELEGIN. I'm afraid the temperature has dropped considerably in the samovar.

YELENA. Never mind, Ivan Ivanych, we'll drink it cold.

TELEGIN. Beg your pardon, ma'am, but I'm not Ivan Ivanych. I'm Ilya Ilyich—er—Ilya Ilyich Telegin, ma'am, or just Waffles, as some people call me because of my pock-marked face. I stood godfather to Sonia, and your husband knows me very well. I live here now, ma'am, on your estate. I expect—er—the fact that I dine with you every day has not escaped your notice.

SONIA. Mr. Telegin is our assistant, our right-hand man. [*Tenderly.*] Won't you have another cup, dear Godfather?

MARIA. Good heavens!

SONIA. What's the matter, Granny?

MARIA. I forgot to tell Alexander—I'm afraid it must have slipped my memory—I had a letter from Kharkov today —from Pavel Alexandrovich. He's sent me his new pamphlet.

ASTROV. Interesting?

MARIA. Yes, but rather peculiar. He flatly contradicts everything he defended seven years ago. This is terrible!

VOYNITSKY. There's nothing terrible about it. Drink your tea, Mother.

MARIA. But I want to talk!

VOYNITSKY. You've been talking for fifty years, talking and reading pamphlets. Time you put a stop to it.

MARIA. I don't know why you always seem to find my conversation disagreeable. I'm sorry, Jean, but you've changed so much during the last year that I simply cannot recognize you. You used to be a man of definite convictions, a man of enlightened views.

VOYNITSKY. Oh, yes, to be sure! I was a man of enlightened views which did not enlighten anyone. [*Pause.*] A man of enlightened views! What a cruel joke! I'm forty-seven now. Till a year ago I did my best to hoodwink myself with that pedantic stuff of yours so as not to see what real life was like. And I thought I was doing the right thing! And now, if you only knew! I can't sleep at night, so vexed, so furious, am I with myself for having so stupidly frittered away my time when I could have had everything that my age now denies me.

SONIA. Uncle Vanya, this is boring!

MARIA [*to her son*]. You seem to be putting all the blame for something on your former convictions. But it is not they that are at fault but yourself. You seem to forget that convictions are nothing by themselves, a dead letter. You should have been doing some real work.

VOYNITSKY. Some real work? Not everyone has the ability to be some sort of scribbling *perpetuum mobile* like that Herr Professor of yours.

MARIA. What are you suggesting by that, pray?

SONIA [*imploringly*]. Granny, Uncle Vanya, please!

VOYNITSKY. All right, all right. I shut up and apologize.

Pause.

YELENA. It's such a lovely day today. . . . Not too hot.

VOYNITSKY. A lovely day to hang oneself.

TELEGIN *tunes his guitar.* MARINA *walks near the house, calling a hen.*

MARINA. Chuck-chuck-chuck . . .

SONIA. What did the peasants come for, Nanny?

MARINA. Oh, always the same thing. About the wasteland again. Chuck-chuck-chuck . . .

SONIA. Which one are you calling?

MARINA. Old Speckly has gone off with her chicks. The crows might get them. . . . [*Goes out.*]

TELEGIN *plays a polka; they all listen in silence; enter a* LABORER.

LABORER. Is the Doctor here? [*To* ASTROV.] If you please, sir, they've sent for you.

ASTROV. Where from?

LABORER. From the factory.

ASTROV [*with vexation*]. Thank you very much. Well, I suppose I'd better go. [*Looks around for his cap.*] A pity, though, damn it.

SONIA. What a shame you have to go. Do come back to dinner from the factory.

ASTROV. Afraid it'll be too late. Yes, afraid so . . . afraid so . . . [*To the* LABORER.] Look here, be a good chap and fetch me a glass of vodka. [*The* LABORER *goes out.*] Where on earth . . . ? Where . . . ? [*Finds his cap.*] There's a character in one of Ostrovsky's plays who has a big mustache but little wit. . . . Well, that's me. Oh, well, good-bye, ladies and gentlemen. [*To* YELENA.] If you care to look me up sometimes with Sonia, I'd be delighted to see you. I have a little estate of about eighty acres, but if you're interested, there's a model orchard and nursery such as you wouldn't find within a thousand miles. Next to my estate is the government plantation. The forester there is old and always ill, so it's I who have really to look after things there.

YELENA. I've been told already that you make a hobby of forestry. I suppose it could be of the greatest use, but don't you think it interferes with your real work? After all, you're a doctor.

ASTROV. God alone knows what our real work is.

YELENA. Do you find it interesting?

ASTROV. Yes, it's interesting work.

VOYNITSKY [*ironically*]. Very!

YELENA [*to* ASTROV]. You're still a young man. You don't look more than, well, thirty-six or thirty-seven, and I don't suppose it's really as interesting as you say. Nothing but trees and trees. Must be awfully monotonous, I should think.

SONIA. Oh no, it's extremely interesting. Dr. Astrov is planting new forests every year, and already he's been awarded a bronze medal and a diploma. He does his best to prevent the destruction of the old forests. If you listen to him, you'll agree with him entirely. He says forests adorn the earth, teach man to understand the beautiful, and instill in him a lofty attitude of mind. Forests temper the severity of the climate. In countries with a mild climate less energy is spent in the struggle with nature, and that is why men there are beautiful, supple, more sensitive, their speech refined, and their movements graceful. Art and learning flourish there. Their outlook on life is not so gloomy, and their attitude to women is full of exquisite refinement.

VOYNITSKY [*laughing*]. Bravo, bravo! All this is charming but hardly convincing, so that [*to* ASTROV], allow me, my friend, to go on stoking my stoves with logs and building my barns of wood.

ASTROV. You can stoke your stoves with peat and build your barns of brick. Well, all right, cut down the woods if you have to, but why destroy them? The Russian forests echo with the sound of the ax, millions of trees are perishing, the homes of wild animals and birds are being laid waste, the rivers are growing shallow and running dry, exquisite scenery is disappearing forever, and all because men are too lazy and too stupid to bend down and pick up their fuel from the ground. [*To* YELENA.] Isn't that so, madam? One has to be a barbarian to burn this beauty in one's stove, to destroy what we cannot create. Man has been endowed with reason and creative powers to increase what has been given him, but so far he has not created but destroyed. There are fewer and fewer forests, the rivers are drying up, the game birds are becoming extinct, the climate is ruined, and every day the earth is becoming poorer and more hideous. [*To* VOYNITSKY.] Here you're looking at me ironically, and you don't think that what I am telling you is serious—and perhaps I really am a crank, but when I walk past the peasants' woods I saved from the ax, or when I hear a young wood planted with my own hands rustling over my head, I realize that the climate is to some extent in my power and that if in a thousand years men are happy and contented, I shall have done my bit toward it. When I plant a birch tree and then see its green branches swaying in the wind, I cannot help feeling proud and thrilled with the thought that I—[*Seeing the* LABORER, *who has brought a glass of vodka on a tray.*] However [*Drinks.*] it's time I was going. All that is, I suppose, just the talk of a crank when all is said and done. Good-bye! [*Goes toward the house.*]

SONIA [*takes his arm and goes with him*]. When are you coming again?

ASTROV. Don't know.

SONIA. Not for another month again?

ASTROV *and* SONIA *go into the house;* MARIA *and* TELEGIN *remain sitting at the table;* YELENA *and* VOYNITSKY *go toward the veranda.*

YELENA. And you, Vanya, have again been behaving disgracefully. What did you want to irritate your mother for with your talk about the *perpetuum mobile?* And at lunch today you quarreled with Alexander again. All this is so petty!

VOYNITSKY. But if I hate him!

YELENA. There's no reason why you should hate Alexander. He's just like everybody else. No worse than you.

VOYNITSKY. Oh, if you could only see your face, your movements! You're too lazy to be alive! Too lazy!

YELENA. Oh, dear, lazy and bored! Everyone's abusing my husband; everyone looks at me with compassion: Poor woman, she has an old husband! This tender concern for me—oh, how well I understand it! As Astrov said just now: You're all recklessly destroying the forests, and soon there will be nothing left on the earth. And in the same way you're recklessly destroying human beings, and thanks to you, there will be no more loyalty, no more purity, nor any capacity for self-sacrifice. Why can't you ever look with indifference at a woman if she doesn't happen to belong to you? Why? Because—again the Doctor is right—there's a devil of destruction in all of you. You don't care what happens to the forests, nor to the birds, nor to women, nor to one another.

VOYNITSKY. I don't like this sort of talk!

Pause.

YELENA. That Doctor has a tired, sensitive face. An interesting face. Sonia quite obviously finds him attractive. She's in love with him, and I quite understand her. This is the third time he's been here since we arrived, but I feel shy with him, and I have never really been nice to him or spoken to him as I should have liked. He must think I'm a detestable creature. I expect the reason why we are such good friends is that we are both such tiresome, such dull people! Tiresome! Don't look at me like that! I don't like it!

VOYNITSKY. How else can I look at you if I love you? You're my happiness, my life, my youth! I know the chances that you should return my feeling are nil, but I'm not asking for anything. All I want is to be allowed to look at you, to listen to your voice——

YELENA. Shh . . . They might hear you! [*Goes toward the house.*]

VOYNITSKY [*following her*]. Let me talk to you of my love. Don't drive me away. That alone will make me the happiest man on earth——

YELENA. This has gone far enough!

YELENA *and* VOYNITSKY *go into the house;* TELEGIN *strikes a chord on the guitar and plays a polka;* MARIA *writes something on the margin of the pamphlet.*

Curtain.

ACT TWO

A dining room in SEREBRYAKOV'S *house. Night. The watchman can be heard knocking in the garden.*

SEREBRYAKOV *is sitting in an armchair before an open window, dozing.* YELENA *is sitting beside him, also dozing.*

SEREBRYAKOV [*waking*]. Who's there? You, Sonia?

YELENA. It's me.

SEREBRYAKOV. You, darling . . . Oh, what excruciating pain!

YELENA. Your rug has fallen on the floor. [*Wraps the rug around his legs.*] I think I'd better close the window, Alexander.

SEREBRYAKOV. No, don't. I can't breathe. I dropped off just now, and I dreamed that my left leg did not belong to me. I was awakened by the frightful pain. No, it's not gout. More likely rheumatism. What's the time?

YELENA. Twenty past twelve.

Pause.

SEREBRYAKOV. Please find Batyushkov for me in the library in the morning. I believe we've got his works.

YELENA. I'm sorry, what did you say?

SEREBRYAKOV. See if you can find Batyushkov for me in the morning. I seem to remember we had his works. But why can't I breathe?

YELENA. You're tired. You haven't slept for two nights.

SEREBRYAKOV. I've been told Turgenev got angina pectoris from gout. I'm afraid I may get it, too. This damnable, disgusting old age! The devil take it. Ever since I've become ill, I've become disgusting to myself. And I shouldn't be in the least surprised if you all find me repugnant.

YELENA. You talk of your old age as though it were our fault that you are old.

SEREBRYAKOV. You most of all, I expect, must find me odious.

YELENA *gets up and sits down farther away.*

SEREBRYAKOV. And you're quite right, of course. I'm not a fool and I understand. You're a young, healthy, beautiful woman. You want to live. And I'm an old man, practically a corpse. Isn't that so? Don't I realize it? And, of course, it's stupid of me to go on living. But wait, I shall soon set you all free. I shan't last much longer.

YELENA. I can't stand it any more. For God's sake, be quiet.

SEREBRYAKOV. What it comes to is that, thanks to me, everyone is worn out, bored, wasting their youth, and only I am satisfied and enjoying life. Why, of course!

YELENA. Do be quiet! You've exhausted me!

SEREBRYAKOV. I've exhausted everyone. Of course.

YELENA [*through tears*]. It's unbearable! Tell me, what do you want of me?

SEREBRYAKOV. Nothing.

YELENA. Well, in that case be quiet. I beg you.

SEREBRYAKOV. It's a funny thing, but every time Ivan or that old idiot Maria starts talking, no one objects, everyone listens. But I've only to open my mouth, and everyone begins to feel miserable. Even my voice disgusts them. Well, suppose I am disgusting, suppose I am an egoist, a despot, but haven't I got some right to be an egoist even in my old age? Haven't I earned it? Haven't I the right, I ask, to enjoy a quiet old age, to be treated with consideration by the people around me?

YELENA. No one's disputing your rights. [*The window bangs in the wind.*] The wind is rising. I'd better close the window. [*Closes window.*] It's going to rain soon. No one disputes your rights.

A pause; the watchman in the garden knocks and sings.

SEREBRYAKOV. All my life I've worked in the interests of learning; I got used to my study, my lecture room, my colleagues, and now I find myself buried alive in this tomb, and every day I'm obliged to see stupid people and listen to their absurd talk. I want to live! I like success, I like fame, I like people to talk about me, and here—why, it's like living in exile! Every minute to be grieving for the past, watching others making a name for themselves, being afraid of death . . . I can't put up with it! I haven't the strength. And here they won't even forgive me for being old!

Enter SONIA.

SONIA. You told me to send for Dr. Astrov yourself, Father, and now that he's here, you won't see him. It's not nice. We seem to have troubled him for nothing.

SEREBRYAKOV. What good is your Astrov to me? He knows as much about medicine as I do about astronomy.

SONIA. You don't want us to send for the whole medical faculty for your gout, do you?

SEREBRYAKOV. I refuse even to talk to that crazy fellow.

SONIA. Just as you like. [*Sits down.*] I don't care.

SEREBRYAKOV. What's the time?

YELENA. Nearly one o'clock.

SEREBRYAKOV. I can't breathe. . . . Sonia, fetch me the drops from the table!

SONIA. Here you are. [*Gives him the drops.*]

SEREBRYAKOV [*irritably*]. Good Lord, not those! You can't ask anyone for anything!

SONIA. Kindly keep your temper. Some people may put up with it, but I won't. So spare me, for goodness' sake. I haven't the time, either. I have to get up early in the morning. We are haymaking.

Enter VOYNITSKY *in dressing gown with a candle.*

VOYNITSKY. There's going to be a storm. [*Lightning.*] Dear me, what a flash! Helen, Sonia, go to bed. I've come to take your place.

SEREBRYAKOV [*frightened*]. No, no! Don't leave him with me. He'll talk me to death!

VOYNITSKY. But you must let them have some rest! It's the second night they've had no sleep.

SEREBRYAKOV. Let them go to bed, but you go, too. Thank you. I implore you. In the name of our past friendship don't raise any objections. We'll talk another time.

VOYNITSKY [*with a grin*]. Our past friendship . . . Past——

SONIA. Do be quiet, Uncle Vanya.

SEREBRYAKOV [*to his wife*]. Darling, don't leave me alone with him! He'll talk me to death.

VOYNITSKY. This is really becoming absurd.

Enter MARINA *with a candle.*

SONIA. Why don't you go to bed, Nanny? It's late.

MARINA. I can't very well go to bed while the samovar's still on the table, can I?

SEREBRYAKOV. No one's asleep, everyone's exhausted. I'm the only one to have a hell of a good time.

MARINA [*goes up to* SEREBRYAKOV, *tenderly*]. What's the matter, sir? Does it hurt very badly? I've a gnawing pain in my legs, too; it keeps on gnawing something terrible. [*Puts his rug right.*] You've had this trouble for a long time, sir. I remember Sonia's mother sitting up night after night with you. She took it so much to heart, poor dear. Aye, she was very fond of you, she was. [*Pause.*] The old are just like children. They want someone to be sorry for them. But no one ever cares for the old. [*Kisses* SEREBRYAKOV *on the shoulder.*] Come along, sir, come along to bed. . . . Come along, love. I'll give you some lime tea and warm your poor legs. . . . Say a prayer for you, I will. . . .

SEREBRYAKOV [*deeply touched*]. Let's go, Marina.

MARINA. I've a gnawing pain in my legs, too, sir. Keeps on gnawing something terrible. [*Leads him away together with* SONIA.] Sonia's mother used to worry over you so much, poor dear. Cried her heart out, she did. You were only a silly little girl then, Sonia. . . . Come along, sir, come along. . . .

SEREBRYAKOV, SONIA, *and* MARINA *go out.*

YELENA. I'm absolutely worn out with him. I can hardly stand on my feet.

VOYNITSKY. You with him and I with myself. This is the third night I've had no sleep.

YELENA. There's something the matter with this house. Your mother hates everything except her pamphlets and the Professor. The Professor is in a state of exasperation: he doesn't trust me and he's afraid of you. Sonia is angry with her father, angry with me, and hasn't spoken to me for a fortnight. You hate my husband and don't conceal your contempt for your mother. I am exasperated and was about to burst into tears a dozen times today. . . . There's something the matter with this house.

VOYNITSKY. Let's drop this silly talk!

YELENA. You, Vanya, are an educated and intelligent person, and I should have thought you ought to understand that the world is not being destroyed by bandits and by fires, but by hatred, enmity, and all these petty squabblings. You ought to stop grumbling and try to reconcile everyone.

VOYNITSKY. Reconcile me to myself first! Oh, my dear—— [*Presses his lips to her hand.*]

YELENA. Don't do that! [*Takes her hand away.*] Go away!

VOYNITSKY. The rain will be over in a moment, and everything in nature will be refreshed and breathe freely. I alone will not be refreshed by the storm. Day and night the thought that my life has been hopelessly wasted weighs upon me like a nightmare. I have no past. It has been stupidly wasted on trifles. And the present frightens me by its senselessness. That's what my life and my love are like. What on earth am I to do with them? My whole inner life is being wasted to no purpose, like a ray of sunshine in a pit, and I'm running to waste, too.

YELENA. When you talk to me about your love, it somehow makes me go all dead inside and I don't know what to say. I'm sorry, but I've nothing to say to you. [*Is about to go out.*] Good night.

VOYNITSKY [*barring her way*]. Oh, if you knew how miserable I am at the thought that by my side in this very house another life is being wasted—yours! What is it you're waiting for? What damned reason prevents you from doing something? Understand, do understand. . . .

YELENA [*looks at him intently*]. Vanya, you're drunk!

VOYNITSKY. Possibly, possibly . . .

YELENA. Where's the Doctor?

VOYNITSKY. He's in there. He's staying the night with me. Possibly, possibly—everything is possible!

YELENA. Have you been drinking today again? Why do you do it?

VOYNITSKY. At least it's something like life. Don't stop me, Helen.

YELENA. You never used to drink before, and you never used to talk so much before. Go to bed. You bore me.

VOYNITSKY [*presses his lips to her hand*]. My darling—my wonderful one!

YELENA [*with vexation*]. Leave me alone, please. This really is the end! [*Goes out.*]

VOYNITSKY [*alone*]. She's gone. [*Pause.*] Ten years ago I used to meet her at my sister's. She was seventeen then and I—thirty-seven. Why didn't I fall in love with her then and propose to her? I could have married her easily. And now she would have been my wife. . . . Yes. . . . Now we should have both been awakened by the storm. She'd have been frightened by the thunder, and I'd have held her in my arms and whispered: "Don't be afraid, darling, I'm here." Oh, what wonderful thoughts! I can't help laughing, so happy do they make me feel. Oh, dear, I'm getting all confused. Why am I old? Why doesn't she understand me? Her fine phrases, her lazy morals, her absurd, her lazy ideas about the destruction of the world—oh, I hate it all so much! [*Pause.*] Oh, how I've been cheated! I adored that Professor, that miserable, gouty nonentity; I worked for him like a horse. Sonia and I squeezed the last penny out of the estate. Like greedy peasants we haggled over linseed oil, peas, curds, half starving ourselves to save up every farthing and send him thousands of rubles. I was proud of him and his learning. He was everything in the world to me. Everything he wrote, every word he uttered, seemed the highest achievement of genius to me. . . . Good God, and now? Now he has retired and now one can see what his life's work amounts to. He won't leave behind a single worthwhile page; he is a mere cipher—a soap bubble! And I have been cheated. I can see it now. Stupidly cheated. . . .

Enter ASTROV, *without waistcoat and tie; he is tipsy; he is followed by* TELEGIN *with the guitar.*

ASTROV. Play!

TELEGIN. But everyone's asleep.

ASTROV. Play, damn you! [TELEGIN *begins to play softly. To* VOYNITSKY.] All alone? No ladies? [*Arms akimbo, sings softly.*] "Dance cottage, dance stove, dance bed, I've nowhere to lay my head. . . ." You see, the storm woke me. Lovely drop of rain. What's the time?

VOYNITSKY. Hanged if I know.

ASTROV. I thought I heard Helen's voice.

VOYNITSKY. She was here a minute ago.

ASTROV. A gorgeous woman. [*Examines bottles on table.*] Medicines. Good Lord, look at these prescriptions! From Kharkov, from Moscow, from Tula . . . Every town must be sick and tired of his gout. Is he ill or is he shamming?

VOYNITSKY. He's ill.

Pause.

ASTROV. Why are you so down in the mouth today? Not sorry for the Professor, are you?

VOYNITSKY. Leave me alone.

ASTROV. Or can it be that you're in love with the Professor's wife?

VOYNITSKY. She's my friend.

ASTROV. Already?

VOYNITSKY. What do you mean—already?

ASTROV. A woman can be a man's friend in the following sequence: first a good companion, then a mistress, and only then a friend.

VOYNITSKY. What a vulgar idea!

ASTROV. Oh? Well, yes, I admit I'm growing vulgar. Besides, as you see, I'm drunk, too. As a rule, I get drunk like this once a month. When in this condition, I become as brazen and insolent as you please. I don't care a damn for anything then. I don't hesitate to do the most difficult operations, and I do them beautifully. I make the most ambitious plans for the future. At such a time I do not think of myself as a crank, and I believe that I'm being of enormous service to humanity—enormous! At such a time, too, I have my own special philosophic system, and all of you, my friends, seem to me such teeny-weeny insects—such microbes. [*To* TELEGIN.] Play, Waffles!

TELEGIN. My dear chap, I'd be only too glad to play for you, but please understand—everyone's asleep!

ASTROV. Play, damn you! [TELEGIN *plays softly.*] We really must have a drink. Come along, we've still got some brandy left. And as soon as it's daylight, we'll go to my place. All right? [*Seeing* SONIA *entering*.] Excuse my dishabille.

He goes out quickly; TELEGIN *follows after him.*

SONIA. And you have again got drunk with the Doctor, Uncle Vanya. Birds of a feather. Thick as thieves. Oh, well, he's always like that, but what made you do it? At your age it certainly doesn't suit you.

VOYNITSKY. Age has nothing to do with it. When there's no real life, one has to live on illusions. It's better than nothing, anyway.

SONIA. The hay is all cut, it rains every day, it's all rotting, and you're amusing yourself with illusions. You don't care about the estate at all any more. I'm the only one who does any work here, and I'm all done up. [*Alarmed*.] Uncle, you have tears in your eyes.

VOYNITSKY. Tears? Not at all—nonsense. You looked at me just now as your mother used to do. My dear! [*Kisses her hands and face*.] My sister, my dear, dear sister. . . . Where is she now? Oh, if she knew! If only she knew!

SONIA. What? Knew what, Uncle?

VOYNITSKY. Oh, I feel so miserable—so unhappy. . . . Never mind. . . . Later . . . I'm going. . . . [*Goes out*.]

SONIA [*knocks on the door*]. Doctor, you're not asleep, are you? Please come out for a minute.

ASTROV [*behind the door*]. One moment! [*A minute later comes out with waistcoat and tie on*.] What can I do for you?

SONIA. You can drink yourself if you don't think it's disgusting, but please don't let my uncle drink. It's bad for him.

ASTROV. All right. We won't drink any more. [*Pause*.] Not a drop. I'm going home now. By the time the horses are harnessed, it will be daylight.

SONIA. It's raining. Wait till morning.

ASTROV. The storm is passing over; we shall get only the tail end of it. I'm going. And please don't send for me to see your father again. I tell him it's gout, and he tells me it's rheumatism. I ask him to stay in bed, and he will sit in a chair. And today he refused to talk to me at all.

SONIA. He's spoiled. [*Looks in the sideboard.*] Won't you have something to eat?

ASTROV. Thank you, I think I will.

SONIA. I like to have a bite of something at night. I think we shall find something here. They say Father has been a great favorite with the ladies and they've spoiled him. Here, have some cheese.

Both of them stand at the sideboard and eat.

ASTROV. I've had nothing to eat today. I've only been drinking. Your father is a very difficult man. [*Takes a bottle from the sideboard.*] May I? There's no one here, so I can speak frankly. You know, I don't think I'd survive a month in your house. The atmosphere would stifle me. Your father can think of nothing but his gout and his books, Uncle Vanya with his depressions, your grandmother, and last but not least, your stepmother . . .

SONIA. What's wrong with my stepmother?

ASTROV. In a human being everything ought to be beautiful: face, dress, soul, thoughts. She is very beautiful, there's no denying it, but all she does is eat, sleep, go for walks, fascinate us all by her beauty and—nothing more. She has no duties. Other people work for her. Isn't that so? And an idle life cannot be pure. [*Pause.*] However, I may be too hard on her. Like your Uncle Vanya, I'm dissatisfied with life, and both of us have become a pair of old grumblers.

SONIA. Are *you* dissatisfied with life?

ASTROV. I love life in general, but I simply can't stand our Russian provincial, philistine life. I have the utmost contempt for it. And as for my own personal life, I wish to goodness I could say there was something good in it. But there's absolutely nothing. You know, if there's only one glimmer of light in the distance as you walk through the woods on a dark night, you don't notice your weariness, nor the darkness, nor the thorns and twigs that strike your face as you pass. . . . I work harder than anyone in our district, fate is forever hitting out at me and sometimes I suffer unbearably, but there's no light gleaming in the distance for me. I don't expect anything for myself any more. I dislike people and it's years since I cared for anyone.

SONIA. Not for anyone?

ASTROV. No, not for anyone. I feel a certain affection only for your old nurse—for old times' sake. There doesn't seem to be much to distinguish one peasant from another. They're all uncivilized, and they all live in squalor; and I find it difficult to get on with our educated people. They make me tired. Our dear old friends all have petty minds and petty feelings, and they don't see further than their noses. In fact, they are simply stupid. And those who are bigger and more intelligent are hysterical, given to self-analysis and morbid introspection. They whine, hate, and slander each other, sidle up to a man, look at him askance, and decide: "He has a bee in his bonnet!" or "He's a windbag!" And when they don't know what label to stick on me, they say: "He's a queer fellow, a queer one!" I like forests, that's queer; I don't eat meat, that's queer, too. They no longer have a spontaneous, pure, and objective attitude to nature or to men. None whatever! [*Is about to drink.*]

SONIA [*prevents him*]. Don't, please. I beg you. Don't drink any more.

ASTROV. Why not?

SONIA. Because you're not that kind of man. You have such natural good manners, such a nice, gentle voice, and—and more than that. You're unlike anyone I know: You are—the salt of the earth! Why do you want to be like ordinary people, who drink and play cards? Oh, please, don't do it, I beseech you! You keep on saying that people do not create but only destroy what Heaven has given them. Then why do you destroy yourself? You mustn't, you mustn't—I beseech you, I beg you!

ASTROV [*holds out his hand to her*]. I won't drink any more.

SONIA. Give me your word.

ASTROV. My word of honor.

SONIA [*presses his hand warmly*]. Thank you!

ASTROV. No more! I've come to my senses. You see I'm quite sober now, and I shall remain sober to the end of my days. [*Looks at his watch.*] And so, let's continue. I say: My time is over, it's too late for me. . . . I've grown old, I've worked too hard, I've become vulgar, all my feelings have become blunted, and I don't think I could form an attachment to anyone any more. I don't love anyone and I don't think I shall ever love anyone. The only thing that still continues to exercise the strongest possible appeal on me is beauty. I can't remain indifferent to it. I can't help feeling that if, for example, Helen wanted to, she could turn my head in one day. . . . But then that's not love. That's not affection. [*Covers his eyes with his hands and shudders.*]

SONIA. What's the matter?

ASTROV. Oh, nothing. . . . In Lent one of my patients died under chloroform.

SONIA. It's time you forgot about it. [*Pause.*] Tell me, if —if I had a friend or a younger sister, and if you were to discover that—well, that she had fallen in love with you, what would your reaction be to that?

ASTROV [*shrugging*]. Don't know. I'd give her to understand that I couldn't care for her and—er—that I had other things on my mind. Well, if I am to go, I must go now. Good-bye, my dear child, or we shall not finish till morning. [*Presses her hand.*] I'll go through the drawing room, if I may. I'm afraid your uncle will detain me. [*Goes out.*]

SONIA [*alone*]. He has said nothing to me. . . . His heart and his mind are still hidden from me, but why do I feel so happy? [*Laughs happily.*] I told him: You're fine, you're noble, you have such a gentle voice. . . . Shouldn't I have said that? His voice trembles, it is so caressing. I—I can still almost feel it in the air. But when I spoke to him about a younger sister, he didn't understand. . . . [*Wringing her hands.*] Oh, how awful it is not to be beautiful! How awful! And I know that I'm not beautiful. I know. I know. Last Sunday when people were coming out of church, I heard them talking about me, and one woman said: "She's such a good and generous girl, but what a pity she is so plain." So plain . . .

Enter YELENA.

YELENA [*opens the window*]. The storm is over. What sweet air! [*Pause.*] Where's the Doctor?

SONIA. Gone.

Pause.

YELENA. Sophia!

SONIA. Yes?

YELENA. How long are you going to be cross with me? We've done one another no harm. Why should we be enemies? Don't you think it's time we made it up?

SONIA. Oh, I've been wishing it myself. [*Embraces her.*] Don't let's be cross ever again.

YELENA. That's different.

Both are agitated.

SONIA. Has Father gone to bed?

YELENA. No, he's sitting in the drawing room. . . . You and I haven't been speaking to one another for weeks, and goodness only knows why. . . . [*Seeing that the sideboard is open.*] What's this?

SONIA. The Doctor has had something to eat.

YELENA. And there's wine, too. Come, let's drink to our friendship.

SONIA. Yes, let's.

YELENA. Out of one glass . . . [*Fills it.*] That's better. Well, so now we're friends?

SONIA. Yes. [*They drink and kiss each other.*] I've been wanting to make it up with you for so long, but I felt ashamed, somehow. [*Cries.*]

YELENA. So what are you crying for?

SONIA. Oh, nothing. I—I can't help it.

YELENA. There, there. [*Cries.*] Oh, dear, I'm so silly, I'm crying too. [*Pause.*] You're angry with me because you think I married your father for selfish reasons. But please believe me, I swear I married him for love. I fell in love with him because he was such a famous man. It was not real love. It was all so insincere, so artificial, but, you see, it seemed real to me at the time. It's not my fault. And since our marriage you have never stopped accusing me with those clever, suspicious eyes of yours.

SONIA. Well, we've made it up now, so let's forget it.

YELENA. You mustn't look at people like that—it's not at all like you. One must trust people, or life becomes impossible.

Pause.

SONIA. Tell me honestly, as a friend—are you happy?

YELENA. No, I'm not.

SONIA. I knew that. One more question. Tell me frankly. Don't you wish your husband were young?

YELENA. What a child you are! Of course, I do! [*Laughs.*] Well, ask me another one—come on.

SONIA. Do you like the Doctor?

YELENA. Yes, I like him very much.

SONIA [*laughs*]. I have such a silly look on my face, haven't I? You see, he's gone, but I can still hear his voice and his footsteps, and I have only to look at the dark window and I see his face. Do let me tell you more about it. . . . But I can't speak so loud—I feel ashamed. Let's go to my room and talk there. Do you think I'm being silly? Tell me truly. Tell me something about him.

YELENA. What do you want me to tell you?

SONIA. Well, he's clever—he knows everything—he can do everything. . . . He's not only a doctor, he plants forests, too.

YELENA. It's not only a question of forests or medicine. My dear, don't you understand? It's his genius that matters! And do you know what that means? Courage, an independent mind, bold initiative . . . He plants a tree and already he's thinking what will be the result of it in a thousand years. Already he's dreaming of the happiness of humanity. . . . Such people are rare; one must love them. . . . He drinks and occasionally he is a little coarse, but what does that matter? A gifted man cannot keep himself entirely spotless in Russia. Just think what sort of life that Doctor has! Muddy, impassable roads, frosts, blizzards, enormous distances, coarse, savage peasants, widespread poverty, diseases—how can you expect a man of forty to have kept himself sober and spotless working and struggling like that, day in, day out, and in such surroundings? [*Kisses her.*] I wish you all the happiness in the world, my dear—you deserve it. [*Gets up.*] As for me, I'm just a tiresome character—an episodic character. . . . In my music, in my husband's house, in all my love affairs —everywhere, in fact—I was only an episodic character. Come to think of it, Sonia, and I mean it seriously, I'm very, very unhappy. [*Paces up and down the stage in agitation.*] There's no happiness for me in this world—none whatever! What are you laughing at?

SONIA [*laughs, hiding her face*]. I'm so happy—so happy!

YELENA. I'd like to have some music. I'd like to play something.

SONIA. Yes, do! [*Embraces her.*] I don't feel like going to bed. Please play!

YELENA. I will in a moment. Your father isn't asleep. Music irritates him when he is not well. Go and ask him if I may. If he agrees, I'll play. Go on.

SONIA. All right. [*Goes out.*]

The watchman is knocking in the garden.

YELENA. I haven't played for ages. I'll play and cry, cry like a fool. [*In the window.*] Is that you, Yefim?

VOICE OF WATCHMAN. Yes, ma'am, it's me.

YELENA. Don't knock, the master's ill.

VOICE OF WATCHMAN. All right, ma'am. I'll be on my way now. [*Whistles.*] Here, good dog. Here, lad! Good dog!

Pause.

SONIA [*returning*]. No!

Curtain.

ACT THREE

Drawing room in SEREBRYAKOV'S *house. Three doors: one on the right, one on the left, and one in the middle. Daytime.*

VOYNITSKY *and* SONIA *seated, and* YELENA *pacing up and down the stage, deep in thought about something.*

VOYNITSKY. The Herr Professor has been so good as to express the wish that we should meet him in this room at one o'clock today. [*Looks at his watch.*] It's a quarter to one. He wishes to make some communication to the world.

YELENA. I suppose it's some business matter.

VOYNITSKY. He has no business matters. All he does is write rubbish, grumble, and be jealous. Nothing else.

SONIA [*in a reproachful voice*]. Uncle!

VOYNITSKY. All right, all right, I'm sorry. [*Motioning toward* YELENA.] Look at her: a sight for the gods! Walks about, swaying lazily. Very charming! Very!

YELENA. You sit there buzzing and buzzing all day long—aren't you sick of it? [*Miserably.*] I'm bored to death. I don't know what to do.

SONIA [*shrugging*]. There's plenty to do if you really wanted to.

YELENA. For instance?

SONIA. You could do some of the work on the estate. You could teach. You could take up nursing. Plenty of things you could do. When Father and you weren't here, Uncle Vanya and I used to go to the market and sell flour.

YELENA. I'm afraid I'm not much good at that sort of thing. And, besides, it's not interesting. It's only in serious novels that people teach and nurse sick peasants. How on earth do you expect me to become a nurse or a teacher just like that?

SONIA. Well, and I just can't understand how one can refuse to go and teach the peasants. You wait. You'll soon be doing it yourself. [*Puts her arm around her.*] Don't be bored, my dear. [*Laughing.*] You're bored, you don't know what to do with yourself, and boredom and idleness are catching. Look: Uncle Vanya does nothing but follow you about like a shadow. I've left my work and come to talk to you. Oh, dear, I've grown lazy, and the worst of it is, I can't help it! Dr. Astrov used to come and see us very rarely before—once a month. It was difficult to coax him into coming. But now he's here every day. Neglects his forests and his patients. You must be a witch.

VOYNITSKY. Why are you in such a state? [*Eagerly.*] Come, my dear, my precious one, be sensible! You have mermaid blood in your veins—well, then, be a mermaid! Let yourself go for once in your life: Fall head over ears in love with some water goblin, plunge headlong into the whirlpool with him, and leave the Herr Professor and all of us gasping with surprise.

YELENA [*angrily*]. Leave me alone! How can you be so cruel? [*Is about to go out.*]

VOYNITSKY [*barring her way*]. Come, come, my sweet, forgive me. I'm sorry. [*Kisses her hand.*] Peace.

YELENA. You must admit, you'd try the patience of a saint.

VOYNITSKY. As a sign of peace and harmony, I'll fetch you a bunch of roses. I gathered them for you this morning. Autumn roses: so sad and so lovely . . . [*Goes out.*]

SONIA. Autumn roses: so sad and so lovely . . .

Both look out of the window.

YELENA. September already. How are we going to live through the winter here? [*Pause.*] Where's the Doctor?

SONIA. In Uncle Vanya's room. He's writing something. I'm glad Uncle Vanya has gone out. I want to talk to you.

YELENA. What about?

SONIA. What about? [*Lays her head on* YELENA'*s bosom.*]

YELENA. There—there. [*Stroking her head.*] There. . . .

SONIA. I'm not beautiful.

YELENA. You have beautiful hair.

SONIA. No! [*Turning her head to have a look at herself in the looking glass.*] No! When a woman is not good-looking, she's told: You've beautiful eyes, you've beautiful hair. I've loved him for six years. I love him more than my own mother. Every minute I can hear his voice, feel the touch of his hand. I keep looking at the door and waiting—expecting him to come in. And—well—you see, I always come running to you to talk about him. Now he's here every day, but he doesn't look at me—doesn't see me. Oh, I can't bear it! I have no hope—no hope at all! [*In despair.*] Oh, God, give me strength. . . . I've been praying all night. . . . I often go up to him, begin talking to him, look into his eyes. . . . I've lost all my pride, I've lost control over my feelings. . . . I told Uncle Vanya yesterday that I loved him. Couldn't help myself. And all the servants know that I love him. Everybody knows.

YELENA. Does he?

SONIA. No. He doesn't notice me.

YELENA [*pondering*]. He's a strange man. . . . Look, why not let me talk to him? I'll be very careful—just a hint. [*Pause.*] Honestly, how much longer are you to remain uncertain? Please, let me. [SONIA *nods.*] That's settled then. It won't be difficult to find out whether he loves you or not. Don't worry, darling. Don't be uneasy. I'll sound him out so discreetly that he won't even notice it. All we have to find out is—yes or no. [*Pause.*] If it's no, then he'd better stop coming here. Don't you think so? [SONIA *nods.*] It would be much better not to see him. It's no use putting it off; I shall question him right away. He promised to show me some maps. Go and tell him that I want to see him.

SONIA [*in violent agitation*]. You will tell me the whole truth, won't you?

YELENA. Yes, of course. I can't help thinking that truth, however unpalatable, is not so dreadful as uncertainty. You can rely on me, my dear.

SONIA. Yes, yes. . . . I'll tell him that you want to see his maps. [*Is going but stops at the door.*] No, uncertainty is much better. . . . At least, there's hope. . . .

YELENA. What did you say?

SONIA. Nothing. [*Goes out.*]

YELENA [*alone*]. There's nothing worse than knowing somebody else's secret and being unable to help. [*Musing.*] He's not in love with her—that's clear—but why shouldn't he marry her? She's not good-looking, but for a country doctor at his age she'll make a splendid wife. She's so intelligent, so kind, and so pure-minded. . . . No, no, that's not the point. [*Pause.*] I understand the poor child. In the midst of so much desperate boredom, living among walking gray shadows instead of men and women, listening to vulgar talk of people whose only aim in life is to eat, drink, and sleep; and here's a man who is so unlike the others: handsome, interesting, fascinating—like a bright moon rising in the darkness. To fall under the spell of such a man, to forget oneself . . . I believe I'm a little in love with him myself. Yes, I certainly feel bored when he's not here. I find myself smiling when I think of him. That Uncle Vanya says I've mermaid blood in my veins. "Let yourself go for once in your life. . . ." Well, why not? Perhaps that's what I really ought to do. Oh, if I could fly away like a bird from you all, from your somnolent faces, from your talk—forget your very existence! But I'm timid, cowardly. . . . My conscience will not let me rest. . . . He comes here every day, and I can guess why he's here, and already I've got a guilty feeling. I'm ready to throw myself on my knees before Sonia and beg her to forgive me.

ASTROV [*comes in with a map of the district*]. How do you do? [*Shakes hands with her.*] You wanted to see my drawings?

YELENA. You promised yesterday to show me your work. Can you spare the time?

ASTROV. Yes, of course. [*Spreads the map on a card table and fastens it with drawing pins.*] Where were you born?

YELENA [*helping him*]. In Petersburg.

ASTROV. And where did you study?

YELENA. At the conservatoire.

ASTROV. I'm afraid you won't find this interesting.

YELENA. Why not? It's true I don't know anything about country life, but I've read a lot about it.

ASTROV. I have my own table in this house. In Vanya's room. When I'm thoroughly exhausted, to the point of stupor, I leave everything and run over here and amuse myself for an hour or two with this. Vanya and Sonia click away at their counting frame, and I sit beside them at my table daubing—and I feel warm and cozy, and the cricket keeps singing. . . . But I don't allow myself to indulge in this pleasant pastime too often—only once a month. [*Pointing to the map.*] Now, look here. This is a picture of our district as it was fifty years ago. The dark and light green show the forests; half of the whole area was covered with forest. Where those red lines crisscross each other over the green, elks and wild goats used to roam. . . . I show both the flora and the fauna here. On this lake there were swans, geese, and ducks and, according to the old people, "a power" of all sorts of birds, thousands of them, clouds of them flying about. Besides the villages and hamlets, as you can see, little settlements were dotted about here and there, small farms, hermitages of Old Believers, water mills. . . . There were lots of cattle and horses. It's all shown in blue. Now, for instance, in this small administrative area, comprising only a few farmsteads, there's a thick smudge of blue: There were whole droves of horses here, and every homestead had on the average three horses. [*Pause.*] Now look lower down. That's what the district was like twenty-five years ago. There was only a third of the area under timber. There are no wild goats, but there are still some elks left. The blue and green colors are paler. And so on. Now let's have a look at the third section. This is the map of the district as it is now. There are still bits of green here and there, but only in small patches. The elks, the swans, and the capercaillies have disappeared. There's no trace left of the old settlements and farms and hermitages and water mills. It is, as a matter of fact, a picture of gradual and unmistakable degeneration, which, I suppose, will be complete in another ten or fifteen years. You may say this shows the influence of civilization, that the old life must naturally give way to the new. Well, I admit that if there were highroads and railways on the site of these ruined forests, if factories, workshops, and schools were built there, the common people would be healthier, better off, and more intelligent. But there's nothing of the kind here! There are still the same swamps and mosquitoes, the same impassable roads, the same poverty, typhus, diphtheria, and the same outbreaks of fire. It is, I'm afraid, a case of degeneration as a result of too severe a struggle for existence. A degeneration caused by apathy, ignorance, and the complete absence of a sense of responsibility. The sort of thing a cold, hungry, and sick man does to save what is left of his life and to keep his children alive when he clutches instinctively and unconsciously at anything that will warm him and relieve his hunger, and destroys everything without thinking of the future. Nearly everything has been destroyed already, but nothing has as yet been created to take its place. [*Coldly.*] I can see from your face that this doesn't interest you.

YELENA. I'm afraid I understand so little about it.

ASTROV. There's nothing to understand. You're simply not interested.

YELENA. To tell the truth, I was thinking of something else. I'm sorry. I ought to put you through a little interrogation, and I'm not quite sure how to begin.

ASTROV. An interrogation?

YELENA. Yes, an interrogation, but—a rather harmless one. Let's sit down. [*They sit down.*] It concerns a certain young lady. We will talk like honest people, like good friends, without beating about the bush. We'll have our talk and then forget all about it. Agreed?

ASTROV. Agreed.

YELENA. What I want to talk to you about is my stepdaughter, Sonia. Do you like her?

ASTROV. Yes, I think highly of her.

YELENA. But do you like her as a woman?

ASTROV [*after a short pause*]. No.

YELENA. A few words more and I've done. You've noticed nothing?

ASTROV. No.

YELENA [*taking him by the hand*]. You don't love her. I can see it from your eyes. She's terribly unhappy. Please understand that and—stop coming here.

ASTROV [*gets up*]. I'm afraid I'm too old for this sort of thing. I have no time for it, anyway. [*Shrugging.*] When could I . . . ? [*He looks embarrassed.*]

YELENA. Oh, dear, what an unpleasant conversation! I'm shaking all over just as though I'd been dragging a ton weight. Well, thank goodness, that's over. Let's forget it just as though we'd never spoken about it, and please go away. You're an intelligent man. You'll understand. [*Pause.*] Goodness, I'm hot all over.

ASTROV. If you'd told me that two or three months ago, I might perhaps have considered it, but now . . . [*Shrugs.*] But if she's unhappy, then of course . . . There's one thing I can't understand, though. What made you undertake this interrogation? [*Looks into her eyes and shakes a finger at her.*] You're a sly one!

YELENA. What do you mean?

ASTROV [*laughing*]. A sly one! Suppose Sonia is unhappy. I'm quite ready to admit it, but what did you want this interrogation for? [*Not letting her speak, eagerly.*] Please don't look so surprised. You know perfectly well why I'm here every day. Why I am here and who brings me here. You know that perfectly well. You sweet little beast of prey, don't look at me like that! I'm an old hand at this sort of game.

YELENA [*bewildered*]. Beast of prey? I don't know what you're talking about.

ASTROV. A beautiful, furry little beast of prey . . . You must have your victims. Here I've dropped everything and done nothing for a whole month. I'm mad with desire for you, and you're awfully pleased about it—awfully! Well, I'm conquered. You knew that even before your interrogation. [*Folding his arms and bowing his head.*] I surrender. Come and eat me up!

YELENA. You're crazy!

ASTROV [*laughs through his teeth*]. And you are—afraid. . . .

YELENA. Oh, I'm much better and more honorable than you think, I assure you! [*Tries to go out.*]

ASTROV [*barring her way*]. I'm going away today. I won't come here again, but—[*takes her hand and looks around*] tell me: Where can we meet? Where? Tell me quickly. Someone may come in. Tell me quickly. [*Passionately.*] Oh, you're so beautiful, so lovely. . . . One kiss . . . Let me just kiss your fragrant hair. . . .

YELENA. I assure you——

ASTROV [*not letting her speak*]. Why assure me? There's no need. No need of unnecessary words . . . Oh, how beautiful you are! What lovely hands! [*Kisses her hands.*]

YELENA. That's enough—go away, please. [*Takes her hands away.*] You're forgetting yourself.

ASTROV. But tell me, tell me, where shall we meet tomorrow? [*Puts his hand around her waist.*] Darling, you see it's inevitable. We must meet.

He kisses her; at that moment VOYNITSKY *enters with a bunch of roses and stops dead at the door.*

YELENA [*not seeing* VOYNITSKY]. For pity's sake let me go. . . . [*Puts her head on* ASTROV*'s chest.*] No! [*Tries to go out.*]

ASTROV [*holding her back by the waist*]. Come to the plantation tomorrow—at two o'clock. . . . Yes? Yes? Darling, you will come, won't you?

YELENA [*seeing* VOYNITSKY]. Let me go! [*In great confusion goes to the window.*] This is awful!

VOYNITSKY [*puts down the bunch of flowers on a chair; agitatedly wipes his face and his neck with his handkerchief*]. It's all right—yes—it's quite all right. . . .

ASTROV [*trying to brazen it out*]. Not a bad day today, my dear sir. A bit cloudy in the morning, looked like rain, but it's nice and sunny now. . . . To be quite fair, we haven't had such a bad autumn this year—the winter corn isn't too bad at all. [*Rolls up the map.*] There's one thing, though: The days are drawing in. . . . [*Goes out.*]

YELENA [*goes quickly up to* VOYNITSKY]. You must see to it; you must do your utmost to arrange that my husband and I leave here today. Do you hear? Today!

VOYNITSKY [*wiping his face*]. What? Why, yes, of course. . . . I saw it all, Helen, all. . . .

YELENA [*tensely*]. You understand? I must get away from here today—today!

Enter SEREBRYAKOV, SONIA, TELEGIN, *and* MARINA.

TELEGIN. I'm afraid, sir, I am not feeling very well myself. Been out of sorts for the last two days. My head's not quite——

SEREBRYAKOV. Where are the others? I hate this house. It's a sort of labyrinth. Twenty-six huge rooms, people are all over the place, and you can never find anyone you want. [*Rings.*] Ask my mother-in-law and my wife to come here.

YELENA. I am here.

SEREBRYAKOV. Please sit down, everybody.

SONIA [*going up to* YELENA, *impatiently*]. Well, what did he say?

YELENA. I'll tell you later.

SONIA. You're trembling? You're agitated? [*Looks searchingly at her.*] I see. . . . He said he won't come here again. . . . Yes? [*Pause.*] Tell me—yes?

YELENA *nods.*

SEREBRYAKOV [*to* TELEGIN]. I don't mind ill health so much—after all, one can't help that, can one?—what I can't stand is the way people live in the country. I have a feeling as though I've dropped off the earth and landed on a strange planet. Sit down, please, all of you. Sonia! [SONIA *does not hear him; she stands with her head bowed sorrowfully.*] Sonia! [*Pause.*] She doesn't hear. [*To* MARINA.] You, too, Nurse, sit down. [*The nurse sits down, knitting a sock.*] Now, if you please, suspend, as it were, your ears on the nail of attention. [*Laughs.*]

VOYNITSKY [*agitated*]. You don't want me here, do you? Do you mind if I go?

SEREBRYAKOV. Yes, it's you I want here most of all.

VOYNITSKY. What do you want with me, sir?

SEREBRYAKOV. Sir? Why are you so cross? [*Pause.*] If I'm to blame for anything I did to you, then I'm deeply sorry.

VOYNITSKY. Drop that tone. Let's get down to business. . . . What do you want?

Enter MARIA VOYNITSKY.

SEREBRYAKOV. Ah, here's Mother-in-law at last. Now I can begin. [*Pause.*] I have invited you here, ladies and gentlemen, to announce that the Government Inspector is about to pay us a visit. However, this is no time for joking. This is a serious matter. I've invited you here to ask for your help and advice, and knowing your unfailing kindness, I feel sure that I shall receive both. I am a scholar; I have spent all my life among books and have always been a stranger to practical affairs. I cannot dispense with the assistance of people who've had practical experience of business, and I beg you, Ivan, you, Mr. Telegin, and you, Mother-in-law—er—— You see, what I'm driving at is that *manet omnes una nox;* I mean, that we are all in God's hands. . . . I'm old and ill, and so I think that the time has come when I ought to settle my worldly affairs in so far as they concern my family. My life's over. I'm not thinking of myself. But I have a young wife and an unmarried daughter. [*Pause.*] I'm afraid I cannot possibly go on living in the country. We are not made for country life. On the other hand, to live in town on the income we derive from this estate is impossible. If, for instance, we were to sell the woods, it's just an emergency measure that cannot be repeated every year. We have, therefore, to look for some means which would ensure us a permanent and more or less stable income. I have thought of one such scheme, and I shall be glad to submit it for your consideration. Leaving aside the details, I shall give you a general idea of it. Our estate returns on average not more than two per cent of its capital value. I propose to sell it. By investing the money in gilt-edged securities, we should get from four to five per cent. I think there might be even a surplus of a few thousand, which will enable us to buy a small country house in Finland.

VOYNITSKY. One moment . . . I think my ears must be deceiving me. Repeat what you've said.

SEREBRYAKOV. Invest the money in gilt-edged securities and use the surplus to buy a small country house in Finland.

VOYNITSKY. Never mind Finland. There was something else you said.

SEREBRYAKOV. I propose to sell the estate.

VOYNITSKY. Yes, that's it. You're going to sell the estate. That's rich! An excellent idea! And how do you propose to dispose of me and my old mother and Sonia here?

SEREBRYAKOV. We shall discuss it all in good time. You don't expect me to settle everything at once, do you?

VOYNITSKY. One moment. It seems to me that up to now I haven't shown a grain of common sense. Up to now I've been fool enough to believe that the estate belonged to Sonia. My father bought this estate as a dowry for my sister. Up to now I've been so naïve as to believe that our laws were not made in Turkey and that the estate passed from my sister to Sonia.

SEREBRYAKOV. Yes, the estate belongs to Sonia. I'm not disputing it. Without Sonia's consent I shouldn't dream of selling it. Besides, I'm proposing to do it for Sonia's benefit.

VOYNITSKY. It's beyond everything—beyond everything! Either I've gone stark staring mad, or——

MARIA. Don't contradict Alexander, Jean. Believe me, he knows much better than you or me what's good and what isn't.

VOYNITSKY. No, he doesn't! Give me some water, please. [*Drinks water.*] Say what you like, what you like!

SEREBRYAKOV. I don't understand why you're so upset. I don't say that my plan is ideal. If all of you think it's no good, I will not insist on it.

Pause.

TELEGIN [*looking embarrassed*]. I've always had a great reverence for learning, sir, and if I may say so, my feelings for it have a certain family connection. You see, sir, my brother's wife's brother, Konstantin Lacedaemonov, as you perhaps know, is an M.A.

VOYNITSKY. Just a moment, Waffles, we're discussing business. Wait a little—later. . . . [*To* SEREBRYAKOV.] Just ask him. The estate was bought from his uncle.

SEREBRYAKOV. Why should I ask him? Whatever for?

VOYNITSKY. The estate was bought at the prices current at the time for ninety-five thousand. My father paid only seventy thousand and twenty-five thousand remained on mortgage. Now, listen . . . this estate would not have been bought if I hadn't given up my share in the inheritance in favor of my sister, whom I loved dearly. What's more, for ten years I've worked like a horse and paid off all the mortgage.

SEREBRYAKOV. I'm sorry I ever started this discussion.

VOYNITSKY. The estate is clear of debt and is in good order thanks only to my own personal exertions. And now, when I'm beginning to get old, I'm to be kicked out of it!

SEREBRYAKOV. I don't see what you're getting at.

VOYNITSKY. I've been managing this estate for twenty-five years. I've worked and sent you the money like a most conscientious agent, and not once during all that time has it occurred to you to thank me. All that time—both when I was young and now—I've received from you five hundred rubles a year in salary, a mere pittance! And not once did it occur to you to add a ruble to it!

SEREBRYAKOV. My dear fellow, how was I to know? I'm not a practical man and I don't understand anything about these things. You could have increased your salary by as much as you pleased.

VOYNITSKY. You mean, why didn't I steal? Why don't you all despise me because I didn't steal? That would be only fair, and I shouldn't have been a pauper now!

MARIA [*sternly*]. Jean!

TELEGIN. Vanya, my dear chap, don't—don't—I'm trembling all over. . . . Why spoil good relations? [*Kisses him.*] Please, don't.

VOYNITSKY. For twenty-five years I sat like a mole within these four walls with this mother of mine. All our thoughts and feelings belonged to you alone. By day we talked about you and your work. We were proud of you. We uttered your name with reverence. We wasted our nights reading books and periodicals for which I have now the utmost contempt!

TELEGIN. Don't, Vanya, don't. . . . I can't stand it.

SEREBRYAKOV [*angrily*]. What is it you want?

VOYNITSKY. We looked upon you as a being of a higher order, and we knew your articles by heart. . . . But now my eyes are opened. I see it all. You write about art, but you don't understand a thing about art. All those works of yours which I used to love aren't worth a brass farthing! You've humbugged us!

SEREBRYAKOV. Won't any one of you stop him? I—I'm going!

YELENA. Be silent, Vanya! I insist. Do you hear?

VOYNITSKY. I won't be silent! [*Stopping in front of* SEREBRYAKOV *and barring his way.*] Wait, I haven't finished! You've ruined my life! I haven't lived! I haven't lived at all! Thanks to you I've wasted, destroyed, the best years of my life! You're my worst enemy!

TELEGIN. I can't stand it—I can't. . . . I'm going. . . . [*Goes out in great agitation.*]

SEREBRYAKOV. What do you want from me? And what

right have you to talk to me like this? Nonentity! If the estate is yours, take it! I don't want it!

YELENA. I shall run away from this hell this very minute! [*Screams.*] I can't stand it any longer!

VOYNITSKY. My life's ruined! I'm gifted, I'm intelligent, I have courage. . . . If I had lived a normal life, I might have been a Schopenhauer, a Dostoyevsky—but I'm talking nonsense! I'm going mad. Mother, I'm in despair! Mother!

MARIA [*sternly*]. Do as Alexander tells you!

SONIA [*kneels before* MARINA *and clings to her*]. Darling Nanny! Darling Nanny!

VOYNITSKY. Mother, what am I to do? Oh, never mind, don't tell me! I know myself what I must do. [*To* SEREBRYAKOV.] You will not forget me in a hurry! [*Goes out through middle door.*]

MARIA *follows him.*

SEREBRYAKOV. This is really going a bit too far! Take that lunatic away! I can't live under the same roof as he. He's always there [*Points to the middle door.*], almost beside me. . . . Let him move into the village or to the cottage on the grounds, or I will move myself, but stay in the same house as he, I cannot!

YELENA [*to her husband*]. We're leaving this place today! We must make all the arrangements at once.

SEREBRYAKOV. An utter nonentity!

SONIA [*on her knees, turns to her father, talking excitedly*]. You must be charitable, Father! Uncle Vanya and I are so unhappy! [*Restraining her despair.*] One must be charitable! Remember how, when you were younger, Uncle Vanya and Granny sat up all night translating books for you, copying your papers—they used to do it every night, every night! Uncle Vanya and I worked without a moment's rest, afraid to spend a penny on ourselves, and sent it all to you. . . . We earned our keep! I'm sorry, I seem to be saying it all wrong, but you must understand us, Father. One must be charitable!

YELENA [*agitatedly, to her husband*]. For heaven's sake, Alexander, go and talk it over with him. . . . I beg you.

SEREBRYAKOV. Very well, I'll have a talk with him. I'm not accusing him of anything, and I'm not angry. But you must admit that, to say the least, his behavior is extraordinary. Very well, I'll go to him. [*Goes out through middle door.*]

YELENA. Be gentle with him. Try to calm him. [*Follows him.*]

SONIA [*clinging to nurse*]. Darling Nanny! Darling Nanny!

MARINA. Don't worry, child. The ganders will gaggle and get tired of it. Gaggle and—get tired of it.

SONIA. Darling Nanny!

MARINA [*stroking her head*]. You're trembling as though you were out in the frost. There, there, my orphan child, the Lord's merciful. A cup of lime tea or raspberry tea, and it will pass. . . . Don't grieve, child. . . . [*Looking at the middle door, angrily.*] What a row these ganders make, drat 'em! [*A shot behind the scenes; a shriek is heard from* YELENA; SONIA *shudders.*] Oh, drat 'em!

SEREBRYAKOV [*runs staggering in, looking terrified*]. Stop him! Stop him! He's gone mad!

YELENA *and* VOYNITSKY *struggle in the doorway.*

YELENA [*trying to snatch the revolver away from him*]. Give it me! Give it me, I tell you!

VOYNITSKY. Let go of me, Helen! Let go of me! [*Freeing himself, runs in and looks for* SEREBRYAKOV.] Where is he? Ah, there he is! [*Fires at him.*] Bang! [*Pause.*] Missed him! Missed him again! [*Furiously.*] Oh, damn, damn, damn! [*Bangs revolver on the floor and sinks exhausted into a chair.*]

SEREBRYAKOV *is stunned;* YELENA *leans against the wall, almost fainting.*

YELENA. Take me away from here! Take me away—kill me. . . . I can't stay here. . . . I can't!

VOYNITSKY [*in despair*]. Oh, what am I doing! What am I doing!

SONIA [*softly*]. Darling Nanny! Darling Nanny!

Curtain.

ACT FOUR

VOYNITSKY's room; it is his bedroom as well as the estate office. At the window, a large table with account books and all sorts of papers, a bureau, cupboards, scales. A smaller table for ASTROV *with paints and drawing materials; beside it, a portfolio. A cage with a starling in it. On the wall, a map of Africa, apparently of no use to anyone. An enormous sofa covered with American cloth. On the left, a door leading to the inner rooms; on the right, a door leading into the hall; near the door on the right, a doormat for the peasants to wipe their feet on.*

An autumn evening. All is quiet. TELEGIN *and* MARINA *sit facing each other, winding wool.*

TELEGIN. You'd better hurry up, Marina, or they'll soon be calling us to say good-bye. The carriage has already been ordered.

MARINA [*trying to wind more rapidly*]. There's not much more of it left.

TELEGIN. They're going to Kharkov. They're going to live there.

MARINA. So much the better.

TELEGIN. Got scared. Helen keeps saying, "I won't stay here another hour—let's go—let's go at once. In Kharkov," she says, "we'll have a good look around and then send for our things." They're not taking many things with them. So it seems, Marina, they're not going to stay here. No, they're not. A divine dispensation of Providence.

MARINA. So much the better. All that row this morning, shooting and God knows what—the disgrace of it!

TELEGIN. Yes, a subject worthy of the brush of Ayvazovsky.

MARINA. Never seen the like of it before. [*Pause.*] We'll live again as we used to do in the old days. Tea at eight o'clock in the morning, dinner at one, and sit down to supper in the evening. Everything as it should be, like other folk, like good Christians. [*With a sigh.*] Haven't tasted noodles for a long time, sinner that I am.

TELEGIN. Aye, it's a very long time since we've had noodles for dinner. [*Pause.*] A long time. As I was walking through the village this morning, Marina, the shopkeeper shouted after me, "Hey, you, sponger!" It made me feel bad, I can tell you.

MARINA. You shouldn't take any notice of that, dear. We're all spongers in the sight of God. You, Sonia, the master—none of us sits about doing nothing. We all work hard, we do. All of us. Where is Sonia?

TELEGIN. In the garden. Still going around with the Doctor looking for Vanya. They're afraid he may lay hands on himself.

MARINA. And where's his pistol?

TELEGIN [*in a whisper*]. I've hidden it in the cellar!

MARINA [*with a smile*]. Such goings-on!

VOYNITSKY and ASTROV come in from outside.

VOYNITSKY. Leave me alone. [*To* MARINA *and* TELEGIN.] And you, too, please go. Can't I be left alone for a single hour? I hate being kept under observation.

TELEGIN. I'll go at once, Vanya. [*Goes out on tiptoe.*]

MARINA. Look at the gander: ga-ga-ga! [*Gathers her wool and goes out.*]

VOYNITSKY. Won't you go?

ASTROV. With the greatest of pleasure. I ought to have gone long ago, but I tell you again, I won't go till you give me back what you took from me.

VOYNITSKY. I took nothing from you.

ASTROV. Seriously, don't detain me. I ought to have gone hours ago.

VOYNITSKY. I tell you, I took nothing from you.

Both sit down.

ASTROV. No? Well, I'll give you a little longer, and I hope you won't mind too much if I have to use force then. We'll tie you up and search you. I'm quite serious about it, I tell you.

VOYNITSKY. As you please! [*Pause.*] To have made such a

fool of myself: fired twice and missed him! That I shall never forgive myself!

ASTROV. If you're so keen on shooting people, why don't you go and shoot yourself?

VOYNITSKY [*shrugs*]. Here I make an attempt to commit murder, and no one thinks of arresting me and putting me on trial. Which, of course, can only mean that I'm regarded as a madman. [*With a bitter laugh.*] It is I who am mad but not those who hide their stupidity, their mediocrity, and their flagrant heartlessness under the mask of a professor, a learned pundit. Those who marry old men and then deceive them under the eyes of everyone are not mad—oh no! I saw you kissing her! I saw!

ASTROV. Yes, I did kiss her, and be damned to you!

VOYNITSKY [*glancing at the door*]. No, it's the earth that's mad to let such people as you go on living on it.

ASTROV. That's a damned silly thing to say.

VOYNITSKY. Well, I'm mad, I'm not responsible for my actions, so I have a right to say damned silly things.

ASTROV. That's an old trick. You're not mad. You're just a crank. A damned fool. Before, I used to regard every crank as a mental case, as abnormal, but now I've come to the conclusion that it is the normal condition of a man to be a crank. You're quite normal.

VOYNITSKY [*buries his face in his hands*]. Oh, the shame of it! Oh, if only you knew how ashamed I am! No pain can be compared with this acute feeling of shame. [*Miserably.*] It's unbearable! [*Bends over the table.*] What am I to do? What am I to do?

ASTROV. Nothing.

VOYNITSKY. Give me something! Oh, God! I'm forty-seven; if I live to be sixty, I have another thirteen years. It's devilishly long! How can I live through those thirteen years? What shall I do? What shall I fill them with? You see [*Squeezing* ASTROV'*s hand convulsively.*], you see, if only you could live what is left of your life in some new way. Wake up on a still, sunny morning and feel that you've begun your life all over again, that all your past was forgotten, vanished like a puff of smoke. [*Weeps.*] To begin a new life . . . Tell me how to begin it—what to begin it with.

ASTROV [*with vexation*]. Oh, you and your new life! A new life indeed! My dear fellow, our position—yours and mine—is hopeless.

VOYNITSKY. Are you sure?

ASTROV. I'm quite sure of it.

VOYNITSKY. Give me something. . . . [*Pointing to his heart.*] I've a burning pain here.

ASTROV [*shouts angrily*]. Stop it! [*Softening.*] Those who will live a hundred or two hundred years after us and who will despise us for living such damned stupid, such insipid lives, will perhaps discover a way of being happy. But as for us . . . there's only one hope left for you and me, one hope only. The hope that when we are at rest in our graves, we may, perhaps, be visited by visions that will not be unpleasant. [*With a sigh.*] Yes, old man, in the whole of this district there were only two decent, intelligent men, you and I. But in the course of some ten years this humdrum, this rotten life has worn us down. Its foul vapors have poisoned our blood, and we've become just as vulgar as the rest. [*Eagerly.*] But don't you try to put me off! Give me what you took from me.

VOYNITSKY. I took nothing from you.

ASTROV. Yes, you did. You took a bottle of morphia out of my traveling medicine case. [*Pause.*] Look here, if you've really made up your mind to make an end of yourself, why don't you go into the woods and blow your brains out? But you must give me back my morphia or else people will start talking, putting two and two together, and end up by saying that I gave it to you. . . . It will be quite enough if I have to do your post-mortem. You don't suppose I shall enjoy that, do you?

Enter SONIA.

VOYNITSKY. Leave me alone.

ASTROV [*to* SONIA]. Your uncle has filched a bottle of morphia from my medicine case, and he refuses to give it back. Tell him that it's—well, not very clever. Besides, I'm in a hurry. I ought to be going.

SONIA. Uncle Vanya, did you take the morphia?

Pause.

ASTROV. He did. I'm certain of it.

SONIA. Give it back. Why do you frighten us? [*Tenderly.*] Give it back, Uncle Vanya! I may be just as unhappy as you, but I don't give way to despair. I can bear it and I shall go on bearing it until my life comes to its natural end. You must bear it, too. [*Pause.*] Give it back! [*Kisses his hands.*] Darling Uncle, give it back! [*Cries.*] You are kind; you will have pity on us and give it back, won't you? Bear up, Uncle! Bear up!

VOYNITSKY [*takes the bottle out of the table drawer and gives it to* ASTROV]. Here, take it! [*To* SONIA.] I must set to work at once, I must do something immediately, or I can't bear it—I can't. . . .

SONIA. Yes, yes, work. As soon as we've seen them off, we shall sit down to work. [*Nervously sorting out the papers on the table.*] We've let everything go. . . .

ASTROV [*puts the bottle into his medicine case and tightens the straps*]. Now I can set off.

YELENA [*enters*]. Vanya, are you here? We're leaving now. Go to Alexander. He wants to say something to you.

SONIA. Go, Uncle Vanya. [*Takes* VOYNITSKY *by the arm.*] Let's go. Father and you must make it up. It must be done.

SONIA *and* VOYNITSKY *go out.*

YELENA. I'm going away. [*Gives* ASTROV *her hand.*] Good-bye!

ASTROV. So soon?

YELENA. The carriage is at the door.

ASTROV. Good-bye.

YELENA. You promised me today that you'd go away.

ASTROV. I haven't forgotten. I'm just going. [*Pause.*] Frightened? [*Takes her hand.*] Is it so terrible?

YELENA. Yes.

ASTROV. Why not stay? What do you say? And tomorrow on the plantation . . .

YELENA. No. . . . It's all settled. . . . And I look at you so bravely because it is settled. . . . There's only one thing I'd like to ask you: Think well of me. Yes, I'd like you to respect me.

ASTROV. Oh, blast! [*Makes a gesture of impatience.*] Do stay. Please! You must realize that there's nothing in the world you can do, that you've no aim in life, that you've nothing to occupy your mind, and that sooner or later your feelings will get the better of you—that's inevitable. So don't you think it had better be here in the country and not in Kharkov or somewhere in Kursk? It's more poetical, at all events. And the autumn here is beautiful. There's the plantation and the half-ruined country houses Turgenev was so fond of describing.

YELENA. How absurd you are! I'm angry with you, but—I shall remember you with pleasure all the same. You're an interesting, an original man. We shall never meet again, so—why conceal it? I was a little in love with you—that's quite true. So let's shake hands and part friends. Don't think too badly of me.

ASTROV [*pressing her hand*]. Yes, I suppose you'd better go. [*Musingly.*] I believe you're a good, warmhearted person, and yet there seems to be something peculiar about you, something that is part of your very nature. The moment you came here with your husband, all of us, instead of going on with our work, instead of doing something, creating something, leave everything and do nothing all the summer except attend to you and your husband's gout. You and your husband have infected us all with your idleness. I became infatuated with you and have done nothing for a whole month, and all the time people have been ill and the peasants have been grazing their herds in my newly planted woods. And so, wherever you and your husband go, you bring ruin and destruction in your wake. . . . I'm joking, of course, but all the same it's—it's strange, and I'm quite sure that if you had stayed here much longer, the devastation would have been enormous. I should have been done for, but—you, too, would not have got off scot free. Well, go. *Finita la commedia!*

YELENA [*takes a pencil from his table and hides it quickly*]. I shall keep this pencil to remember you by.

ASTROV. It's all so strange. . . . We've met and, suddenly, for some unknown reason, we shall never see each other again. Everything in the world is like that. . . . But while there's no one here, before Uncle Vanya comes in with his bunch of flowers, let me—kiss you. . . . A farewell kiss. . . . Yes? [*Kisses her on the cheek.*] Well—that's the end of that.

YELENA. I wish you all the happiness in the world. [*Looking around.*] Oh, I don't care! For once in my life! [*Embraces him impulsively and both at once draw quickly away from each other.*] I must go.

ASTROV. Hurry up and go. If the carriage is ready, you'd better set off.

YELENA. I think they're coming.

Both listen.

ASTROV. *Finita!*

Enter SEREBRYAKOV, VOYNITSKY, MARIA VOYNITSKY *with a book,* TELEGIN, *and* SONIA.

SEREBRYAKOV [*to* VOYNITSKY]. Let bygones be bygones. After all that has happened, during these few hours I've been through so much and I've thought over so much that I believe I could write a whole treatise on the art of living for the benefit of posterity. I gladly accept your apologies and I apologize myself. Good-bye.

SEREBRYAKOV *and* VOYNITSKY *kiss each other three times.*

VOYNITSKY. You will receive the same amount you received before, regularly in the future. Everything will be as it used to be.

YELENA *embraces* SONIA.

SEREBRYAKOV [*kisses* MARIA VOYNITSKY'*s hand*]. Mother-in-law . . .

MARIA. Do have your photograph taken again, Alexander, and send it to me. You know how dear you are to me.

TELEGIN. Good-bye, sir. Don't forget us!

SEREBRYAKOV [*kissing his daughter*]. Good-bye. . . . Good-bye, everyone! [*Shaking hands with* ASTROV.] Thank you for the pleasure of your company. I respect your way of looking at things, your enthusiasms, your impulses, but please permit an old man like me to add just one single observation to my farewell: We must work, ladies and gentlemen, we must work! Good-bye!

SEREBRYAKOV *goes out, followed by* MARIA VOYNITSKY *and* SONIA.

VOYNITSKY [*kisses* YELENA'*s hand warmly*]. Good-bye. . . . Forgive me. . . . We shall never meet again. . . .

YELENA [*deeply moved*]. Good-bye, my dear. [*Kisses him on the head and goes out.*]

ASTROV [*to* TELEGIN]. Tell them, Waffles, to bring my carriage around, too.

TELEGIN. Certainly, my dear fellow. [*Goes out. Only* ASTROV *and* VOYNITSKY *remain.*]

ASTROV [*collects his paints from the table and puts them away in his suitcase*]. Why don't you go and see them off?

VOYNITSKY. Let them go. I—I can't. . . . I'm sick at heart. . . . I must get to work quickly. Do something—anything. . . . To work, to work! [*Rummages among the papers on the table.*]

Pause; the sound of harness bells can be heard.

ASTROV. They've gone. The Professor must be jolly glad, I shouldn't wonder. You won't get him to come here again for all the tea in China.

MARINA [*comes in*]. They've gone. [*Sits down in an easy chair and knits her sock.*]

SONIA [*comes in*]. They've gone. [*Wipes her eyes.*] I hope they'll be all right. [*To her uncle.*] Well, Uncle Vanya, let's do something. . . .

VOYNITSKY. Work, work . . .

SONIA. It seems ages since we sat at this table together. [*Lights the lamp on the table.*] I don't think there's any ink. . . . [*Takes the inkstand, goes to the cupboard, and fills it with ink.*] I can't help feeling sad now that they've gone.

MARIA [*comes in slowly*]. They've gone! [*Sits down and becomes absorbed in her pamphlet.*]

SONIA [*sits down at the table and turns the pages of the account book*]. First of all, Uncle Vanya, let's make up the accounts. We've neglected them terribly. Today someone sent for his account again. Let's start. You do one account and I another.

VOYNITSKY [*writes*]. To the account of . . . Mr. . . .

Both write in silence.

MARINA [*yawns*]. I'm ready for bye-byes. . . .

ASTROV. Silence. The pens scratch and the cricket sings. Warm, cozy . . . No, I don't want to go. . . . [*The sound of harness bells is heard.*] There's my carriage. . . . Well, my friends, all that's left for me to do is to say good-bye to you, say good-bye to my table, and—be off! [*Puts away maps in portfolio.*]

MARINA. What's the hurry? Sit down.

ASTROV. Sorry, Nanny, I can't.

VOYNITSKY [*writes*]. Balance from previous account two rubles, seventy-five kopecks. . . .

Enter LABORER.

LABORER. Your carriage is waiting, Doctor.

ASTROV. I know. [*Hands him the medicine case, the suit-case, and the portfolio.*] Take these, and mind, don't crush the portfolio.

LABORER. Very good, sir. [*Goes out.*]

ASTROV. Well, that's that. [*Goes to say good-bye.*]

SONIA. When shall we see you again?

ASTROV. Not before next summer, I'm afraid. Hardly in the winter. Naturally, if anything should happen, you'll let me know and I'll come. [*Shakes hands.*] Thank you for your hospitality and for your kindness, for everything, in fact. [*Goes up to the nurse and kisses her on the head.*] Good-bye, old woman.

MARINA. You're not going without tea?

ASTROV. I don't want any, Nanny.

MARINA. You'll have a glass of vodka, though, won't you?

ASTROV [*hesitantly*]. Thank you. Perhaps I will. . . . [MARINA *goes out. Pause.*] My trace horse is limping a bit. I noticed it yesterday when Petrushka was taking it to water.

VOYNITSKY. You must change its shoes.

ASTROV. I suppose I'd better call at the blacksmith's in Rozhdestveny. Yes, I'll have to, it seems. [*Goes up to the map of Africa and looks at it.*] I expect down there in Africa the heat must be simply terrific now. Terrific!

VOYNITSKY. I expect so.

MARINA [*comes back with a tray on which there is a glass of vodka and a piece of bread*]. Here you are! [ASTROV *drinks the vodka.*] To your health, dear. [*Makes a low bow.*] Have some bread with it.

ASTROV. No, thank you, I like it as it is. Well, good-bye all! [*To* MARINA.] Don't bother to see me off, Nanny. There's no need.

He goes out; SONIA *follows him with a candle to see him off;* MARINA *sits down in her easy chair.*

VOYNITSKY [*writes*]. February the second: linseed oil, twenty pounds. . . . February the sixteenth: linseed oil again, twenty pounds. . . . Buckwheat meal . . .

Pause. The sound of harness bells is heard.

MARINA. He's gone.

Pause.

SONIA [*comes back, puts candle on table*]. He's gone. . . .

VOYNITSKY [*counts on the abacus and writes*]. Total: fifteen —twenty-five . . .

SONIA *sits down and writes.*

MARINA [*yawns*]. Mercy on us. . . .

TELEGIN *comes in on tiptoe, sits down near the door, and softly tunes the guitar.*

VOYNITSKY [*to* SONIA, *passing his hand over her hair*]. My child, I'm so unhappy! Oh, if only you knew how unhappy I am!

SONIA. It can't be helped, we must go on living however unhappy we are! [*Pause.*] We shall go on living, Uncle Vanya. We shall live through a long, long round of days and dreary evenings; we shall bear with patience the trials which fate has in store for us; we shall work without resting for others now and in our old age, and when our time comes, we shall die without complaining; and there, beyond the grave, we shall say that we have wept and suffered, that we had a hard, bitter struggle; and God will have pity on us, and you and I, Uncle dear, will see a new life, a bright, lovely, and happy life; and we shall rejoice and shall look back with a deep feeling of tenderness and a smile upon our present sufferings and tribulations, and —and we shall rest. . . . I believe that, Uncle, fervently, passionately believe it! [TELEGIN *plays softly on the gui-*

tar.] We shall rest! We shall hear the angels; we shall see all heaven bright with many stars, shining like diamonds; we shall see all our sufferings and all earthly evil dissolve in mercy that will fill the whole world, and our life will be peaceful, tender, and sweet as a caress. I believe that, I do, I believe it. [*Wipes away his tears with her handkerchief.*] Poor, poor Uncle Vanya, you are crying. . . . [*Through tears.*] You knew no happiness in your life, but wait, Uncle Vanya, wait. . . . We shall rest. . . . [*Embraces him.*] We shall rest! [TELEGIN *plays softly;* MARIA VOYNITSKY *writes on the margin of her pamphlet;* MARINA *knits her sock.*] We shall rest!

The curtain descends slowly.

THE THREE SISTERS

A Drama in Four Acts

CHARACTERS

ANDREY SERGYEEVICH PROZOROV
NATASHA (NATALIE IVANOVNA), *his fiancée, afterwards his wife*
OLGA
MASHA (MARIA) } *his sisters*
IRINA
FYODOR ILYICH KULYGIN, *secondary school teacher, Masha's husband*
ALEXANDER IGNATYEVICH VERSHININ, *lieutenant colonel, battery commander*
NIKOLAI (NICHOLAS) LVOVICH TUSENBACH, *Baron, lieutenant*
VASILY VASILYEVICH SOLYONY, *subaltern*
IVAN ROMANOVICH CHEBUTYKIN, *army doctor*
ALEXEY PETROVICH FEDOTIK, *second lieutenant*
VLADIMIR KARLOVICH RODÉ, *second lieutenant*
FERAPONT, *an old District Council porter*
ANFISA, *a nurse, an old woman of eighty*
TWO ARMY OFFICERS
TWO MUSICIANS
A SOLDIER
A MAID

The action takes place in a provincial capital.

THE THREE SISTERS

ACT ONE

A drawing room in the Prozorovs' house, separated from a large ballroom by a row of columns. Noon; it is a bright, sunny day. In the ballroom the table is being laid for lunch.

Olga, *wearing the dark-blue regulation dress of a secondary school mistress, is correcting her pupils' exercise books, standing or walking about the room;* Masha, *in a black dress, is sitting reading a book, her hat on her lap;* Irina, *in white, stands lost in thought.*

Olga. It is just a year since Father died, on this very day, the fifth of May—your birthday, Irina. It was dreadfully cold; it was snowing then. I felt as though I'd never be able to live through it, and you were lying in a dead faint. But now a whole year has gone by and the thought of it no longer troubles us. You're wearing a white dress again; you look so radiant. [*The clock strikes twelve.*] Then, too, the clock struck twelve. [*Pause.*] I remember the military band playing at Father's funeral, and they fired a salute at the cemetery. Though Father was a general and a brigade commander, there were not many people at his funeral. It is true, it was raining then. Pouring with rain, and snowing.

Irina. Why must you talk about it?

In the ballroom, behind the columns, Baron Tusenbach, Chebutykin, *and* Solyony *appear near the table.*

Olga. It is warm today—the windows can be opened wide—but the birch trees have not opened up yet. It is eleven years since Father was given his brigade and left Moscow with us, and I distinctly remember it, the flowers were in bloom in Moscow just at this time—the beginning of May. Oh, it was so warm then, and everything was drenched in sunlight. Eleven years have passed, but I can remember everything just as if we had left Moscow only yesterday. My goodness! When I woke up this morning and saw the bright sunshine, saw the spring, my heart leapt for joy, and I felt such a passionate longing to be back home!

CHEBUTYKIN. The devil you did!

TUSENBACH. It's all nonsense, of course!

MASHA, *daydreaming over her book, whistles a tune softly.*

OLGA. Don't whistle, Masha. How can you? [*Pause.*] I suppose it's because I'm at school all day and giving private lessons in the evenings that I'm getting these constant headaches and these thoughts, just as if I were old already. And really, all these four years while I've been working at school, I've felt as though my strength and my youth were draining out of me drop by drop. And one's longing only grows stronger and stronger——

IRINA. To go to Moscow. Sell the house, finish with everything here, and leave for Moscow.

OLGA. Yes! To Moscow, as soon as possible.

CHEBUTYKIN *and* TUSENBACH *laugh.*

IRINA. I expect Andrey will get a professorship soon, and anyway, he's not going to live here much longer. The only difficulty is poor old Masha.

OLGA. Masha could come to Moscow every year and stay with us the whole summer.

MASHA *continues whistling her tune softly.*

IRINA. Let's hope everything will turn out all right. [*Looking through the window.*] Oh, what a beautiful day! I don't know why I'm feeling so calm and serene. This morning I remembered that it was my birthday, and suddenly, I felt so happy. I remembered our childhood, when Mother was still alive, and such wonderful, exciting thoughts kept flashing through my mind. Oh, what wonderful thoughts!

OLGA. You look so radiant today, more beautiful than ever. Masha, too, is beautiful. Andrey would have been quite good-looking if he had not put on so much weight. It doesn't suit him at all. As for me, I've grown old and a lot thinner. I suppose it must be because I get so irritable with the girls at school. Today I'm free, I'm at home, I haven't got a headache, and I feel much younger than I did yesterday. After all, I'm only twenty-eight, except that . . . Everything's all right, everything's as God wills, but I can't help thinking that if I'd got married and stayed at home all day, things would be much better. [*Pause.*] I'd have loved my husband.

TUSENBACH [*to* SOLYONY]. What nonsense you talk. I'm sick of listening to you. [*Going into the drawing room.*] I forgot to tell you: Vershinin, our new battery commander, will be calling on you today. [*Sits down at the piano.*]

OLGA. Will he? He'll be very welcome.

IRINA. Is he old?

TUSENBACH. No, not really. Forty—forty-five at most. [*Plays quietly.*] An excellent fellow by all accounts. Not a fool by any means, that's certain. He talks too much, though.

IRINA. Is he an interesting man?

TUSENBACH. Yes, I should say so, only, you see, he's got a wife, a mother-in-law, and two little girls. You see, it's his second wife. He calls on people and tells everybody that he has a wife and two little girls. He's sure to tell you all about it too. His second wife, I'm sorry to say, does not seem to be altogether in her right mind. She wears a long plait like a girl, uses very grandiloquent language, philosophizes, and every now and again tries to commit suicide. Apparently, to annoy her husband. I'd have left a woman like that long ago, but he puts up with it. Just keeps on complaining.

SOLYONY [*enters the drawing room with* CHEBUTYKIN]. I can only lift half a hundredweight with one hand, but with two I can lift a hundredweight and more. From which I infer that two men are not only twice but three or even more times as strong as one.

CHEBUTYKIN [*reads a newspaper while he comes in*]. For falling hair: one hundred and thirty grains of naphthalene in half a bottle of spirits. Dissolve and apply daily. [*Writes it down in his notebook.*] Let's make a note of it. [*To* SOLYONY.] Well, as I was saying, you put a cork into the bottle and pass a glass tube through the cork. . . . Then you take a pinch of ordinary powdered alum——

IRINA. Doctor, dear Doctor . . .

CHEBUTYKIN. What is it, child? What is it, my sweet?

IRINA. Tell me, why am I so happy today? I feel as if I

were sailing under a wide blue sky and great white birds were flying above me. Why is it? Why?

CHEBUTYKIN [*kissing both her hands, tenderly*]. My lovely white bird . . .

IRINA. When I awoke this morning, got up, and washed, I suddenly felt as if everything in the world had become clear to me and I knew how one ought to live. Dear Doctor, I do know everything. Man must work, work by the sweat of his brow, whoever he might be. That alone gives a meaning and a purpose to his life, his happiness, his success. Oh, how wonderful it must be to be a laborer who gets up with the sun and breaks stones by the roadside, or a shepherd, or a schoolmaster teaching children, or a driver of a railway engine. Why, dear Lord, better be an ox or a horse and go on working than a young woman who wakes up at twelve, drinks her coffee in bed, then takes two hours dressing. . . . Oh, how dreadful! Just as one is sometimes dying for a drink of water on a hot day, so I'm dying to do some work. Why, if I don't get up early and do some real work, don't count me among your friends any more, Doctor.

CHEBUTYKIN [*tenderly*]. I won't. . . . I won't. . . .

OLGA. Father trained us to get up at seven o'clock. That is why Irina always wakes up at seven and lies in bed at least till nine thinking about all sorts of things. How serious she looks! [*Laughs.*]

IRINA. You're so used to looking on me as a little girl that it seems strange to you when I look serious.

TUSENBACH. Dear Lord, how well I understand this craving for work. I've never done a stroke of work in my life. I was born in Petersburg, a cold and idle city. My family never knew what work or worry meant. I remember when I came home from the military academy, a valet would pull off my boots while I swore at him. My mother looked at me with adoring eyes and was genuinely surprised when people looked differently at me. I was carefully guarded against work. But they did not succeed in shielding me from it. Not now, at any rate. The time is coming when something huge is about to overwhelm us. A mighty hurricane is on the way; it is quite near already, and soon, very soon, it will sweep away from our society idleness, complacency, prejudice against work, and effete boredom.

I shall work and in another twenty-five or thirty years everyone will work—everyone!

CHEBUTYKIN. I won't work.

TUSENBACH. You don't count.

SOLYONY. In twenty-five years you won't be alive, thank goodness. In a couple of years you will die of a stroke or I'll lose my temper and put a bullet through your head, dear fellow. [*Takes a perfume bottle from his pocket and sprinkles the perfume over his chest and hands.*]

CHEBUTYKIN [*laughs*]. It's quite true, I have never done a stroke of work in my life. As soon as I left the university, I never lifted a finger or opened a book. I only read newspapers. [*Takes another newspaper out of his pocket.*] Here. . . . I know from the papers that we had—er—a critic by the name of Dobrolyubov, but I'm hanged if I know what he wrote about. [*Somebody is heard knocking on the floor from downstairs.*] There. . . . Somebody wants to see me downstairs. They're calling me to come down. I'll be back in a moment. I won't be long. [*Goes out hurriedly, stroking his beard.*]

IRINA. He's up to something.

TUSENBACH. I think so too. He's gone out looking very solemn. I expect he's gone to fetch your present.

IRINA. Oh, how I hate it!

OLGA. Yes, it is dreadful. He's always doing something silly.

MASHA. "For he on honey-dew hath fed, and drunk the milk of Paradise . . . and drunk the milk of Paradise" . . .* [*Gets up, humming quietly.*]

OLGA. You're not very cheerful today, Masha. [MASHA *puts on her hat, humming.*] Where are you off to?

* The first two lines from Pushkin's epilogue to *Ruslan and Lyudmila*, which Masha repeats once in Act One and twice in Act Four, are full of magic and mystery. But this is only apparent in the original and can only be perceived by a Russian audience familiar with those lines from childhood. When translated—"A green oak tree grows at the bay/A golden chain is on that oak tree"—they are meaningless. To convey this feeling, I have chosen two lines from Coleridge's "Kubla Khan," which are not only similar but which also help us to understand Masha's sudden attraction to the idealist Vershinin, the man who fits most closely the two lines of Coleridge's poem. It must be remembered that Masha knew English and would most certainly have read "Kubla Khan" in the original—not that it matters, since the important thing is to convey Masha's feeling and mood to an English-speaking audience [D.M.].

MASHA. Home.

IRINA. Strange!

TUSENBACH. Leave a birthday party!

MASHA. What does it matter? I'll be back this evening. Good-bye, darling. [*Kisses* IRINA.] Let me wish you again good health and happiness. In the old days, when Father was alive, we always used to have thirty or forty army officers at our birthday parties—such noisy parties—but today we've only got a man and a half, and it's quiet as a desert. I'm going home. I'm in a terribly melancholy mood today. I'm not feeling particularly cheerful, so you'd better not listen to me. [*Laughing through tears.*] We'll have a good talk later; good-bye for now, my darling. I'll just go somewhere, anywhere.

IRINA [*displeased*]. Really, Masha . . .

OLGA [*tearfully*]. I understand you, Masha.

SOLYONY. If a man philosophizes, it is philosophistry or, if you like, sophistry, but if a woman or a couple of women start philosophizing, it's all a lot of nonsense.

MASHA. What do you mean by that, you frightfully terrible man?

SOLYONY. Nothing. "He had barely time to catch his breath before the bear was hugging him to death."

MASHA [*to* OLGA, *crossly*]. Don't howl.

Enter ANFISA *and* FERAPONT *with a cake.*

ANFISA. This way, my good man. Come in, your boots are clean. [*To* IRINA.] From the District Council, my dear, from Mr. Protopopov, Mikhail Ivanovich, a cake.

IRINA. Thank you. Please give my thanks to Mr. Protopopov. [*Accepts the cake.*]

FERAPONT. Beg pardon, miss?

IRINA [*louder*]. Thank Mr. Protopopov.

OLGA. Nanny, let him have some pie. Go to the kitchen, Ferapont. They'll give you some pie there.

FERAPONT. Beg pardon, miss?

ANFISA. Come along, my dear, come along. [*Goes out with* FERAPONT.]

MASHA. I don't like this Protopopov, this Mikhail Potapych or Ivanych.* I don't think we ought to invite him.

IRINA. I didn't invite him.

MASHA. Good!

Enter CHEBUTYKIN, *followed by a* SOLDIER *carrying a silver samovar; murmurs of astonishment and displeasure.* OLGA *covers her face.*

OLGA. A samovar! This is awful. [*Goes through to the ballroom and stands by the table.*]

IRINA. Oh, dear Doctor, what are you doing?

TUSENBACH [*laughs*]. I told you so.

MASHA. Really, Doctor, you ought to be ashamed of yourself!

CHEBUTYKIN. My dear sweet darlings, you're all I have, you're all I hold most dear in the world. I shall soon be sixty. I'm an old man, a lonely, worthless old man. There's nothing good about me except my love for you. But for you I'd have been dead long ago. [*To* IRINA.] My darling, my dear child, I've known you ever since you were born. . . . I used to carry you about in my arms. . . . I loved your mother. . . .

IRINA. But why such expensive presents?

CHEBUTYKIN [*through tears, crossly*]. Expensive presents! Don't talk such nonsense. [*To his orderly.*] Take the samovar to the other room. [*In a mocking voice.*] Expensive presents!

The orderly carries off the samovar to the ballroom.

ANFISA [*crossing the drawing room*]. My dears, a strange colonel's just arrived. He's taken off his coat and he's coming here now. Irina, darling, be nice and polite to him. [*Going out.*] Lunch should have been served long ago. Dear, oh dear. [*Goes out.*]

TUSENBACH. I expect it must be Vershinin. [*Enter* VERSHININ.] Lieutenant Colonel Vershinin!

* The Russian folk name for a bear is Mishka, a pet name for Mikhail. Sometimes the patronymic Potapych is added. Protopopov's name is also Mikhail, but his patronymic is Ivanovich or Ivanych. Coming so quickly after Solyony's quotation from Krylov's fable *The Peasant and the Bear*, the indirect implication is that the bear Protopopov will, in the end, bring about the ruin of the three sisters [D.M.].

VERSHININ [*to* MASHA *and* IRINA]. Allow me to introduce myself: Vershinin. I'm very glad, very glad indeed, that I'm here at last. Good heavens, how you've grown!

IRINA. Please be seated. We're very pleased to meet you, Colonel.

VERSHININ [*gaily*]. I'm so glad, so glad! But surely there are three of you, three sisters. I remember three little girls. I don't remember their faces, but I do remember that your father, Colonel Prozorov, had three little girls. I remember it very well. I saw them myself. How time flies! Dear me, how time flies!

TUSENBACH. The Colonel comes from Moscow.

IRINA. Moscow? Are you from Moscow?

VERSHININ. Yes, I'm from Moscow. Your father was a battery commander there, and I served in the same brigade. [*To* MASHA.] I seem to remember your face a little.

MASHA. I'm afraid I don't remember you.

IRINA. Olga! Olga! [*Shouts into the ballroom.*] Olga! Do come! [OLGA *comes in from the ballroom.*] Lieutenant Colonel Vershinin, it seems, comes from Moscow.

VERSHININ. So you're Olga, the eldest sister. And you are Maria. And you are Irina, the youngest.

OLGA. You are from Moscow?

VERSHININ. Yes. I went to school in Moscow and began my service in Moscow. I served there a long time and, at last, was put in command of the battery here. Moved over here, as you see. I do not really remember you. All I remember is that there were three sisters. I remember your father very well. I have only to shut my eyes to see him just as if he were alive. I used to visit you in Moscow.

OLGA. I thought I remembered everybody, and suddenly——

VERSHININ. My Christian name is Alexander.

IRINA. Alexander Vershinin, and you are from Moscow. What a surprise!

OLGA. You see, we're going to live there.

IRINA. Yes, we hope to be there by autumn. It's our home town. We were born there, in Old Basmanny Street.

OLGA *and* IRINA *laugh happily.*

MASHA. Meeting a fellow townsman so unexpectedly . . .

[*With animation.*] Now I remember! Do you remember, Olga, there was someone we used to call "the lovesick major"? You were only a lieutenant then and you were in love with some girl, and for some reason, we all nicknamed you, teasingly, the major.

VERSHININ [*laughs*]. That's it! That's it! The lovesick major. Yes, that's true.

MASHA. In those days you only had a mustache. Oh, you look so much older! [*Through tears.*] So much older!

VERSHININ. Yes, when I was known as the lovesick major, I was still a young man. I was in love then. It's different now.

OLGA. But you haven't got a single gray hair. You've grown older, but you're not an old man.

VERSHININ. I shall soon be forty-three all the same. How long have you been away from Moscow?

IRINA. Eleven years. What are you crying for, Masha? You funny girl! [*Through tears.*] You're making me cry, too.

MASHA. I'm all right. And where did you live?

VERSHININ. In Old Basmanny Street.

OLGA. We lived there, too.

VERSHININ. At one time I lived in German Street. I used to walk from there to the barracks. I had to cross a gloomy bridge on the way; the water rushed so noisily under it. It made me feel so sad when walking over it by myself. [*Pause.*] But here you have such a fine river, such a wonderful river!

OLGA. Yes, only it's very cold. It's very cold here and lots of mosquitoes.

VERSHININ. You can't mean it! Here you have such a good, healthy climate, a real Russian climate. Forest, river . . . and also birch trees. Dear, modest birch trees. I love them more than any other trees. It's nice living here. The only trouble is that the railway is fifteen miles from the town. Nobody seems to know why.

SOLYONY. I know why. [*Everyone looks at him.*] Because, you see, if the railway station had been near, it wouldn't have been far, and if it's far, it's because it is not near.

An awkward silence.

TUSENBACH. He likes his little joke, our subaltern does.

OLGA. Now I've remembered you, too. Yes, I remember you.

VERSHININ. I knew your mother.

CHEBUTYKIN. She was a good woman, God rest her soul.

IRINA. Mother was buried in Moscow.

OLGA. At the Novo-Devichy Monastery.

MASHA. I'm afraid I'm already beginning to forget what she looked like. I suppose people will forget us, too, in the same way. They'll forget us.

VERSHININ. Yes, they'll forget us. Such is our fate. There's nothing we can do about it. The things that seem great, significant, and very important to us now will no more seem to be important with time. [*Pause.*] It's certainly an interesting fact that we cannot possibly know today what in the future will be considered great and important or just pitiful and ridiculous. Didn't the discoveries of Copernicus or, let's say, Columbus appear to be useless and ridiculous at the time, while some utter drivel, written by some crank, seemed to be a great truth? It is quite likely that our present life, to which we are so reconciled, will in time appear to be odd, uncomfortable, stupid, not particularly clean and, perhaps, even immoral.

TUSENBACH. Who knows? Perhaps our life will be considered to have been noble and will be remembered with respect. We no longer have tortures, public executions, or invasions, and yet there's still so much suffering.

SOLYONY [*in a high-pitched voice*]. Cluck, cluck, cluck . . . No need to scatter corn for the Baron; just give him a chance to philosophize.

TUSENBACH. Leave me alone, will you? [*Changes his place.*] It's getting rather boring.

SOLYONY [*in a high-pitched voice*]. Cluck, cluck, cluck.

TUSENBACH [*to* VERSHININ]. The suffering that we can observe today—and there's so much of it—still shows a certain degree of moral uplift already achieved by our society.

VERSHININ. Yes, yes, of course.

CHEBUTYKIN. You've said just now, Baron, that our present life may be called great, but people are rather small all the same. [*Gets up.*] Look how small I am. It's to console me that one should say my life is noble. That, I think, is clear enough.

A violin is played offstage.

MASHA. It's our brother, Andrey, playing the violin.

IRINA. He's our scholar. We hope he's going to be a professor one day. Father was a soldier, but his son has chosen an academic career.

MASHA. It was Father's wish.

OLGA. We've been teasing him today. We think he's a little in love.

IRINA. With a local girl. She'll be calling on us today, most probably.

MASHA. Heavens, how she dresses! It isn't that her clothes are not pretty or fashionable—they are just pathetic. Some sort of bright-yellow frock with a cheap-looking fringe and a red blouse. Her cheeks, too, are so thoroughly scrubbed! Andrey's not in love with her. I just can't believe it, for after all, he has got some taste. I think he's simply doing it to tease us. It's his way of playing the fool. I was told yesterday that she was going to marry Protopopov, the chairman of our District Council. And an excellent thing, too! [*Calls through the side door.*] Andrey, come here! Just for a moment, dear!

Enter ANDREY.

OLGA. This is my brother, Andrey.

VERSHININ. Vershinin.

ANDREY. Prozorov. [*Wipes the perspiration from his face.*] Are you our new battery commander?

OLGA. Just imagine! Colonel Vershinin comes from Moscow.

ANDREY. Oh? Well, I congratulate you. Now my sisters won't give you any peace.

VERSHININ. I'm afraid your sisters must be getting bored with me already.

IRINA. Look what a lovely picture frame Andrey gave me today for a present. [*Shows him the frame.*] Andrey made it himself.

VERSHININ [*looks at the picture frame and is at a loss for what to say*]. Well, yes, er—it's—er—very nice.

IRINA. And the little frame over the piano, he made that too.

ANDREY *waves his hand deprecatingly and walks off.*

OLGA. He's our scholar, he plays the violin, and he's very clever with a fret saw. In fact, he can turn his hand to anything. Andrey, don't go. He has a habit of always walking away. Come here!

MASHA *and* IRINA *take* ANDREY *by the arms and, laughing, lead him back.*

MASHA. Come on, come on!

ANDREY. Leave me alone, please.

MASHA. You are funny! We used to call Colonel Vershinin the lovesick major, and he was never cross.

VERSHININ. Not a bit!

MASHA. I'd like to call you the lovesick fiddler!

IRINA. Or the lovesick professor.

OLGA. He's fallen in love. Our little Andrey has fallen in love. [*Clapping her hands.*] Bravo, bravo! Encore! Our little brother is in love!

CHEBUTYKIN [*walks up behind* ANDREY *and puts his arms round* ANDREY'*s waist*]. It's for love alone that nature has created us. [*Bursts out laughing, still holding his newspaper in his hand.*]

ANDREY. All right, that'll do, that'll do. [*Wipes his face.*] I didn't sleep a wink last night, and I'm not in top form now, as they say. I read till four o'clock and then went to bed. But it was no use. I kept thinking of one thing and another, and before I knew it, it was dawn and the sun was simply pouring into the bedroom. I'd like to translate a book from the English during the summer while I'm here.

VERSHININ. Do you read English?

ANDREY. Yes. Father, may he rest in peace, inflicted education upon us. This may sound silly and ridiculous, but I must confess all the same that since he died, I've been putting on weight. Indeed, in one year I've put on so much weight that it is as if my body had burst its bonds. But thanks to Father, my sisters and I know French, German, and English, and Irina knows Italian too. But at what a cost!

MASHA. To speak three languages in this town is an unnecessary luxury. Why, it isn't even a luxury, just a sort of useless appendage, like a sixth finger. We know a lot that is of no use to us.

VERSHININ. Good heavens! [*Laughs.*] You know a lot that is of no use to you. Well, I can't help thinking there's no town so dull and depressing that an intelligent, educated man would be superfluous in it. Let's assume that among the hundred thousand people in this town, who, I admit, are rather backward and coarse, there are only three people like you. It stands to reason that you won't be able to convert the uneducated mass of people around you. In the course of your life you will have to make some concessions till, little by little, you'll get lost among these hundred thousand people. Life will stifle you, but nevertheless, you'll not be lost entirely. Neither will you be gone without having exerted some influence. Six people like you will perhaps emerge after you, then twelve, and so on, until the majority of people will have become like you. In two or three hundred years life on earth will become incredibly beautiful and marvelous. Man must have a life like that. If it isn't here yet, he must be able to anticipate it, to wait for it, to dream about it, and to prepare himself for it. To make sure of it, he must be able to see and know more than his father and grandfather did. [*Laughs.*] And you're complaining that you know a lot that's of no use to you.

MASHA [*takes off her hat*]. I'm staying to lunch.

IRINA [*with a sigh*]. Really, someone should have written it all down.

ANDREY *has left the room, unnoticed.*

TUSENBACH. You say that many years later life on earth will be beautiful, marvelous. That's true. But to take part in it now, even at a distance, one has to prepare for it, one has to work for it.

VERSHININ [*gets up*]. Yes, indeed. What a lot of flowers you have here! [*Looks round.*] And what a wonderful place you have here! I envy you. All my life I've lived in lodgings with two chairs, a sofa, and a stove which invariably smoked. What I missed most in my life were just such flowers. [*Rubs his hands.*] Oh, well, what's the use? . . .

TUSENBACH. Yes, we must work. I expect you must be thinking: That German has grown sentimental all of a sudden. But I assure you, I'm a Russian. I don't speak a word of German. My father was Greek Orthodox.

Pause.

VERSHININ [*walks up and down the stage*]. I often wonder what it would be like if we were to start our life all over again. Consciously, I mean. If our first life had been, as it were, only a rough copy and our second, a fair one. In that case, I believe, every one of us would first of all do his utmost not to repeat himself. At least he would create a different environment for himself. He would, for instance, get himself a place like this, with flowers and full of light. I have a wife and two little girls. My wife, I'm sorry to say, always complains of being poorly, and so on and so forth. Well, if I had to start my life all over again, I wouldn't get married. . . . No, certainly not.

Enter KULYGIN, *wearing his schoolmaster's uniform.*

KULYGIN [*walks up to* IRINA]. Congratulations, dear sister. Many happy returns. I wish you good health and everything a girl of your age ought to have. Let me, finally, present you with this book. [*Hands her a book.*] It's the history of our school for the last fifty years. I wrote it myself. Not a very important book, I admit. I wrote it in my spare time, having nothing better to do, but you should read it all the same. Good morning, ladies and gentlemen. [*To* VERSHININ.] Let me introduce myself: Kulygin, a master at the secondary school here, civil servant of the seventh rank. [*To* IRINA.] In this book you'll find a list of all the pupils who've completed their course of studies at our school during the last fifty years. *Feci, quod potui, faciant meliora potentes.* [*Kisses* MASHA.]

IRINA. But you gave me this book as a present last Easter!

KULYGIN [*laughs*]. Impossible! In that case, you'd better give it back to me, or, no, better give it to the Colonel. Please take it, Colonel. You may read it one day when you've nothing better to do.

VERSHININ. Thank you. [*Is about to leave.*] I'm very glad to have made your acquaintance.

OLGA. You're not going, are you? Please don't.

IRINA. You must stay and have lunch with us. Please!

OLGA. Please do.

VERSHININ [*bows*]. I seem to have dropped in on your birthday party. I'm sorry, I didn't know. I didn't offer you my congratulations.

He goes into the ballroom with OLGA.

KULYGIN. Today, ladies and gentlemen, is Sunday, a day of rest. Let us, therefore, rest. Let us make merry, each in accordance with his age and position in life. The carpets will have to be taken up for the summer and put away till the winter. Must sprinkle them first with Persian powder or naphthalene. The Romans were healthy because they knew how to work and how to rest. They had *mens sana in corpore sano*. Their life ran according to well-established forms. Our headmaster says the main thing in life is form. Anything that loses its form is finished. It's the same in our everyday life. [*Takes* MASHA *by the waist, laughing.*] Masha loves me. My wife loves me. The curtains, too, will have to be put away with the carpets. . . . Today I'm happy. I'm in excellent spirits. [*To* MASHA.] At four o'clock, my dear, we have to be at the headmaster's. An outing has been arranged for the teachers and their families.

MASHA. Sorry, I'm not going.

KULYGIN [*chagrined*]. My dear Masha, why not?

MASHA. We'll talk about it later. . . . [*Crossly.*] Oh, very well, I'll come. Only leave me alone, please. [*Walks away.*]

KULYGIN. Afterwards, we'll spend the evening at the headmaster's. Though in bad health, that man is doing his best to be sociable above all. A fine man, a man of irreproachable conduct. A most excellent man! After the staff meeting yesterday he said to me: "I'm tired, my dear fellow, I'm tired!" [*Looks at the clock, then at his watch.*] Your clock is seven minutes fast. Yes, he said: "I'm tired."

Someone is playing a violin offstage.

OLGA. Please, gentlemen, lunch is served. We're having a pie!

KULYGIN. My dear, dear Olga, yesterday I began work in the morning and I went on working till eleven o'clock at night. I felt tired, but now I feel happy. [*Goes into the ballroom to the table.*] Dear Olga!

CHEBUTYKIN [*puts the newspaper in his pocket and combs his beard*]. A pie! Excellent!

MASHA [*to* CHEBUTYKIN, *sternly*]. Mind, no drinking today. Do you hear? It's bad for you.

CHEBUTYKIN. Don't worry. That's all in the past. Haven't had a real drinking bout for two years. [*Impatiently.*] Good Lord, my dear woman, does it really matter so much?

MASHA. All the same, don't you dare to drink. Don't you dare! [*Crossly, but trying not to be overheard by her husband.*] Damnation, another boring evening at the headmaster's.

TUSENBACH. If I were you, I wouldn't go. Very simple.

CHEBUTYKIN. Don't go, my dear.

MASHA. Don't go, indeed! A damnable, unbearable life! [*Goes into the ballroom.*]

CHEBUTYKIN [*goes after her*]. Oh, well!

SOLYONY [*crossing into the ballroom*]. Cluck, cluck, cluck.

TUSENBACH. Chuck it, my dear sir, chuck it!

SOLYONY. Cluck, cluck, cluck . . .

KULYGIN [*gaily*]. Your health, Colonel. I'm a schoolmaster and quite at home here. I'm Masha's husband. She's a good woman, a very good woman.

VERSHININ. I'll have some of that dark brandy. [*Drinks.*] Your health! [*To* OLGA.] I feel so happy here.

Only IRINA *and* TUSENBACH *remain in the drawing room.*

IRINA. Masha's in a bad mood today. She got married when she was eighteen. At the time, her husband seemed the most intelligent man in the world to her. It's quite different now. He's the most good-natured but not the most intelligent of men.

OLGA [*impatiently*]. Andrey, are you coming?

ANDREY [*offstage*]. One moment. [*Comes in and goes to the table.*]

TUSENBACH. What are you thinking about?

IRINA. Oh, I don't know. I don't like that Solyony of yours. I'm afraid of him. He says such stupid things.

TUSENBACH. He's a strange fellow. I'm both sorry for him and annoyed by him. Mostly sorry, though. I think he's shy. When I'm alone with him, he's very intelligent and friendly, but in company he's coarse, a bully. Don't go in there yet, not before they've taken their places at the table. Stay with me a little longer. What are you thinking about? [*Pause.*] You're twenty, and I'm not yet thirty. Think of the years we still have ahead of us. A long succession of days, each one full of my love for you.

IRINA. Please don't talk to me about love.

TUSENBACH [*not listening*]. I've such a passionate yearning for life, for work, to strive for a better life. This yearning has, somehow, become mingled with my love for you, Irina. And as luck would have it, you are beautiful, and life also seems to be so beautiful to me. What are you thinking about?

IRINA. You say life is beautiful. Yes, but what if it only seems so? Our life, I mean the lives of us three sisters, has not been particularly beautiful so far. Life has stifled us like a weed. I'm sorry, I'm crying. I mustn't. [*Quickly dries her eyes and smiles.*] We must work, work! We are so unhappy and we have so gloomy a view of life because we don't know the meaning of work. We're the children of people who despised work.

NATASHA *enters wearing a pink dress with a green belt.*

NATASHA. Good heavens, they've gone in to lunch already. . . . I'm late. . . . [*Throws a quick glance at herself in the mirror and tidies herself up.*] My hair's all right, I think. [*Catches sight of* IRINA.] Dear Irina, congratulations. [*Gives her a hearty and drawn-out kiss.*] You've got such a lot of visitors. . . . I feel quite shy. . . . Good morning, Baron.

OLGA [*enters the drawing room*]. Ah, here you are, Natasha. How are you, my dear? [*They kiss.*]

NATASHA. Congratulations. You've such a lot of people. I'm so shy.

OLGA. It's all right, they're all old friends. [*Lowering her voice, startled.*] My dear, you're wearing a green belt. That's not nice.

NATASHA. Is it unlucky?

OLGA. No, it simply doesn't suit you and—er—it looks a little out of place.

NATASHA [*in a tearful voice*]. Does it? It isn't really green, you know. It's not shiny. [*Follows* OLGA *into the ballroom.*]

They are all seated at the table now. The drawing room is empty.

KULYGIN. I wish you a good husband, Irina. It's time you got married.

CHEBUTYKIN. I wish you a nice fiancé too, Natasha.

KULYGIN. Natasha has one already, I believe.

MASHA [*strikes her plate with a fork*]. Let's have a glass of vodka! Oh, life is sweet! What the hell!

KULYGIN. You get Unsatisfactory for conduct.

VERSHININ. The brandy's excellent. What is it made of?

SOLYONY. Cockroaches!

IRINA [*tearfully*]. Ugh! How disgusting!

OLGA. We're having roast turkey for dinner tonight and an apple turnover for dessert. Thank goodness I'm at home all day today. At home this evening, too. Please, you must all come this evening.

VERSHININ. I'd like to come this evening if you don't mind.

IRINA. Please do.

NATASHA. They don't stand on ceremony here.

CHEBUTYKIN. It's for love alone that nature has created us. [*Laughs.*]

ANDREY [*crossly*]. Do stop it, please. Haven't you had enough?

FEDOTIK *and* RODÉ *come in with a large basket of flowers.*

FEDOTIK. We're late. They're having lunch.

RODÉ [*in a loud voice and speaking with a burr*]. Are they? Good Lord, yes, so they are!

FEDOTIK. One moment, please. [*Takes a snapshot.*] One! One moment. [*Takes another snapshot.*] Two! That's all!

They pick up the basket and go into the ballroom, where they get a noisy reception.

RODÉ [*in a loud voice*]. Congratulations! I wish you all the best. Gorgeous weather today. Simply marvelous! I spent the morning with some schoolboys. I'm a gym teacher, you see.

FEDOTIK. You can move now, Irina, if you want to. [*Taking a snapshot.*] You look lovely today. [*Takes a humming top out of his pocket.*] Here, by the way, is a top. It's got a marvelous hum.

IRINA. It's lovely!

MASHA. "For he on honey-dew hath fed, and drunk the milk of Paradise . . . and drunk the milk of Paradise." [*Tearfully.*] Why do I go on saying this? Can't get these lines out of my head.

KULYGIN. Thirteen at table!

RODÉ [*in a loud voice*]. Surely you're not superstitious, are you?

Laughter.

KULYGIN. When there are thirteen at table, it means that some of them are in love. It isn't you, Doctor, by any chance?

Laughter.

CHEBUTYKIN. I'm an old sinner, but why Natasha should look so embarrassed, I simply fail to understand.

Loud laughter; NATASHA *runs out of the ballroom into the drawing room.* ANDREY *follows her.*

ANDREY. Please don't pay any attention to them. Don't go, I beg you.

NATASHA. I feel so ashamed. I don't know what I've done wrong, and they're just laughing at me. I know it wasn't nice to leave the table like that, but I couldn't help it. [*Covers her face with her hands.*]

ANDREY. Oh, my dear, I beg you, I implore you, don't be upset. I assure you, they're only joking. They don't mean to be unkind. My dear, my dear, my beautiful one! They're all nice, kindly people, and they're fond of us both. Come over to the window. They won't be able to see us there. [*Looks round.*]

NATASHA. I'm so unaccustomed to being with people!

ANDREY. Oh, you're so young, so beautifully, so splendidly

young. My dear, my darling, don't be upset. Do believe me. Believe me. I'm so happy, my heart is so full of love, of ecstasy. . . . No, they can't see us from here, they can't! Why, why did I fall in love with you? When did I fall in love with you? Oh, I don't understand anything. My darling, my beautiful darling, my pure one, be my wife! I love you, I love you as I've never loved anyone before.

A *kiss.*

TWO ARMY OFFICERS *come in, and seeing the kissing couple, stop dead in amazement.*

Curtain.

ACT TWO

The scene is the same as in Act One.

It is eight o'clock in the evening. Offstage, in the street, the sound of an accordion can be heard faintly. The stage is dark. Enter NATASHA *in a dressing gown, carrying a candle; she walks across the stage and stops at the door leading to* ANDREY'S *room.*

NATASHA. What are you doing, Andrey dear? Reading? Never mind, I just . . . [*Goes to another door, opens it, looks into the room, and shuts it again.*] Must make sure there's no light left burning.

ANDREY [*comes in with a book in his hand*]. What's the matter, Natasha?

NATASHA. I'm just making sure no one's left a light burning. It's Shrovetide—carnival time. The servants are all excited, and you have to make sure that nothing goes wrong. About twelve o'clock last night I walked through the dining room and there was a candle burning on the table. I just couldn't find out who lit it. [*Puts the candle down.*] What's the time?

ANDREY [*glancing at the clock*]. A quarter past eight.

NATASHA. Olga and Irina are out. Not back yet. Still hard at work, poor darlings. Olga at her staff meeting and Irina at the telegraph office. [*Sighs.*] Only this morning I said to your sister: "You must take more care of yourself, Irina darling." But she won't listen to me. A quarter past eight, did you say? I'm afraid our Bobby isn't at all well. Why is he so cold? Yesterday he had a temperature. But today he's quite cold. I'm so worried.

ANDREY. Don't worry, Natasha. The boy's well enough.

NATASHA. All the same I think we ought to be more careful about his diet. I'm worried. I'm told, dear, that after nine o'clock some carnival dancers are expected to come. I wish they weren't coming, Andrey dear.

ANDREY. Well, I don't know. They've been invited, you see.

NATASHA. This morning our little darling woke up, looked at me, and suddenly smiled. He must have recognized me. "Good morning, Bobby," I said. "Good morning, darling." He laughed. Little children understand, oh, they understand everything. You don't mind, Andrey dear, if I tell the servants not to let the dancers in, do you?

ANDREY [*hesitatingly*]. But you see, it depends on my sisters. It's their house.

NATASHA. Yes, it's their house, too, I suppose. I'll tell them. They're so kind. [*Going.*] I've ordered sour milk for supper. The doctor says you ought to eat nothing but sour milk. Otherwise you won't lose weight. [*Stops.*] Bobby is so cold. I'm afraid his room is too cold. We'll have to find him another room. At least till the warm weather. Now, Irina's room is just right for a baby. It's dry and it gets the sun all day long. I must tell her. She could share Olga's room for the time being. She isn't at home during the day, anyway. She only sleeps here. [*Pause.*] Darling, why don't you say anything?

ANDREY. Oh, I was thinking. . . . There's nothing really I can say, is there?

NATASHA. Now, what is it I wanted to tell you? Oh, yes. Ferapont from the District Council is here. He wants to see you about something.

ANDREY [*yawns*]. Tell him to come in. [NATASHA *goes out.* ANDREY, *bending over the candle she has left behind, is reading his book. Enter* FERAPONT. *He wears a shabby old overcoat with a turned-up collar. His ears are muffled.*] Hello, old man. What have you got to tell me?

FERAPONT. The chairman, sir, sent you this register and a document. Here. [*Hands him the book and the document.*]

ANDREY. Thanks. That's all right. But why are you so late? It's past eight o'clock.

FERAPONT. Beg pardon, sir?

ANDREY [*louder*]. I said you've come too late. It's after eight.

FERAPONT. That's right, sir. When I came here, it was still daylight, but they wouldn't let me in. "The master's busy," they said. Well, I thought to myself, if he's busy, he's busy. I'm in no hurry. [*Thinking that* ANDREY *has asked him about something.*] Beg pardon, sir?

ANDREY. Nothing. [*Turning over the pages of the book.*] Tomorrow's Friday. There's no Council meeting, but I'll go to the office just the same. Do some work. It's boring at home. [*Pause.*] My dear old fellow, how strangely everything changes, how life deceives us! Today I picked up this book (I was bored, you see, had nothing else to do), my old university lectures, and I couldn't help laughing. Good Lord, I am the secretary of the District Council, the Council of which Protopopov is chairman. I am a secretary, and the most I can hope for is to become a member of the Council. A member of a District Council! I, who used to dream every night that I was a professor of Moscow University, a famous scholar of whom the whole of Russia was proud.

FERAPONT. Afraid I don't know, sir. Don't hear very well.

ANDREY. If you could hear properly, I might not be talking to you like this. I must talk to someone. My wife does not understand me, and for some reason I'm afraid of my sisters. I'm afraid they will ridicule me, make me feel ashamed of myself. . . . I don't drink and I don't like going to pubs, but, my dear fellow, you can't imagine how I'd love to spend some time in Moscow at Testov's or at The Great Moscow Restaurant.

FERAPONT. Did you say Moscow, sir? A contractor was telling us at the office the other day about some business-men who were eating pancakes in Moscow. One of them who ate forty pancakes apparently died. Was it forty or fifty? Don't remember.

ANDREY. You sit in a big dining room of a restaurant in Moscow—you know no one, no one knows you, but you don't feel you're a stranger. Here, you know everyone and everyone knows you, but you're a stranger, a stranger. . . . A stranger and all alone.

FERAPONT. Beg pardon, sir? [*Pause.*] The same contractor said—he may be lying for all I know—that a rope is stretched right across the whole of Moscow.

ANDREY. Whatever for?

FERAPONT. Don't know, sir. The contractor said so.

ANDREY. Nonsense! [*Reads his book.*] Have you ever been to Moscow?

FERAPONT [*after a pause*]. No, sir. It wasn't God's will that I should go there, I suppose. [*Pause.*] Can I go now, sir?

ANDREY. You can go. Good-bye. [FERAPONT *goes out.*] Good-bye. [*Reads.*] Come and take the papers tomorrow morning. You can go now. [*Pause.*] He's gone. [*A bell rings.*] Yes, that's how it is. . . . [*Stretches and goes back to his room unhurriedly.*]

Offstage the nurse is heard singing while rocking the baby to sleep. Enter MASHA *and* VERSHININ. *While they talk, a maid lights a lamp and candles.*

MASHA. I don't know. [*Pause.*] I don't know. Habit's very important, of course. For instance, after Father died, it took us a long time to get accustomed to the idea that we no longer had any orderlies. But quite apart from habit, it seems to me that what I said was only fair. It may be different somewhere else, but in our town the military are the most well-bred and well-educated people.

VERSHININ. I'm thirsty. I'd love some tea.

MASHA [*glancing at the clock*]. They'll bring it in presently. I was married off when I was eighteen. I was afraid of my husband because he was a schoolmaster and I had only just left school. He seemed to me frightfully learned, clever, and distinguished. Now, I'm sorry to say, it's quite different.

VERSHININ. Yes, I see.

MASHA. But I'm not discussing my husband. I've got used to him. You see, there are so many coarse, ill-bred, uneducated people among the civilians. Coarseness upsets and offends me. I suffer physically in the presence of a man who is not sufficiently well-bred, not sufficiently delicate or courteous. I suffer agonies in the company of schoolmasters, my husband's colleagues.

VERSHININ. Well, yes, but I should have thought that in a town like this there was nothing to choose between a civilian and an army officer. It really makes no difference. Listen to any educated person here, civilian or army officer, and he'll tell you that he's sick and tired of his wife or his family or his estate or his horses. A Russian is particularly susceptible to high thinking, but tell me, why does he aim so low in life? Why?

MASHA. Why?

VERSHININ. Why is he sick and tired of his children, sick and tired of his wife, and why are his wife and children sick and tired of him?

MASHA. You're not in a very good mood today, are you?

VERSHININ. Perhaps not. I haven't had any lunch today. I haven't had anything to eat since morning. One of my daughters is not very well, and when my little girls are not well, I'm worried. You see, I can't help thinking that it's my fault they have such a mother. Oh, if you'd seen her today—what a nonentity! We started quarreling at seven o'clock and at nine I walked out, slamming the door behind me. [*Pause.*] I never talk about it to anyone, and curiously enough, it's to you alone that I complain. [*Kisses her hand.*] Don't be angry with me. I've no one but you. No one.

MASHA. Listen to that noise in the chimney! Before Father died the wind howled in the chimney just like that. Exactly like that.

VERSHININ. You're not superstitious, are you?

MASHA. Yes, I am.

VERSHININ. That's strange. [*Kisses her hand.*] You're a magnificent, wonderful woman. Magnificent, wonderful! It's dark here, but I can see your eyes gleaming.

MASHA [*sits down on another chair*]. There's more light here.

VERSHININ. I love you, I love you, I love you! I love your eyes, your movements. I dream about them. Magnificent, wonderful woman!

MASHA [*laughing softly*]. When you talk to me like that, I somehow cannot help laughing, though I'm terrified. Don't say it again, I beg you. [*In an undertone.*] Yes, yes, do go on. [*Covers her face with her hands.*] I don't mind. Someone's coming. Talk about something else.

IRINA *and* TUSENBACH *come in through the ballroom.*

TUSENBACH. I have a triple-barreled name: Baron Tusenbach-Krone-Altschauer, but I'm a Russian, a Greek Orthodox like you. There's little of the German left in me, except perhaps patience and the obstinacy with which I'm boring you. I see you home every night.

IRINA. I'm so tired!

TUSENBACH. And I'll go on coming to the telegraph office and seeing you home every day for ten or twenty years if necessary, until you drive me away. [*Catching sight of* MASHA *and* VERSHININ, *joyfully*.] Is it you? Good evening.

IRINA. At home at last. [*To* MASHA.] A woman came to the telegraph office an hour or so ago. She wanted to send a telegram to her brother in Saratov to tell him that her son had died today, but she just couldn't remember the address. So I sent on the telegram without an address. Simply to Saratov. She was crying. I was rude to her. I don't know why. "I'm sorry," I said, "I'm in a hurry." It was so stupid. We are having the carnival dancers in today, aren't we?

MASHA. Yes.

IRINA [*sits down in an armchair*]. Must rest. Awfully tired.

TUSENBACH [*with a smile*]. Every time you come back from the office, you look so young, so unhappy.

Pause.

IRINA. I'm tired. I'm afraid I don't like the telegraph office. Don't like it at all.

MASHA. You've grown thinner. [*Whistles a tune.*] And you look younger. You look like a boy.

TUSENBACH. That's because of the way she does her hair.

IRINA. I'll have to find another job. This one doesn't suit me. It isn't what I was looking for, what I was dreaming of. Work without poetry, without thought. [*A knock on the floor from below.*] The Doctor's knocking. [*To* TUSENBACH.] Please be an angel and answer him. I can't. I'm tired. [TUSENBACH *knocks on the floor.*] He'll be here in a moment. We must do something. Yesterday the Doctor and Andrey went to the club and lost at cards again. Apparently, Andrey lost two hundred rubles.

MASHA [*with indifference*]. It's a little late to do anything about it.

IRINA. Two weeks ago he lost; in December he lost. I wish he'd hurry up and lose everything he's got. Perhaps we'd leave for Moscow then. Dear Lord, every night I dream of Moscow. I'm going quite off my head. [*Laughs.*] We shall be going there in June, but before June there's still—February, March, April, May—nearly half a year!

MASHA. We must make sure Natasha doesn't find out about his losses.

IRINA. I don't think she cares.

CHEBUTYKIN, *who has only just got out of bed—he had a nap after dinner—enters the ballroom combing his beard. He sits down at the table and takes a newspaper out of his pocket.*

MASHA. Just look at him! Has he paid his rent?

IRINA [*laughs*]. Good Lord, no. Not a penny for the last eight months. Forgotten all about it, I daresay.

MASHA [*laughs*]. How importantly he sits!

They all laugh; pause.

IRINA. Why so silent, Colonel?

VERSHININ. Don't know. I'm dying for a cup of tea. Half a life for a cup of tea! Haven't had a bite since morning.

CHEBUTYKIN. Irina, my dear.

IRINA. What is it?

CHEBUTYKIN. Please come here. *Venez ici.* [IRINA *goes over and sits at the table.*] You must help me.

IRINA *lays out the cards for a game of patience.*

VERSHININ. Well, if we can't have any tea, let's at least have a talk.

TUSENBACH. Let's. What about?

VERSHININ. What about? Let's just—er—imagine what life will be like after we're gone—er—say, in two or three hundred years.

TUSENBACH. Well, I suppose after us, people will fly about in balloons, wear a different cut of coat, perhaps discover and develop a sixth sense, but life will still remain the same as ever: a hard life, a life full of all sorts of mysteries and . . . a happy life. A thousand years hence, man will still be sighing: "Oh, life is hard!" At the same time he'll be just as afraid of death, just as unwilling to die as he is now.

VERSHININ [*thinking it over*]. Now, how shall I put it? I can't help thinking that everything on earth must change little by little. Indeed it is already changing before our very eyes. In two hundred, three hundred, or even a thousand years—the actual time doesn't matter—a new and happy life will begin. We shan't take part in it, of course, but we're living for it now . . . working and . . . well . . . suffering for it, creating it. . . . This alone is the goal of our existence and, if you like, our happiness.

MASHA *laughs quietly.*

TUSENBACH. What's the matter?

MASHA. Don't know. I've been laughing all day today. Ever since morning.

VERSHININ. I went to the same school as you. I did not go to the Military Academy. I read a lot, but I don't know what books to choose. I shouldn't be at all surprised if I read all the wrong books. Yet the longer I live, the more I want to know. My hair's turning gray, I'm almost an old man, but I know little—oh, how little! Nevertheless, I think I know what matters most now. I'm certain of that. What I'd most like to prove to you is that there is no such thing as happiness, that there must not be, and that it will not be for us. All we must do is work, work, and work. Happiness is for our distant descendants. [*Pause.*] If not for me, then at least for the descendants of my descendants.

FEDOTIK *and* RODÉ *come into the ballroom; they sit down and sing softly, strumming a guitar.*

TUSENBACH. According to you, one oughtn't even to dream of happiness. But what if I am happy!

VERSHININ. You're not.

TUSENBACH [*flinging up his hands and laughing*]. I'm afraid we don't understand one another. How am I to convince you? [MASHA *laughs quietly. He points a finger at her.*] Laugh! [*To* VERSHININ.] Life will be the same, not only in two or three hundred years, but in a million years. It never changes, it remains constant. It follows its own laws regardless of us. At least those laws will always remain a mystery to you. Migrant birds, cranes for instance, fly and fly, and whatever thoughts—great or little—

might be drifting through their heads, they will go on flying without knowing where or why. They'll fly and go on flying, however many philosophers may be born among them. Indeed, let them philosophize as much as they like so long as they go on flying.

MASHA. But there must be some meaning, mustn't there?

TUSENBACH. A meaning . . . Look, it's snowing. What meaning is there in that?

Pause.

MASHA. It seems to me that a man must be either religious or seeking some religion. Otherwise, his life is empty, empty. To live and not to know why cranes fly, why children are born, why there are stars in the sky . . . You must either know what you live for or else nothing matters any more. It's all meaningless nonsense.

Pause.

VERSHININ. All the same, it is a pity that I'm no longer young.

MASHA. Gogol says: "It's a boring world, my friends."

TUSENBACH. And I say: "It's difficult to agree with you, my friends." Let's drop the subject.

CHEBUTYKIN [*reading his paper*]. Balzac was married in Berdichev. [IRINA *hums softly.*] In a hole like Berdichev! I think I'll make a note of that. [*Writes down in his notebook.*] Balzac was married in Berdichev. [*Reads his paper.*]

IRINA [*laying out patience, reflectively*]. Balzac was married in Berdichev.

TUSENBACH. The die is cast. I've sent in my resignation. Did you know that, Masha?

MASHA. Yes, I did. I must say, I can't see anything good about it. I don't like civilians.

TUSENBACH. Makes no difference. [*Gets up.*] I'm not handsome—what sort of a soldier am I? Well, anyway, it makes no difference. I'll work. . . . Spend at least one day of my life working so hard that when I come home in the evening, I'll fall on my bed dead tired and go to sleep at once. [*Going into the ballroom.*] I expect workers sleep soundly.

FEDOTIK [*to* IRINA]. I've just bought some colored pencils for you at Pyzhikov's in the Moscow Road. And this penknife.

IRINA. You still go on treating me like a child. You forget I'm a grown-up woman. [*Accepts pencils and penknife joyfully.*] They're lovely!

FEDOTIK. I bought a knife for myself. Have a look: one blade, another blade, a third for scooping out your ears, a fourth for cleaning your nails——

RODÉ [*loudly*]. Doctor, how old are you?

CHEBUTYKIN. Me? Thirty-two.

Laughter.

FEDOTIK. Let me show you another game of patience. [*Lays out the cards.*]

A *samovar is put on the table.* ANFISA *is busy at the samovar.* A *little later* NATASHA *comes in and also busies herself at the table. Enter* SOLYONY, *who, after greeting everybody, sits down at the table.*

VERSHININ. What a wind, though!

MASHA. Yes. I'm tired of winter. I've already forgotten what summer's like.

IRINA. I can see it's working out. We shall be in Moscow.

FEDOTIK. It's not working out. See! The eight has to cover the two of spades. [*Laughs.*] Which means, you won't be in Moscow.

CHEBUTYKIN [*reads his paper*]. Tsitsihar. Smallpox is raging here.

ANFISA [*going up to* MASHA]. Masha, tea, darling. [*To* VERSHININ.] Please, sir. I'm sorry I've forgotten your name.

MASHA. Bring it here, Nanny. I'm not going over there.

IRINA. Nanny!

ANFISA. Coming, dear.

NATASHA [*to* SOLYONY]. Little babies understand very well. "Good morning, Bobby," I said. "Good morning, darling!" He gave me a knowing look. You think it's the mother in me speaking, don't you? It isn't. Believe me, it isn't! It's quite an extraordinary child.

SOLYONY. If it was my child, I'd roast him in a frying pan

and eat him. [*Goes into the drawing room with his glass of tea and sits down in a corner.*]

NATASHA [*covering her face with her hands*]. What a coarse, ill-bred fellow!

MASHA. Anyone who doesn't notice whether it's summer or winter now is a happy man. I can't help thinking that if I were in Moscow, I'd be indifferent to the weather.

VERSHININ. The other day I read the diary of a French Cabinet Minister. He wrote it in prison. He'd been sentenced for the Panama affair. With what rapturous delight does he mention the birds he sees through the prison window, the birds he never noticed before when he was a Minister. Of course, now that he's been released, he doesn't notice the birds any more. Neither will you notice Moscow when living there. Happiness doesn't exist. It cannot exist. We merely desire it.

TUSENBACH [*takes a chocolate box from the table*]. Where are the chocolates?

IRINA. Solyony's eaten them.

TUSENBACH. All of them?

ANFISA [*serving tea*]. Here's a letter for you, sir.

VERSHININ. For me? [*Takes the letter.*] From my daughter. [*Reads.*] Yes, of course. . . . Excuse me, Masha, I'll slip out quietly. I won't have any tea. [*Gets up, excitedly.*] Always the same thing.

MASHA. What is it? It's not a secret, is it?

VERSHININ [*in a low voice*]. My wife's taken poison again. I must go. I'll go out unobserved. Terribly unpleasant, all this. [*Kisses* MASHA'*s hand.*] My dear one, you're so good, so sweet. . . . I'll go this way . . . quietly. [*Goes out.*]

ANFISA. Where is he off to? I've just given him tea. Well, I must say . . .

MASHA [*angrily*]. Leave me alone! Pestering me! Not a moment's peace! [*Goes to the table with her cup of tea.*] I'm tired of you, old woman!

ANFISA. Why are you so cross, my dear?

ANDREY [*offstage*]. Anfisa!

ANFISA [*mimicking*]. Anfisa! Sitting there . . . [*Goes out.*]

MASHA [*in the ballroom, crossly*]. Let me sit down, will you?

[*Mixing up the cards on the table.*] Sprawling all over the place with your cards. Why don't you drink your tea?

IRINA. You've got a foul temper, Masha.

MASHA. Don't talk to me if I've a foul temper. Leave me alone!

CHEBUTYKIN [*laughing*]. Leave her alone, leave her alone——

MASHA. You're sixty, but you're always talking some damned nonsense as if you were a silly little boy.

NATASHA [*sighs*]. My dear Masha, why must you use such language? I assure you that with your attractive appearance you'd be simply bewitching in any refined society if it were not for your language. *Je vous prie, pardonnez-moi, Marie, mais vous avez des manières un peu grossières.*

TUSENBACH [*restraining his laughter*]. Please . . . please . . . pass me. . . . There's some brandy, I think.

NATASHA. *Il paraît que mon Bobby déjà ne dort pas*—he's awake. I'm afraid he isn't well today. I'd better go and see. Excuse me. [*Goes out.*]

IRINA. And where has the Colonel gone?

MASHA. Home. He's having some trouble with his wife again.

TUSENBACH [*goes up to* SOLYONY *with a decanter of brandy*]. You always sit alone thinking, goodness knows what about. Come, let's make it up. Let's have some brandy. [*They drink.*] I expect I'll have to play the piano all night —all sorts of rubbish. . . . Oh, well!

SOLYONY. Why make it up? We haven't quarreled, have we?

TUSENBACH. You always make me feel as if something's happened between us. You're a strange character, I must say.

SOLYONY [*declaiming*]. I am strange. Who isn't? Do not be angry, Aleko!

TUSENBACH. What's Aleko got to do with it?

Pause.

SOLYONY. When I'm alone with someone, I'm all right. I'm just like the rest. But in company I feel depressed, I'm shy and . . . and I talk a lot of nonsense. But all the same I'm a damn sight better and more honest than a lot of other people. And I can prove it.

TUSENBACH. I'm often angry with you, you continually pick on me when we're in company, but I like you for all that. I don't know why. Anyway, I'm going to get drunk tonight. Let's have another drink!

SOLYONY. Let's. [*They drink.*] I've never had anything against you, Baron. But my character is like Lermontov's. [*In a low voice.*] I even look a little like Lermontov. So I'm told. [*Takes a perfume bottle from his pocket and sprinkles his hands.*]

TUSENBACH. I've sent in my resignation. I've had enough. I've been thinking about it for five years, and I've made up my mind at last. I shall work.

SOLYONY [*declaiming*]. Do not be angry, Aleko. . . . Forget, forget your dreams. . . .

While they are talking, ANDREY *enters quietly with a book and sits down by the candle.*

TUSENBACH. I shall work.

CHEBUTYKIN [*going into the drawing room with* IRINA]. And the food was genuinely Caucasian: onion soup and for a roast—mutton, chekhartma.

SOLYONY. Cheremsha isn't meat at all; it's a plant, something like our onion.

CHEBUTYKIN. No, sir. No, my angel. Chekhartma isn't an onion; it's roast mutton.

SOLYONY. And I'm telling you cheremsha is an onion.

CHEBUTYKIN. And I'm telling you chekhartma is mutton.

SOLYONY. And I'm telling you cheremsha is an onion.

CHEBUTYKIN. What's the use of arguing with you? You've never been to the Caucasus, and you've never eaten chekhartma.

SOLYONY. Haven't eaten it because I can't stand it. Cheremsha reeks like garlic.

ANDREY [*imploringly*]. Enough, gentlemen. Please!

TUSENBACH. When will the carnival dancers come along?

IRINA. They promised to be here by nine, which means any moment now.

TUSENBACH [*embraces* ANDREY]. "Oh, my bright, my beautiful hallway, my beautiful new hallway . . ." *

* A traditional Russian folk song and dance [D.M.].

ANDREY [*dances and sings*]. "My maple-wood hall . . ."

CHEBUTYKIN [*dances*]. "My latticed hall . . ."

Laughter.

TUSENBACH [*kisses* ANDREY]. Hang it all, let's drink! Andrey, my dear fellow, let's drink to our friendship. I'll come to Moscow with you, to the university.

SOLYONY. Which one? There are two universities in Moscow.

ANDREY. There's only one university in Moscow.

SOLYONY. And I tell you there are two.

ANDREY. Three, if you like. So much the better.

SOLYONY. There are two universities in Moscow. [*Murmurs of protest and booing.*] There are two universities in Moscow: the old and the new. But if you don't want to listen to me, if my words annoy you, I'll shut up. I can even go to another room. [*Goes out through one of the doors.*]

TUSENBACH. Bravo, bravo! [*Laughs.*] Let's start, ladies and gentlemen. I'm sitting down at the piano. Funny fellow, that Solyony. [*Sits down at the piano and plays a waltz.*]

MASHA [*dances by herself*]. The Baron's drunk, the Baron's drunk, the Baron's drunk.

Enter NATASHA.

NATASHA [*to* CHEBUTYKIN]. Doctor . . . [*Speaks to* CHEBUTYKIN, *then goes out quietly.*]

CHEBUTYKIN touches TUSENBACH *on the shoulder and whispers something to him.*

IRINA. What is it?

CHEBUTYKIN. Time we were going. Good-bye.

TUSENBACH. Good night. It's time we were off.

IRINA. Wait a minute. What about the carnival dancers?

ANDREY [*greatly embarrassed*]. There won't be any. You see, my dear, Natasha says that Bobby isn't very well, and that's why. . . . Anyway, I don't know. . . . I don't care a damn. . . .

IRINA [*shrugging*]. Bobby isn't well!

MASHA. Oh, all right! If they're kicking us out, we'd better go. [*To* IRINA.] It isn't Bobby who's ill, it's she herself. . . . Here! [*Taps her forehead.*] The stupid, selfish, trivial creature!

ANDREY *goes to his room through the right-hand door.* CHEBUTYKIN *follows him. In the ballroom they are saying good-bye.*

FEDOTIK. What a shame! I counted on spending the evening here, but of course, if the baby's ill . . . I'll bring him some toys tomorrow.

RODÉ [*in a loud voice*]. I had a good sleep after lunch because I thought I was going to dance all night. Why, it's only nine o'clock!

MASHA. Let's go outside. We can talk there. We'll decide what to do.

Voices saying "Good-bye" and "Good night" can be heard. TUSENBACH *is heard laughing gaily. All go out.* ANFISA *and a maid clear the table, put out the lights. The nurse is heard singing a lullaby.* ANDREY, *wearing an overcoat and a hat, and* CHEBUTYKIN *enter quietly.*

CHEBUTYKIN. I never managed to get married because my life flashed by like a streak of lightning. Also because I was madly in love with your mother, a married woman.

ANDREY. One shouldn't marry. One shouldn't because it's so boring.

CHEBUTYKIN. That may be so, but what about the loneliness? Say what you like, but loneliness, my dear fellow, is a terrible thing. Although, as a matter of fact . . . I mean, it makes absolutely no difference, does it?

ANDREY. Let's get out quickly.

CHEBUTYKIN. What's the hurry? Plenty of time.

ANDREY. I'm afraid my wife may stop me.

CHEBUTYKIN. Oh!

ANDREY. I won't gamble today. I'll just sit and watch. Don't feel too well. . . . What am I to do for my asthma, Doctor?

CHEBUTYKIN. Why ask me? I can't remember, dear boy. Don't know.

ANDREY. Let's go through the kitchen.

They go out. The doorbell rings twice; voices and laughter are heard.

IRINA [*comes in*]. What's that?

ANFISA [*in a whisper*]. The mummers!

The doorbell rings.

IRINA. Tell them, Nanny, there's no one at home. Say we're sorry.

ANFISA *goes out.* IRINA *paces the room pensively; she's upset. Enter* SOLYONY.

SOLYONY [*bewildered*]. No one here. Where's everybody?

IRINA. Gone home.

SOLYONY. Strange. Are you alone here?

IRINA. Yes. [*Pause.*] Good-bye.

SOLYONY. I'm sorry I behaved rather tactlessly a short while ago . . . forgot myself. But you're not like the rest. You're high-minded and pure. You see the truth. . . . You alone can understand me. I love you; I love you deeply, passionately——

IRINA. Good-bye. Please go away.

SOLYONY. I can't live without you. [*Going after her.*] Oh, my joy! [*Through tears.*] Oh, my happiness! Lovely, exquisite, wonderful eyes, eyes unlike those of any other woman I've ever known.

IRINA [*coldly*]. Don't, please.

SOLYONY. It's the first time I've spoken to you of my love, and I feel as though I'm not on earth but on another planet. [*Rubs his forehead.*] Oh, never mind. I can't force you to love me, of course. But I shall not put up with any successful rivals. I shan't. I swear to you by all that I hold sacred that I shall kill my rival. Oh, my wonderful one!

NATASHA *enters carrying a candle.*

NATASHA [*glances into one room, then into another, and passes the door leading into her husband's room*]. Andrey's there. Let him read. [*To* SOLYONY.] I'm sorry. I didn't know you were here. Excuse my dressing gown.

SOLYONY. Don't mind me. Good-bye. [*Goes out.*]

NATASHA. You look tired, darling. Oh, you poor child! [*Kisses* IRINA.] You ought to go to bed earlier.

IRINA. Is Bobby asleep?

NATASHA. Yes, he is. But he's very restless. By the way, my

dear, I've been wanting to say something to you, but either you've been out or I've been too busy. I can't help thinking that the nursery is too cold and damp for Bobby. Your room is just what a baby wants. Darling, don't you think you could move into Olga's room? Just for a short time.

IRINA [*not understanding*]. Where?

The harness bells of a troika can be heard as it drives up to the house.

NATASHA. You and Olga will share one room, for the time being, I mean, and Bobby will have your room. He's such a darling! Today I said to him: "Bobby, you're mine! Mine!" And he looked at me with his sweet little eyes. [*The doorbell rings.*] Must be Olga. She *is* late! [*The maid goes up to* NATASHA *and whispers in her ear.*] Protopopov? What a funny man! Protopopov asks me to go for a drive with him in his troika. [*Laughs.*] These men are strange, aren't they? [*The doorbell rings.*] Somebody's come. I suppose I could go for a drive for a quarter of an hour. [*To the maid.*] Tell him I shan't be long. [*The doorbell rings.*] The doorbell again. That must be Olga. [*Goes out.*]

The maid runs off; IRINA *sits lost in thought; enter* KULYGIN *and* OLGA, *followed by* VERSHININ.

KULYGIN. How do you like that? I was told they'd be having a party.

VERSHININ. I must be off. I left not so long ago, half an hour ago to be precise, and they were expecting carnival dancers.

IRINA. They've all gone.

KULYGIN. Masha gone too? What's Protopopov waiting for outside in a troika? Who is he waiting for?

IRINA. Don't ask me. I'm tired.

KULYGIN. Oh, you naughty child!

OLGA. The staff meeting has only just ended. I'm dead tired. Our headmistress is ill and I'm deputizing for her. Oh, my head! My head's aching! [*Sits down.*] Andrey lost two hundred rubles at cards yesterday. The whole town is talking about it.

KULYGIN. Yes, our staff meeting has made me tired too. [*Sits down.*]

VERSHININ. My wife's taken it into her head to frighten me. She nearly poisoned herself. Everything's all right, I'm glad to say. I'm no longer worried, thank goodness. I suppose we must go, mustn't we? Well, in that case, I wish you all the best. What about coming with me, Kulygin? I can't stay at home, I simply can't. Come on!

KULYGIN. Too tired. Sorry I can't go with you. [*Gets up.*] Too tired. Has my wife gone home?

IRINA. I suppose so.

KULYGIN [*kisses* IRINA'*s hand*]. Good-bye. I shall take it easy all day tomorrow and the day after tomorrow. All the best. [*Going.*] I'd love a cup of tea. Counted on spending the evening in pleasant company and—*O, fallacem hominum spem!* The accusative case in exclamations!

VERSHININ. Oh, well, I'll be going somewhere by myself.

Goes out with KULYGIN, *whistling.*

OLGA. My head, my head aches. . . . Andrey lost . . . The whole town's talking. I'll go and lie down. [*Going.*] Tomorrow I'm free. Goodness, that really is lovely! Free tomorrow, free the day after tomorrow. My head aches . . . my head . . . [*Goes out.*]

IRINA [*alone*]. All gone. No one's left.

The sound of an accordion from the street; the nurse sings a lullaby.

NATASHA [*walks across the ballroom in a fur coat, followed by the maid*]. I'll be back in half an hour. Just going out for a little drive. [*Goes out.*]

IRINA [*alone, longingly*]. To Moscow! To Moscow! To Moscow!

Curtain.

ACT THREE

OLGA's and IRINA's room. Screened-off beds on the right and the left. It is past two o'clock in the morning. Offstage a fire alarm bell is ringing on account of a fire that started a long time before. It is clear that no one in the house has yet gone to bed. MASHA is lying on a sofa, dressed, as usual, in black. OLGA and ANFISA come in.

ANFISA. They're downstairs, sitting under the staircase. "Please," I says to them, "come upstairs. You can't carry on like that." But they go on crying. "We don't know where Daddy is," they says. "He's probably been burnt in the fire." The things they think of! In the yard, too, there are some people . . . also in their night clothes.

OLGA [*takes dresses out of the wardrobe*]. Take this gray one . . . this one too . . . also this blouse. And this frock, too, Nanny. Goodness me, how awful! The entire Kirsanov Lane seems to have burned down. . . . Take this too . . . and this. [*Throws clothes into* ANFISA's *hands.*] The poor Vershinins! They were terrified. Their house nearly burned down. Let them spend the night here. They mustn't be allowed to go home. Poor old Fedotik lost everything in the fire. Nothing left.

ANFISA. I think I'd better call Ferapont, dear. I can't carry it all.

OLGA [*rings*]. They never answer. [*Calls through the door.*] Anyone there? Come here, please. [*Through the open door a window, red with the glow of the fire, can be seen; a fire engine can be heard passing the house.*] Oh, the horror of it! And what a mess it is! [*Enter* FERAPONT.] Take all this downstairs. You'll find the Kolotilin girls under the staircase. Give it to them. And this . . .

FERAPONT. Yes'm. In 1812 Moscow was also burnt down. Dear, oh dear, weren't the French surprised!

OLGA. Go on. Hurry up.

FERAPONT. Yes'm. [*Goes out.*]

OLGA. Nanny dear, give everything away. We don't want anything. Give it all away. I'm dead tired. Can hardly stand on my feet. We mustn't let the Vershinins go back home. The girls can sleep in the drawing room, and the Colonel, downstairs with the Baron. Fedotik can also stay with the Baron or else in the ballroom. The Doctor would get drunk, dead drunk, just now, and we can't let anyone go into his room. Vershinin's wife, too, in the drawing room.

ANFISA [*in a tired voice*]. Don't turn me out of the house, Olga dear. Please don't turn me out.

OLGA. Don't talk nonsense, Nanny. No one is turning you out.

ANFISA [*puts her head on* OLGA*'s bosom*]. My darling child, my precious, you know I work as hard as I can. But as soon as I grows too weak for work, they're all sure to say: Out with her! Where could I go? Where? I'm in my eighties. Nearly eighty-two.

OLGA. You'd better sit down, Nanny. You're tired, poor dear. [*Makes her sit down.*] Rest a while, dear. You're so pale.

NATASHA *enters.*

NATASHA. They're saying we ought to form a committee as soon as possible to raise funds for the people made homeless by the fire. Well, why not? It's an excellent idea. Anyway, it's the duty of the rich to help the poor. Bobby and little Sophie are peacefully asleep. The little darlings are asleep as if nothing had happened. There are people everywhere; the house is full of them, whichever way you turn. There's a flu epidemic in town. I'm afraid the children might catch it.

OLGA [*not listening to her*]. We can't see the fire in this room. It's quiet here.

NATASHA. Yes. . . . I must be an awful sight. [*Stands in front of the mirror.*] People say I've got fat—it just isn't true! I'm no fatter. Masha's asleep. She's tired out, poor girl. [*To* ANFISA, *coldly.*] Don't you dare sit down in my presence! Get up! Get out of here! [ANFISA *goes out; pause.*] I simply can't understand why you keep the old woman!

OLGA [*taken aback*]. I'm sorry, but I don't understand——

NATASHA. She's quite useless in the house. She's a peasant and she ought to live in the country. Spoiling her, aren't you? I like order in the house. There should be no superfluous people in the house. [*Strokes* OLGA'*s cheek.*] Oh, you poor thing! You're tired. Our headmistress is tired. When my little Sophie grows up and goes to school, I'll be afraid of you.

OLGA. I shan't be a headmistress.

NATASHA. They're going to appoint you, dearest. It's settled.

OLGA. I'll refuse. I couldn't. . . . It's beyond me. [*Drinks water.*] You treated Nanny so abominably just now. I'm sorry, but I can't bear it. It made me feel quite faint.

NATASHA [*excitedly*]. I'm sorry, Olga, I'm sorry. I didn't want to upset you.

MASHA *gets up, picks up a pillow, and walks out angrily.*

OLGA. Please understand, my dear. We may have been brought up in a rather peculiar way, but I can't bear this sort of thing. Such an attitude cuts me to the quick. It makes me ill. . . . I simply lose heart.

NATASHA. I'm sorry, I'm sorry. . . . [*Kisses her.*]

OLGA. Any rudeness, however slight, any harsh word, upsets me.

NATASHA. I admit I often say things I shouldn't, but, my dear, you must agree that there's no reason why she shouldn't live in the country.

OLGA. She's been with us for thirty years.

NATASHA. But she can't do any work now! Either I don't understand or you don't want to understand me. She's incapable of doing any work. All she does is sleep or sit about.

OLGA. Well, let her sit about.

NATASHA [*in surprise*]. Let her sit about? But she's a servant, isn't she? [*Through tears.*] I don't understand you, Olga. I have a nanny, I have a wet nurse, we have a maid, a cook; whatever do we want this old woman for? What for?

Fire alarm offstage.

OLGA. I've aged ten years tonight.

NATASHA. We must come to an understanding, Olga. You're at school; I'm at home. You've got your teaching; I've got to run the house. And if I talk about it, I know what I'm talking about. I know what I'm talk-ing a-bout! By tomorrow I want that old thief, that old hag, out of my house. [*Stamps her foot.*] The old witch! Don't you dare exasperate me! Don't you dare! [*Recollecting herself.*] Really, Olga, if you don't move downstairs, we'll always be quarreling. This is dreadful!

Enter KULYGIN.

KULYGIN. Where's Masha? Time we went home. They say the fire is subsiding. [*Stretching.*] Only one block has burned down. There was a strong wind, though, and it did seem at first that the whole town was on fire. [*Sits down.*] Oh, I'm tired, dear Olga. I often think that if it hadn't been for Masha, I'd have married you, dear. You're so good. . . . Oh, I'm exhausted. [*Listens.*]

OLGA. What is it?

KULYGIN. The Doctor is on one of his drinking sprees. It would happen just now. Terribly drunk. [*Gets up.*] I believe he's coming here. Listen! Yes, he's coming here. [*Laughs.*] What a man! Really! I'd better hide myself. [*Goes toward the wardrobe and stands in the corner.*] What a bandit!

OLGA. He hasn't been drinking for two years, and now, all of a sudden, he goes and gets drunk.

OLGA *retires, with* NATASHA, *to the back of the room. Enter* CHEBUTYKIN; *he walks across the room without swaying, just as if he were sober, looks round, goes up to the washstand, and starts washing his hands.*

CHEBUTYKIN [*morosely*]. To hell with all of them! To blazes with them! They think I'm a doctor, that I can treat any illness. The truth is, I know absolutely nothing, forgotten everything I ever knew, remember nothing, absolutely nothing. [OLGA *and* NATASHA *go out, unnoticed by him.*] To hell with it! Last Wednesday I attended a woman in Zasyp. She died, and it was my fault that she died. Yes. . . . Twenty-five years ago I knew something or other, but I don't remember a damn thing now. Not a damn thing. Perhaps I'm not a human being at all but merely imagine that I have hands and feet and a head; perhaps

I don't exist at all but merely imagine that I walk, eat, and sleep. [*Weeps.*] Oh, if only I did not exist! [*Stops weeping; morosely.*] Oh, hell! Day before yesterday they were talking at the club. . . . Heard them say: "Shakespeare," "Voltaire . . ." Never read them, not a single word, but I did my best to look as if I had. The others did the same. The vulgarity of it! The baseness! But then I remembered the woman I killed on Wednesday—remembered everything—and I felt dirty, nasty, loathsome. . . . I went and got drunk.

Enter IRINA, VERSHININ, *and* TUSENBACH. TUSENBACH *is wearing a new, fashionable suit.*

IRINA. Let's sit down. No one will come in here.

VERSHININ. If it weren't for the soldiers, the whole town would have burned down. Stout fellows! [*Rubs his hands with pleasure.*] What splendid people! Fine men, every one of them!

KULYGIN [*going up to them*]. What's the time?

TUSENBACH. After three. It's getting light.

IRINA. Everyone's sitting in the ballroom. No one thinks of going home. Your Solyony's there too. [*To* CHEBUTYKIN.] You'd better go to bed, Doctor.

CHEBUTYKIN. Never mind me, thank you. [*Combs his beard.*]

KULYGIN [*laughs*]. Sozzled, eh, Doctor? [*Slaps him on the shoulder.*] Good lad! *In vino veritas*, the ancients used to say.

TUSENBACH. Everyone's asking me to organize a concert in aid of the homeless.

IRINA. But who——

TUSENBACH. It could be arranged if we tried. If you ask me, Masha plays the piano beautifully.

KULYGIN. She plays wonderfully.

IRINA. She's forgotten how to. She hasn't played for three years . . . or four.

TUSENBACH. There's absolutely no one in this town who appreciates music, not a soul, but I do, and I assure you that Masha plays wonderfully, almost like a concert pianist.

KULYGIN. You're quite right, Baron. I love Masha very much. She's a dear.

TUSENBACH. To be able to play so splendidly and to know all the time that there's no one to appreciate you—no one!

KULYGIN [*sighs*]. Yes, but do you think it would be the correct thing for her to take part in a concert? [*Pause.*] I know nothing about such matters, of course. It may be all right. I must say our headmaster is a decent fellow, a very decent fellow indeed, and very intelligent too, but he has—er—well, views. . . . Of course, it isn't his business, but all the same, I might perhaps have a talk with him.

CHEBUTYKIN *picks up a porcelain clock and examines it.*

VERSHININ. I got so filthy at the fire, I look like nothing on earth. [*Pause.*] I heard a rumor yesterday that our brigade is to be transferred somewhere very far away. Some say to Poland, others to Chita.

TUSENBACH. I heard it too. Yes, well, I suppose the town will be quite deserted then.

IRINA. We shall be gone, too!

CHEBUTYKIN [*drops the clock, which breaks*]. Smashed to bits!

Pause; everyone looks upset and embarrassed.

KULYGIN [*picking up the pieces*]. Break an expensive thing like that! Oh, Doctor, Doctor, zero minus for conduct!

IRINA. That was Mother's clock.

CHEBUTYKIN. Possibly. So it was your mother's clock. Perhaps I didn't smash it, but it just seems as though I did. Perhaps we only imagine that we exist, but we don't really exist at all. I don't know anything. Nobody knows anything. [*Stops at the door.*] What are you staring at? Natasha is having a disgusting affair with Protopopov, and you don't see it. You're just sitting about here and don't see anything, while Natasha is having her disgusting affair with Protopopov. [*Sings.*] Won't you accept this little present from me? [*Goes out.*]

VERSHININ. Well, well . . . [*Laughs.*] As a matter of fact, the whole thing is rather odd. [*Pause.*] When the fire broke out, I hurried off home. I got there. . . . Our house wasn't damaged and wasn't in danger, but my two little girls were standing at the front door in their night clothes; their mother wasn't there, people were rushing about, horses galloping past, dogs—and the girls looked upset, frightened, appealing, I don't know what else. My heart sank when I saw their faces. Good Lord, I thought, what else will these girls have to experience during a long life? I snatched them up, started running, and all the time kept thinking one and the same thing: What else would they have to experience in this world? [*Fire alarm; pause.*] I come here, their mother's here . . . angry, shouting.

MASHA *enters with a pillow and sits down on the sofa.*

VERSHININ. When my little girls were standing at the front door in their night clothes and the street was red with the glow of the fire and the noise around was terrifying, the thought occurred to me that something like it must have happened many years ago when an enemy made a sudden raid, looted, burned. . . . And yet, what a difference between what was happening now and what had happened before. When a little more time has passed, say, in two or three hundred years, people will look upon our present life, too, with horror and contempt. Everything we accept now will seem to them clumsy and dreadful, extremely uncomfortable and strange. I'm sure of it! Oh, what a wonderful life it will be, what a life! [*Laughs.*] I'm sorry, I'm off again! Please, let me continue. I'd really like to go on airing my views. I'm in the mood for it now. [*Pause.*] They all seem to be asleep. So, as I was saying, what a wonderful life it will be. You can just imagine it. . . . There are only three like you in the town now, but in the generations to come there will be more and more and more, and the time will come when everything will change as you would have it—people will live as you do now—and then you, too, will become antiquated. People will be born who will be better than you. . . . [*Laughs.*] I'm in a curious kind of mood. Damn it, I want to live and live! [*Sings.*] "To love all ages are in thrall, her impulses are good for all." * [*Laughs.*]

MASHA. Tram-tum-tum.

VERSHININ. Tam-tam.

* The old general's aria from *Eugene Onegin* [D.M.].

MASHA. Tra-ra-ra.

VERSHININ. Tra-ta-ta. . . . [*Laughs.*]

Enter FEDOTIK.

FEDOTIK [*dances*]. Burnt down! Burnt down! To the last cinder!

IRINA. You're joking! Everything burned?

FEDOTIK [*laughs*]. Everything to the last cinder. Nothing left. My guitar, my camera, and all my letters.

Enter SOLYONY.

IRINA [*to* SOLYONY]. Please go away. You can't come in here.

SOLYONY. Why can the Baron and I can't?

VERSHININ. We really ought to go. How's the fire?

SOLYONY. Dying down, I'm told. But I really can't see why the Baron can and I can't. [*Takes out a perfume bottle and sprinkles himself.*]

VERSHININ. Tram-tam-tam.

MASHA. Tam-tam.

VERSHININ [*laughs; to* SOLYONY]. Let's go to the ballroom.

SOLYONY. Very well. We'll make a note of that. "I could make my tale much more clear, but that may irritate the geese, I fear." * [*Looking at* TUSENBACH.] Cluck-cluck-cluck.

SOLYONY *goes out with* VERSHININ *and* FEDOTIK.

IRINA. What a stink Solyony's left behind him. [*Bewildered.*] The Baron's asleep! Baron! Baron!

TUSENBACH [*waking*]. Sorry, I'm terribly tired. . . . The brickworks . . . I'm not talking in my sleep. I really will start work at a brickworks soon. Start work . . . I've discussed it already. [*Tenderly, to* IRINA.] You are so pale, so beautiful, so fascinating. Your pallor, it seems to me, irradiates the dark air like a shaft of light. You're sad, you're dissatisfied with life. Oh, come away with me! Come away and let's work together.

MASHA. Go away, Baron.

TUSENBACH [*laughing*]. You here? I can't see. [*Kisses* IRINA'*s hand.*] Good-bye, I'm going. I look at you now and it comes back to me how a long time ago, on your birthday,

* A quotation from Krylov's fable Geese [D.M.].

you were so bright and cheerful and talked of the joys of life. At the time I, too, looked forward to a happy life. Where is it? [*Kisses her hand.*] There are tears in your eyes. You ought to go to bed. It's getting light, the day's dawning. Oh, if only I were allowed to give my life for you!

MASHA. Go away! Well, really! . . .

TUSENBACH. I'm going. [*Goes out.*]

MASHA [*lying down*]. Are you asleep, Fyodor?

KULYGIN. Eh?

MASHA. Why don't you go home?

KULYGIN. My dear Masha, my darling Masha——

IRINA. She's tired. Let her have a rest.

KULYGIN. I'll go in a minute. My wife's a good, nice woman. I love you, my only one.

MASHA [*angrily*]. *Amo, amas, amat, amamus, amatis, amant.*

KULYGIN [*laughs*]. Isn't she wonderful? I've been married to you for seven years, but it seems as if we only left the church yesterday. On my word of honor! You really are a wonderful woman. I'm content, content, content.

MASHA. I'm bored, bored, bored. [*Sits up.*] I can't get it out of my head. It's simply disgraceful. It preys on my mind. I can't keep silent. I mean about Andrey. He's mortgaged the house to a bank, and his wife's grabbed all the money, but the house doesn't belong to him alone, does it? It belongs to all four of us. He should have known that if he's an honest man.

KULYGIN. Why should you worry, Masha? What do you care? Andrey's up to his neck in debt. Well, let him do what he likes.

MASHA. It's disgraceful, however you look at it. [*Sits down.*]

KULYGIN. You and I aren't poor. I work, I teach at the high school, I give private lessons, I'm an honest man. A plain man. *Omnia mea mecum porto,* as they say.

MASHA. I don't want anything, but I can't bear injustice. [*Pause.*] Go home, Fyodor.

KULYGIN [*kisses her*]. You're tired. Rest for half an hour. I'll sit and wait for you downstairs. Try to sleep. [*Going.*] I'm content, content, content. [*Goes out.*]

IRINA. Our Andrey really has degenerated, gone to seed and

grown old beside that woman. Once upon a time he was thinking of becoming a professor; yesterday he was boasting of having at last been made a member of the local Council. He's a member of the Council, while Protopopov is chairman. The whole town's talking and laughing about it. He alone doesn't see or know anything. Here's everyone rushing off to the fire, but he sits in his room as if nothing were happening. Just plays his fiddle. [*Distractedly.*] Oh, it's awful, awful, awful! [*Weeps.*] I can't, I can't bear it any longer. I can't, I can't. [OLGA *comes in and starts tidying up things on her bedside table.* IRINA *sobs loudly.*] Throw me out, throw me out. I can't bear it any longer!

OLGA [*frightened*]. What's the matter? What is it, darling?

IRINA [*sobbing*]. Where, where has it all gone to? Where is it? Oh, God; oh, God! I've forgotten everything, forgotten. . . . It's got all mixed up in my head. I can't remember the Italian for *window* or for *ceiling.* I'm forgetting everything, every day I'm forgetting, and life's passing and will never return, never! We'll never go to Moscow. I can see that we'll never go.

OLGA. Darling, darling . . .

IRINA [*controlling herself*]. I'm so unhappy. I can't work. I won't work. I've had enough, thank you. I worked as a telegraphist; now I've got a job at the Town Council, and I hate and despise everything I have to do there. I'm twenty-three. I've worked for a long time and my brain's dried up. I'm growing thin, I'm losing my looks, I'm getting old, and there's nothing, nothing I can look forward to, no satisfaction out of life I can hope for. Time's flying past, and I seem to be getting further and further away from real life, from a life that is beautiful, and heading for some horrible disaster. I'm in despair and I simply can't understand how I go on living, how I haven't killed myself before now.

OLGA. Don't cry, darling. I can't bear to see you cry.

IRINA. I'm not crying. I'm not crying. I've stopped now. See? I'm not crying any more. I've stopped. I've stopped.

OLGA. Darling, I'm talking to you as your sister, as your friend. If you take my advice, you'll marry the Baron! [IRINA *cries softly.*] You do respect him, don't you? You think highly of him. It's true he's not handsome, but he's such an honest, decent man. After all, people don't marry for love but to do their duty. At least I think so. I wouldn't hesitate to marry a man I didn't love. I would marry anyone who asked me, provided he was a decent man. I'd even marry an old man.

IRINA. I was always waiting until we moved to Moscow, where I hoped to meet the right man for me, the man I've dreamed of, the man I'd love. . . . But, as it turned out, it was all nonsense . . . all nonsense.

OLGA [*embraces her sister*]. My dear, my sweet sister, I understand, I understand everything. When the Baron left the army and came to see us in civilian clothes, I thought he looked so unprepossessing that I even started crying. He asked me why I was crying, but I couldn't tell him that, could I? But I'd be very happy if he married you. That's quite a different matter, quite different.

NATASHA, *carrying a lighted candle, walks across the stage in silence from the door on the right to the door on the left.*

MASHA. She walks as if she had set the town on fire herself.

OLGA. You're silly, Masha. You're the silliest in our family. I'm sorry.

MASHA. I'd like to confess to you, dear sisters. My heart is heavy. Let me confess to you and never to anyone again, never again. I'll tell you now. [*Softly.*] It's my secret, but you must know everything. I can't be silent any more. [*Pause.*] I love him, I love him, I love that man. You've just seen him. Well, why conceal it? I love Vershinin.

OLGA [*goes behind the screen*]. Don't. I'm not listening anyway.

MASHA. What am I to do? [*Clutches at her head.*] At first I thought him rather strange, then I began to pity him, and then I fell in love with him. . . . I fell in love with his voice, his talk, his misfortunes, his two little daughters.

OLGA [*behind the screen*]. I'm telling you I'm not listening. You can say any stupid thing you like; I'm not listening.

MASHA. Oh, you are stupid, Olga. I love him. Well, you can't do anything about it, can you? It's happened. It's fate. He loves me, too. It's terrible, isn't it? It's not nice, is it? [*Draws* IRINA *to her by her hand.*] Oh, my dear, what's to become of us? What's our life going to be like? When you read some love story, it all seems so old and so obvious, but when you fall in love yourself, you realize that no one knows anything and that everyone has to decide for himself. My dear, dear sisters . . . I've told you everything and now I shall be silent. I shall be like Gogol's madman—silence . . . silence . . .

Enter ANDREY, *followed by* FERAPONT.

ANDREY [*crossly*]. What do you want? I don't understand.

FERAPONT [*in the doorway, impatiently*]. I've told you a dozen times already.

ANDREY. Sir!

FERAPONT. Sir. The firemen, sir, are asking for permission to drive down to the river through your garden. Otherwise they has to drive all the way round, which, they says, sir, is a terrible nuisance.

ANDREY. Oh, all right. Tell them it's all right. [FERAPONT *goes out.*] Fed up! Where's Olga? [OLGA *comes out from behind the screen.*] I've come to ask you for the key to the cupboard. I've lost mine. You've got it. The little key. [OLGA *gives him the key in silence.* IRINA *goes behind the screen in her part of the room. Pause.*] What a terrific fire! It's dying down now. Damn that Ferapont! He made me furious and made me say something silly. Sir! [*Pause.*] Why are you so silent, Olga? [*Pause.*] It's time you dropped this nonsense and stopped sulking like this without rhyme or reason. You're here, Masha, and so are you, Irina. Excellent! Let's have a frank talk—once and for all. What have you got against me? What?

OLGA. Leave it, Andrey dear. We'll have our talk tomorrow. [*Agitatedly.*] What an awful night!

ANDREY [*looking very embarrassed*]. Don't get excited. I'm perfectly calm and I'm asking you what you've got against me. Tell me straight.

VERSHININ [*offstage*]. Tram-tam-tam.

MASHA [*gets up; loudly*]. Tra-ta-ta! [*To* OLGA.] Good-bye, Olga. God bless. [*Goes behind the screen and kisses* IRINA.] Sleep well. Good-bye, Andrey. Go away now. They're tired. Talk it over tomorrow. [*Goes out.*]

OLGA. Really, Andrey dear, why not put it off till tomorrow? [*Goes behind the screen to her part of the room.*] Time to go to bed.

ANDREY. Let me say what's on my mind and I'll go at once. To begin with, you've got something against Natasha, my wife. I've noticed it ever since the first day of our marriage. Natasha's a fine and honest person, straightforward and honorable—that's my opinion. I love and respect my wife, understand?—respect—and I demand that others should also respect her. I repeat, she's an honest and decent person, and, I'm sorry to say, the reason why you resent her so much is because you're so eager to find fault with her. [*Pause.*] Secondly, you seem to be angry with me because I'm not a professor and because I've given up my studies. But I work at the District Council and I'm a member of its board. I regard my service there as honorable and as important as service to science. I'm a member of the board of the District Council and I'm proud of it if you want to know. [*Pause.*] Thirdly . . . there's one thing more I'd like to say. I've mortgaged the house without your consent. It was wrong of me—yes. I'm sorry; I was driven to it by my debts . . . thirty-five thousand. I've given up gambling for some time now, but the chief thing I have to say to justify myself is that you girls, you get Father's pension, while I . . . haven't anything—I mean, any income. [*Pause.*]

KULYGIN [*at the door*]. Isn't Masha here? [*Anxiously.*] Where is she? That's funny. . . . [*Goes out.*]

ANDREY. They're not listening. Natasha's an excellent, honest person. [*Paces the stage in silence and then stops dead.*] When I got married, I thought we'd be happy, all of us happy. But, my God . . . [*Weeps.*] My dear sisters, my darling sisters, don't believe me, don't believe . . . [*Goes out.*]

KULYGIN [*at the door; anxiously*]. Where's Masha? Isn't Masha here? Extraordinary business! [*Goes out.*]

Fire alarm; then stage is empty.

IRINA [*behind the screen*]. Olga, who's knocking on the floor?

OLGA. It's the Doctor. He's drunk.

IRINA. What a restless night! [*Pause.*] Olga! [*Looks out from behind the screen.*] Have you heard? The brigade's been ordered to leave. It's being transferred somewhere far away.

OLGA. It's only a rumor.

IRINA. We shall be left all alone then. . . . Olga!

OLGA. Well?

IRINA. Oh, my dear, my darling, I respect the Baron. I think a lot of him. He's a fine man. I will marry him. I agree. Only, let's go to Moscow. Please, please let's go. There's no place like Moscow in the whole world. Let's go, Olga. Let's go!

Curtain.

ACT FOUR

The old garden of the Prozorovs' house. A long avenue of firs, with a river at the end of it. On the other side of the river, a forest. On the right, a veranda; empty bottles and glasses on a table make it obvious that champagne has just been drunk. It is midday. Passers-by occasionally walk through the garden on their way to the river from the street; five soldiers march past rapidly.

CHEBUTYKIN, *in a good-humored frame of mind which doesn't desert him throughout the whole of the act, is sitting in an easy chair in the garden waiting to be called; he is wearing his army cap and holding a walking stick.* IRINA, KULYGIN, *with a decoration round his neck and with his mustache shaved off, and* TUSENBACH, *standing on the veranda, are seeing off* FEDOTIK *and* RODÉ, *who are coming down the steps; both officers are in field dress.*

TUSENBACH [*exchanging kisses with* FEDOTIK]. You're a good fellow. We got on well together. [*Exchanging kisses with* RODÉ.] Again . . . good-bye, dear friend.

IRINA. *Au revoir.*

FEDOTIK. Not *au revoir*, but good-bye. We shall never meet again.

KULYGIN. Who knows? [*Wipes his eyes, smiles.*] Look at me—crying!

IRINA. We shall meet one day.

FEDOTIK. In ten or fifteen years? But we'll hardly know each other then. Exchange cold greetings. [*Takes a snapshot.*] Stand still, please . . . for the last time.

RODÉ [*embraces* TUSENBACH]. We shan't meet again. [*Kisses* IRINA'*s hand.*] Thanks for everything, for everything!

FEDOTIK [*annoyed*]. Wait!

TUSENBACH. Let's hope we shall meet. Write to us. Be sure to write.

RODÉ [*glancing round the garden*]. Good-bye, trees! [*Shouts.*] Ho-ho! [*Pause.*] Good-bye, echo!

KULYGIN. For all we know you may get married there—in Poland. Your Polish wife will throw her arms around you and say: "*Kochany!*" [*Laughs.*]

FEDOTIK [*glancing at his watch*]. There's less than an hour left. Solyony is the only one from our battery who's going on the barge. The rest of us are marching with the troops. Three batteries are leaving today, another three tomorrow—the town will be quiet and peaceful at last.

TUSENBACH. And terribly boring.

RODÉ. Where's Masha?

KULYGIN. In the garden.

FEDOTIK. Must say good-bye to her.

RODÉ. Good-bye. We must go or I'll burst into tears. [*Embraces quickly* TUSENBACH *and* KULYGIN, *and kisses* IRINA'*s hand.*] We've had a lovely time here.

FEDOTIK [*to* KULYGIN]. Here's something to remember me by—a notebook with a pencil. We'll go down to the river from here.

They go away, both looking round several times.

RODÉ [*shouts*]. Ho-ho!

KULYGIN [*shouts*]. Good-bye!

At the back of the stage FEDOTIK *and* RODÉ *meet* MASHA *and take leave of her;* MASHA *goes off with them.*

IRINA. They've gone. [*Sits down on the bottom step of the veranda.*]

CHEBUTYKIN. They forgot to say good-bye to me.

IRINA. What about you?

CHEBUTYKIN. Well, yes, I too forgot, somehow. Still, I shall be seeing them soon. I'm leaving tomorrow. Yes . . . one more day. In another year I shall be put on the retired list. I shall come back here and spend the rest of my life near you. There's only one more year left before I qualify for a pension. [*Puts a newspaper in his pocket and takes out another.*] I'll come back to you here and change my way of life drastically. I shall become a very quiet, well-behaved, decent little man.

IRINA. You jolly well have to change your way of life, dear Doctor. You really must.

CHEBUTYKIN. Yes, I feel it. [*Sings softly.*] Tara-ra-boom-di-ay . . . I'm sitting in a room-di-ay. . . .

KULYGIN. The Doctor's incorrigible. Incorrigible!

CHEBUTYKIN. Why don't you give me a few lessons? I'd become a reformed character then.

IRINA. Fyodor's shaved off his mustache. I can't bear to look at him.

KULYGIN. Why not?

CHEBUTYKIN. I could tell you what your face looks like, only I wouldn't like to.

KULYGIN. Ah, well! I'm afraid it's the accepted thing, the *modus vivendi.* Our headmaster has shaved off his mustache and so have I now that I have become second master. No one likes it, but I don't care. I'm content. Whether with or without a mustache, I'm content. [*Sits down.*]

At the back of the stage ANDREY *is wheeling a pram with a sleeping baby.*

IRINA. Dear Doctor, I'm terribly worried. You were out on the boulevard yesterday. Be a darling and tell me what happened there.

CHEBUTYKIN. What happened? Nothing. Nothing at all. [*Reads his newspaper.*] It's of no importance.

KULYGIN. I'm told Solyony and the Baron met yesterday on the boulevard near the theatre——

TUSENBACH. Do shut up! Really! [*Waves his hand and goes into the house.*]

KULYGIN. . . . near the theatre. Solyony began picking a quarrel with the Baron, and the latter lost his temper and said something offensive.

CHEBUTYKIN. Don't know. It's all nonsense.

KULYGIN. In some seminary a teacher wrote "nonsense" in Russian on an essay, and the pupil thought it was written in Latin but couldn't find the word in a dictionary. [*Laughs.*] Terribly funny. They say that Solyony's in love with Irina and that he's grown to hate the Baron. Well, that's understandable. Irina's a very nice girl. She's very like Masha, just as given to daydreaming. Except that your character, Irina, is more gentle. Though I must say,

Masha, too, has a very good character. I love her. I love my Masha.

At the back of the stage someone shouts: "Coo-ee! Hey!"

IRINA [*shudders*]. Everything seems to startle me today for some reason. [*Pause.*] I've got everything packed. I'm sending my things off after lunch. The Baron and I are getting married tomorrow. We're leaving for the brick-works tomorrow, and the day after I shall be at the school. A new life will begin. May God help me! When I was sitting for my teacher's diploma, I cried for joy, so conscious was I of the importance of the career I was about to embark on. [*Pause.*] The cart will be here in a moment for my things.

KULYGIN. Yes, that's how it is. And yet, it doesn't seem to be serious. All this, I mean. It's all just fine ideas, nothing very serious. Still, I wish you every success with all my heart.

CHEBUTYKIN [*deeply moved*]. My sweet child, my good, my precious girl. . . . You've gone so far ahead of me that I shall never catch up with you. I've been left behind, an old migrant bird that can't fly. Fly, my dear one, fly, and God bless you. [*Pause.*] You shouldn't have shaved off your mustache, Kulygin.

KULYGIN. Drop it for goodness' sake. [*Sighs.*] The soldiers will be gone today, and everything will go on as before. Whatever people may say, Masha's a good, honest woman. I love her very much and I thank my fate. Everyone's fate is different. A certain Kozyryov, an excise officer, was at school with me. He was expelled from the eighth grade because he seemed quite unable to understand *ut consecutivum*. He's terribly hard up now and in bad health too. Every time I meet him I say to him: "How d'you do, *ut consecutivum!*" "Yes, indeed, that's just it: *consecutivum*," he replies, and starts coughing. But I've been lucky all my life. I'm happy, have even been awarded the order of Stanislav, second class, and am now myself teaching others the *ut consecutivum*. Of course, I'm a clever man, much cleverer than most people, but that's no guarantee of happiness.

"The Maiden's Prayer" is being played on the piano in the house.

IRINA. Tomorrow night, thank goodness, I shan't have to listen to "The Maiden's Prayer," shan't have to meet Protopopov. [*Pause.*] Protopopov's sitting there in the drawing room. He's here today, too. . . .

KULYGIN. The headmistress hasn't arrived yet, has she?

IRINA. No. We've sent for her. Oh, if only you knew how difficult it is for me to live here by myself, without Olga. She lives at the school; she's the headmistress, she's busy all day, while I'm alone here. I'm bored, I have nothing to do, and I hate the room I live in. So what I've decided is that if I'm not going to live in Moscow, then I must make the best of it. I suppose it's fate and there's nothing to be done about it. It's all the will of God—that's clear. The Baron proposed to me. Well, I thought it over and decided to accept. He's a good man, it's really quite extraordinary how good he is. It was then that my soul, as it were, suddenly grew a pair of wings. I felt cheerful again, lighthearted, and once more I wanted to work, work. Only something happened yesterday, and some kind of awful uncertainty seems to hang over me.

CHEBUTYKIN. Nonsense!

NATASHA [*through the window*]. The headmistress!

KULYGIN. The headmistress has arrived. Let's go.

He goes with IRINA *into the house.*

CHEBUTYKIN [*reads his papers, humming a tune*]. Tara-ra-boom-di-ay . . . I'm sitting in a room-di-ay. . . .

MASHA *walks up; at the back of the stage* ANDREY *is wheeling the pram.*

MASHA. There he sits, enjoying himself.

CHEBUTYKIN. And why not?

MASHA [*sits down*]. Oh, nothing. [*Pause.*] Were you in love with my mother?

CHEBUTYKIN. Yes, very much.

MASHA. Was she in love with you?

CHEBUTYKIN [*after a pause*]. That, I'm afraid, I don't remember.

MASHA. Is my man here? That's what our cook Marfa used to call her policeman, "my man." Is he here?

CHEBUTYKIN. No, not yet.

MASHA. When you have to snatch your happiness piecemeal, in little bits, and then lose it as I've lost it, you gradually become coarse and bitter. [*Pointing to her breast.*] I feel it seething here. [*Looking at her brother,* ANDREY, *who is wheeling the pram.*] There's old Andrey, our darling brother. All our hopes have perished. Thousands of people were raising a bell, much money and labor was spent on it, and then it suddenly fell and got smashed to bits. That is Andrey!

ANDREY. When are they going to be quiet in the house? Such a noise!

CHEBUTYKIN. Soon. [*Looks at his watch.*] This is a very old watch. It chimes. [*Winds his watch, which chimes.*] The first, second, and fifth battery will be leaving at exactly one o'clock. [*Pause.*] I'm leaving tomorrow.

ANDREY. For good?

CHEBUTYKIN. Don't know. I may return in about a year. Damned if I know. . . . It makes no difference. . . .

Somewhere far away a harp and a violin can be heard being played.

ANDREY. The town will be deserted, just as if a bell glass had been put over it. [*Pause.*] Something happened outside the theatre yesterday. Everyone's talking about it, but I don't know anything.

CHEBUTYKIN. Nothing much. Solyony began picking a quarrel with the Baron, who lost his temper and insulted him. In the end, of course, Solyony was obliged to challenge him to a duel. [*Looks at his watch.*] I think it's time. . . . At half past twelve, in the forest there, on the other side of the river. You can see it from here. Bang-bang! [*Laughs.*] Solyony imagines he's a second Lermontov. He even writes poetry. Joking apart, though, it's his third duel.

MASHA. Whose third duel?

CHEBUTYKIN. Solyony's.

MASHA. And the Baron's?

CHEBUTYKIN. What about the Baron?

MASHA. I'm all confused. Anyway, they shouldn't be allowed to fight. He might wound the Baron, or even kill him.

CHEBUTYKIN. The Baron is an excellent fellow, but one

Baron more or less—what difference does it make? Let them! It makes no difference. [*Beyond the garden somebody shouts: "Coo-ee! Hollo!"*] That's Skvortsov shouting, one of the seconds. He's waiting in the boat. Let him wait.

Pause.

ANDREY. If you ask me, it's simply immoral to fight a duel or to be present at one as a doctor.

CHEBUTYKIN. It only seems so. We don't exist, nothing exists in the world. It only seems that we exist. Besides, what difference does it make?

MASHA. They just talk, talk all day long. [*Going.*] You live in a climate where it may start snowing any moment, and here they go on talking. [*Stopping.*] I won't go into the house. I can't go there. Please tell me when Vershinin comes. [*Walks off along the avenue.*] The birds are already flying away. [*Looks upward.*] Swans or geese. Oh, my dear, my happy birds! . . . [*Goes out.*]

ANDREY. There'll be no one left in the house. The army officers will go, you will go, my sister will get married, and I'll be left alone.

CHEBUTYKIN. What about your wife?

FERAPONT *comes in with papers.*

ANDREY. A wife's a wife. My wife's an honest, decent woman and—well, yes!—a kind woman, but for all that there's something in her that brings her down to the level of a mean, blind animal, a sort of horrible, rough-skinned animal. In any case, she's not a human being. I'm telling you this as a friend, for you're the only person to whom I can open up my heart. I love Natasha, that's quite true. But sometimes she strikes me as extraordinarily vulgar, and then I feel completely lost; I don't understand why —for what reason—I love her so much or, anyway, did love her.

CHEBUTYKIN [*gets up*]. Well, my dear fellow, I'm going away tomorrow, and we may never meet again, so here's my advice to you: Put on your hat, take your walking stick in your hand, and go away—go away and go on walking without looking back. The farther you go the better.

SOLYONY *walks across the back of the stage with* TWO ARMY

OFFICERS; *seeing* CHEBUTYKIN, *he turns toward him; the* OFFICERS *go on.*

SOLYONY. It's time, Doctor. Half past twelve already. [*Exchanges greetings with* ANDREY.]

CHEBUTYKIN. One moment, please. Oh, I'm sick of the lot of you. [*To* ANDREY.] I say, my dear fellow, if anyone should ask for me, tell him I'll be back presently. [*Sighs.*] Dear, oh dear!

SOLYONY. "He had barely time to catch his breath before the bear was hugging him to death." [*Goes with him.*] What are you groaning about, old man?

CHEBUTYKIN. Well!

SOLYONY. How do you feel?

CHEBUTYKIN [*angrily*]. Fit as a fiddle.

SOLYONY. There's nothing to be upset about, old man. I shan't go too far. I'll only wing him like a woodcock. [*Takes out a perfume bottle and sprinkles his hands.*] I've emptied a whole bottle on my hands today and still they smell—smell like a corpse. [*Pause.*] Yes, sir. . . . Remember Lermontov's lines? "And he, the rebel, the raging tempest seeks, as though peace in tempests could be found."

CHEBUTYKIN. Yes. "He had barely time to catch his breath before the bear was hugging him to death."

They go out. Shouts of "Coo-ee! Hollo!" are heard. ANDREY *and* FERAPONT *come in.*

FERAPONT. Papers to sign, sir.

ANDREY [*nervously*]. Leave me alone, will you? Leave me alone. Please! [*Goes off with the pram.*]

FERAPONT. What's papers for if not to be signed? [*Goes off to the back of the stage.*]

Enter IRINA *and* TUSENBACH *in a straw hat.* KULYGIN *walks across the stage shouting: "Coo-ee, Masha, coo-ee!"*

TUSENBACH. He seems to be the only person in town who's glad the soldiers are going away.

IRINA. That's understandable. [*Pause.*] Our town will be deserted.

TUSENBACH. Darling, I'll be back presently.

IRINA. Where are you going?

TUSENBACH. I've something to see to in town. Then I must . . . see off all my colleagues.

IRINA. It's not true. Nicholas, why are you so preoccupied today? [*Pause.*] What happened outside the theatre yesterday?

TUSENBACH [*making an impatient movement*]. I'll be back in an hour and I'll be with you again. [*Kisses her hand.*] My dearest darling . . . [*Gazes into her eyes.*] It's five years since I fell in love with you, and I still can't get used to it. You seem more and more beautiful to me. What lovely, wonderful hair! What lovely eyes! I'm going to take you away tomorrow. We shall work. We shall be rich. My dreams will come true. You will be happy, darling. Only one thing, one thing only, worries me: You don't love me!

IRINA. I can't help that. I shall be your wife, your true and faithful wife, but I don't love you. We can't do anything about it. [*Weeps.*] I've never been in love and, oh, how I dreamed of love, dreamed of it for years and years, night and day, but my heart is like an expensive grand-piano that is locked and the key is lost. [*Pause.*] You look troubled.

TUSENBACH. I didn't sleep last night. There's nothing in my life I'm afraid of; it's only the lost key I'm worried about. Say something to me. [*Pause.*] Say something to me.

IRINA. What? What do you want me to say? What?

TUSENBACH. Just something.

IRINA. Don't fret, dear. Don't please.

Pause.

TUSENBACH. It is strange how sometimes little things, mere stupid trifles, suddenly, without rhyme or reason, become important in our life. One laughs at them, as one always does, one considers them of no importance, but one goes on all the same, and one hasn't got the strength to stop. Oh, don't let's talk about it! I feel fine! I feel as though I were seeing those firs, maples, and birch trees for the first time in my life, as though they were all looking curiously at me and . . . waiting. How beautiful these trees are and how beautiful life ought really to be near them. [*There is a shout: "Coo-ee! Hollo!"*] I must go. It's time. This tree here is dead, but it goes on swaying in the wind with the others. So I, too, can't help feeling that if I should die, I'd go on taking part in life one way or another. Good-bye, darling. [*Kisses her hands.*] The papers that you gave me are on my desk under the calendar.

IRINA. I'm coming with you.

TUSENBACH [*uneasily*]. No, no! [*Walks away quickly but stops in the avenue.*] Irina!

IRINA. What?

TUSENBACH [*not knowing what to say*]. I haven't had my coffee today. Please tell them to get it ready for me. [*Goes off quickly.*]

IRINA *stands, lost in thought, then walks off to the back of the stage and sits down on a swing. Enter* ANDREY *with the pram;* FERAPONT *appears.*

FERAPONT. The papers, sir, belong to the office. They're not mine, sir. I didn't make 'em.

ANDREY. Oh, where's my past? Where's it gone to? Where's the time when I was young, gay, clever, when my dreams and thoughts were so exquisite? When the present and the future were so bright with hope? Why is it that before we even begin to live, we become dull, drab, uninteresting, lazy, indifferent, useless, unhappy? Our town's been in existence for two hundred years, it has a hundred thousand inhabitants, and yet not one of them is different from the others. Not one saint—now or in the past—not one scholar, not one artist. Not one fairly outstanding man who could arouse envy or a passionate desire to emulate him. They just eat, drink, sleep, then die. Others are born and they, too, eat, drink, sleep, or, to avoid lapsing into complete idiocy out of sheer boredom, try to introduce some variety into their lives by nasty gossip, drink, cards, or malicious litigation. The wives deceive their husbands; the husbands tell lies, pretend not to see anything, not to hear anything; and their profoundly vulgar influence has so crushing an effect on their children that the divine spark in them is extinguished and they become just as pitiable corpses, and as like to one another, as their fathers and mothers. . . . [*To* FERAPONT, *crossly.*] What do you want?

FERAPONT. Beg pardon, sir. The papers to sign, sir.

ANDREY. I'm sick and tired of you.

FERAPONT [*handing him the papers*]. The porter of the Tax Collector's Office was telling me just now, sir, that there was two hundred degrees of frost in Petersburg this winter.

ANDREY. The present is hateful, but whenever I think of the future, everything becomes so wonderful! I feel so lighthearted, so unconfined. In the distance I can discern a glimmer of light, I can see freedom, I can see my children becoming free from idleness, from kvass, from geese with cabbage stuffing, from after-dinner naps, from a life of mean sponging.

FERAPONT. He was saying, sir, that two thousand people was frozen to death. Frightened to death, they was. In Petersburg or Moscow—can't remember rightly.

ANDREY [*in an excess of tenderness*]. My dear, dear sisters! My wonderful sisters! [*Through tears.*] Masha, my sister . . .

NATASHA [*at the window*]. Who's talking so loudly out there? Is that you, Andrey dear? You'll wake little Sophie. *Il ne faut pas faire du bruit, la Sophie est dormée déjà. Vous êtes un ours.* [*Getting angry.*] If you must talk, give the pram with the child to someone else. Ferapont, take the pram from the master.

FERAPONT. Yes'm. [*Takes the pram.*]

ANDREY [*embarrassed*]. I was talking quietly.

NATASHA [*behind the window, caressing her little boy*]. Bobby darling! Naughty Bobby! Bad Bobby!

ANDREY [*glancing through the papers*]. All right, I'll go through them, sign if necessary, and you can take them back to the office.

ANDREY *goes into the house, reading the papers;* FERAPONT *is pushing the pram at the back of the stage.*

NATASHA [*behind the window*]. Darling Bobby, what's your Mummy's name? You sweet little darling! And who's this? It's Auntie Olga. Say to your auntie: Good morning, Olga.

Two street musicians, a man and a girl, play on a violin and a harp; VERSHININ, OLGA, *and* ANFISA *come out of the house and stand listening for a moment in silence;* IRINA *comes up to them.*

OLGA. Our garden's like a public thoroughfare. Everyone walks and drives through it. Give something to the musicians, Nanny.

ANFISA [*gives some money to the* MUSICIANS]. Get along with you, my dears. [*The* MUSICIANS *bow and go out.*] Poor wretches! You don't play music in the street on a full stomach. [*To* IRINA.] How are you, my darling? [*Kisses her.*] Well, my little one, I'm having a lovely time now. A lovely time! Living with dear Olga in her flat at school. The Lord has been good to me, dear, in my old age. I've never lived so comfortably before, sinner that I am. It's a large apartment, no rent to pay, and I've got a room to myself and a lovely bed. Nothing to pay. I wakes up at night and—oh, dear God, holy Mother of God, there's no one happier than me.

VERSHININ [*glancing at his watch*]. We shall be leaving soon, Olga. It's time I went. [*Pause.*] I wish you all the best, all the best. Where's Masha?

IRINA. She's somewhere in the garden. I'll go and look for her.

VERSHININ. Thank you. I *am* in a hurry.

ANFISA. I'll go and look for her, too. [*Shouts.*] Masha, coo-ee! [*They go together to the back of the garden.*] Coo-ee! Coo-ee!

VERSHININ. Everything comes to an end. We, too, must part. [*Looks at his watch.*] The town gave us a sort of farewell lunch; we drank champagne, the mayor made a speech, I ate and listened, but in spirit I was here with you. [*Looking round the garden.*] I've got used to you.

OLGA. Shall we ever meet again?

VERSHININ. I don't suppose we shall. [*Pause.*] My wife and my two little girls will be staying here for another two months. Please, if anything happens, if they should need anything——

OLGA. Of course, of course. You needn't worry. [*Pause.*] There won't be a single soldier left in the town tomorrow; it will be all a memory, and of course, a new life will begin for us. [*Pause.*] Nothing happens as we want it to. I didn't want to be a headmistress and yet I'm one now. So we shan't be in Moscow. . . .

VERSHININ. Oh, well, thank you for everything. Forgive me if things haven't turned out exactly as—er . . . I'm afraid I've been talking a lot. Too much, indeed. Please forgive me for that too. Don't think too badly of me.

OLGA [*wipes her tears*]. Why isn't Masha coming?

VERSHININ. What else can I tell you before leaving? Any more views to air? [*Laughs.*] Life is hard. To many of us it seems dull and hopeless, but we must admit nevertheless that it is getting brighter and easier, and I should say that the time is not far off when it will be quite bright. [*Looks at his watch.*] It's time, high time, I went. Before, mankind was busy making war. Its whole existence was taken up with campaigns, invasions, and victories; but now all that is out of date. It's left a huge vacuum behind it, which we don't seem to know how to fill. Mankind is passionately looking for something to fill it with and will, I have no doubt, find it one day. Oh, if only we hadn't to wait too long! [*Pause.*] You know, if only we could add education to diligence and diligence to education. . . . [*Looks at his watch.*] I'm afraid I simply must go. . . .

OLGA. Here she comes!

Enter MASHA.

VERSHININ. I've come to say good-bye.

OLGA *walks away a little so as not to interfere with them.*

MASHA [*gazes at his face*]. Good-bye.

A prolonged kiss.

OLGA. There . . . there . . .

MASHA *sobs bitterly.*

VERSHININ. Write to me. Don't forget me. Let me go now —it's time. Olga, please take her. I have to go. . . . I'm late as it is. [*Deeply moved, he kisses* OLGA'*s hands, then embraces* MASHA *again, and goes out quickly.*]

OLGA. There, there, darling. Don't, don't. . . .

Enter KULYGIN.

KULYGIN [*embarrassed*]. Never mind, let her cry, let her.

My good Masha, my sweet Masha. . . . You're my wife and I'm happy, whatever may have happened. I'm not complaining, I don't reproach you. . . . I don't. Olga's my witness. Let's live again as we used to. You won't hear a word from me, not a hint.

MASHA [*suppressing her sobs*]. "For he on honey-dew hath fed, and drunk the milk of Paradise . . . and drunk the milk of Paradise" . . . I'm going mad. . . . "On honey-dew hath fed . . ."

OLGA. Take hold of yourself, Masha. Take hold of yourself. . . . Give her some water.

MASHA. I'm not crying any more.

KULYGIN. She's not crying. . . . She's good. . . .

A dull report of a distant shot is heard.

MASHA. "For he on honey-dew hath fed, and drunk the milk of Paradise" . . . "singing of Mount Abora." . . . I'm getting all mixed up. [*Drinks water.*] My life's a failure. . . . I don't want anything any more now. . . . I'll be all right in a moment. . . . It doesn't matter. . . . Honey-dew . . . what's honey-dew? Why can't I get this word out of my head? My thoughts are all in a muddle.

IRINA *comes in.*

OLGA. Compose yourself, Masha. That's right. . . . Clever girl. . . . Let's go indoors.

MASHA [*angrily*]. I'm not going into that house. [*Sobs but stops immediately.*] I won't go into that house again—never again!

IRINA. Let's sit down together and, please, don't let's talk. I'm going away tomorrow.

Pause.

KULYGIN. Yesterday I took this false beard and mustache away from a boy in the sixth grade. [*Puts on the false beard and mustache.*] I look like our German master, don't I? [*Laughs.*] Those boys are funny beggars.

MASHA. You do look like your German.

OLGA [*laughs*]. Yes.

MASHA *cries.*

IRINA. Stop it, Masha.

KULYGIN. I certainly look like him.

Enter NATASHA.

NATASHA [*to the maid*]. What? Mr. Protopopov will sit with little Sophie and let your master take out Bobby in the pram. Children are such a bother! [*To* IRINA.] You're leaving tomorrow, aren't you, Irina? What a pity! Why don't you stay here another week? [*Gives a little scream on catching sight of* KULYGIN, *who laughs and takes off the beard and mustache.*] Good heavens, you frightened me to death! [*To* IRINA.] I've got so used to you that it won't be so easy for me to part from you. I'll tell Andrey to move into your room with his fiddle —let him saw away there—and I'll put darling Sophie in his room. Oh, she's such a lovely child! Such a darling little girl! Today she looked at me with such big eyes and said: "Mummy!"

KULYGIN. A lovely child—that's true!

NATASHA. So it seems I shall be alone here tomorrow. [*Sighs.*] First of all, I shall have this avenue of trees cut down, then that maple—it's so unsightly in the evening. [*To* IRINA.] My dear, that belt doesn't suit you at all. It's such bad taste. You ought to get something bright and shiny. And here I shall have flowers, flowers, flowers everywhere, and there'll be such a lovely smell. . . . [*Suddenly.*] Why's this fork left lying about on the seat? [*On the way back to the house, to the maid.*] Why's this fork left lying about on the seat? I asked you. [*Screams.*] Don't answer me back!

KULYGIN. There she goes again!

A march is played offstage; they all listen.

OLGA. They're going away.

CHEBUTYKIN *comes in.*

MASHA. Our friends are going away. Well . . . happy journey to them. [*To her husband.*] We must go home. Where's my hat and cape?

KULYGIN. I left them indoors. I'll fetch them at once.

CHEBUTYKIN. I say, Olga . . .

OLGA. What is it? [*Pause.*] What?

CHEBUTYKIN. Oh, nothing. I don't know how to tell you. . . . [*Whispers in her ear.*]

OLGA [*aghast*]. It can't be!

CHEBUTYKIN. Yes. Too bad. . . . I'm awfully tired—exhausted. I'm not going to say another word. [*Vexed.*] Still, it makes no difference!

MASHA. What's happened?

OLGA [*embraces* IRINA]. What a dreadful day! I don't know how to tell you, my dear.

IRINA. What is it? Tell me quickly; what? For God's sake! [*Bursts into tears.*]

CHEBUTYKIN. The Baron has just been killed in a duel.

IRINA [*cries quietly*]. I knew . . . I knew. . . .

CHEBUTYKIN [*sits down on a garden seat at the back of the stage*]. Tired out . . . [*Takes a newspaper out of his pocket.*] Let her have a good cry. [*Sings softly.*] Tara-ra-boom-di-ay . . . I'm sitting in a room-di-ay. . . . What difference does it make?

The three sisters are standing, clinging to each other.

MASHA. Oh, how gay the music sounds! They're going away from us—one has gone already, gone forever—and we shall be left alone to start our life anew. We must live. . . . We must live.

IRINA [*lays her head on* OLGA'*s breast*]. The time will come when there will be no more secrets, when all that is now hidden will be made plain, and when all will know what these sufferings are for. Till then we must live. We must work, just work! Tomorrow I shall go away alone; I shall teach in a school, and I shall give my life to those who may need it. . . . It is autumn now. It will be winter soon, and everything will be covered with snow. But I shall be working. . . . I shall be working. . . .

OLGA [*embraces her two sisters*]. The music is so cheerful and gay, and I want to live. Dear God! Time will pass and we shall be gone forever. We shall be forgotten, and people will no longer remember our voices or our faces or how many of us there were. But our sufferings will pass into joy for those who live after us. . . . Peace and happiness will reign on earth, and we who live now will be remembered with gratitude and will be blessed. Oh, my dear, dear sisters, our lives are not finished yet. Let us live! The music is so gay, so joyful, and it almost seems that in a little while we shall know why we live and why we suffer. Oh, if only we knew . . . if only we knew!

The music is growing fainter and fainter; KULYGIN, *looking happy and smiling, comes in carrying the hat and cape.* ANDREY *is wheeling the pram, in which Bobby is sitting.*

CHEBUTYKIN [*sings softly*]. Tara-ra-boom-di-ay . . . I'm sitting in a room-di-ay. . . . [*Reads his newspaper.*] It makes no difference! It makes no difference!

OLGA. If only we knew . . . if only we knew!

Curtain.

THE CHERRY ORCHARD

A Comedy in Four Acts

CHARACTERS

LYUBOV (LYUBA) ANDREYEVNA RANEVSKY, *a landowner*
ANYA, *her daughter, aged seventeen*
VARYA, *her adopted daughter, aged twenty-four*
LEONID ANDREYEVICH GAYEV, *Mrs. Ranevsky's brother*
YERMOLAY ALEXEYEVICH LOPAKHIN, *a businessman*
PETER (PYOTR) SERGEYEVICH TROFIMOV, *a student*
BORIS BORISOVICH SIMEONOV-PISHCHIK, *a landowner*
CHARLOTTE IVANOVNA, *a governess*
SIMON PANTELEYEVICH YEPIKHODOV, *a clerk*
DUNYASHA, *a maid*
FIRS, *a manservant, aged eighty-seven*
YASHA, *a young manservant*
A HIKER
A STATIONMASTER
A POST OFFICE CLERK
GUESTS *and* SERVANTS

The action takes place on MRS. RANEVSKY'S *estate.*

THE CHERRY ORCHARD

ACT ONE

A room which is still known as the nursery. One of the doors leads to Anya*'s room. Daybreak; the sun will be rising soon. It is May. The cherry trees are in blossom, but it is cold in the orchard. Morning frost. The windows of the room are shut.*

Enter Dunyasha, *carrying a candle, and* Lopakhin *with a book in his hand.*

Lopakhin. The train's arrived, thank goodness. What's the time?

Dunyasha. Nearly two o'clock, sir. [*Blows out the candle.*] It's light already.

Lopakhin. How late was the train? Two hours at least. [*Yawns and stretches.*] What a damn fool I am! Came here specially to meet them at the station and fell asleep. . . . Sat down in a chair and dropped off. What a nuisance! Why didn't you wake me?

Dunyasha. I thought you'd gone, sir. [*Listens.*] I think they're coming.

Lopakhin [*listening*]. No. . . . I should have been there to help them with the luggage and so on. [*Pause.*] Mrs. Ranevsky's been abroad for five years. I wonder what she's like now. . . . She's such a nice person. Simple, easy-going. I remember when I was a lad of fifteen, my late father—he used to keep a shop in the village—punched me in the face and made my nose bleed. We'd gone into the yard to fetch something, and he was drunk. Mrs. Ranevsky—I remember it as if it happened yesterday, she was such a young girl then and so slim—took me to the washstand in this very room, the nursery. "Don't cry, little peasant," she said, "it won't matter by the time you're wed." [*Pause.*] Little peasant . . . It's quite true my father was a peasant, but here I am wearing a white waistcoat and brown shoes. A dirty peasant in a fashionable shop. . . . Except, of course, that I'm a rich man now, rolling in money. But, come to think of it, I'm a plain peasant still. . . . [*Turns the pages of his book.*] Been reading this book and haven't understood a word. Fell asleep reading it.

Pause.

DUNYASHA. The dogs have been awake all night; they know their masters are coming.

LOPAKHIN. What's the matter, Dunyasha? Why are you in such a state?

DUNYASHA. My hands are shaking. I think I'm going to faint.

LOPAKHIN. A little too refined, aren't you, Dunyasha? Quite the young lady. Dress, hair. It won't do, you know. Remember your place!

Enter YEPIKHODOV *with a bunch of flowers; he wears a jacket and brightly polished high-boots which squeak loudly; on coming in, he drops the flowers.*

YEPIKHODOV [*picking up the flowers*]. The gardener sent these. Said to put them in the dining room. [*Hands the flowers to* DUNYASHA.]

LOPAKHIN. Bring me some kvass while you're about it.

DUNYASHA. Yes, sir. [*Goes out.*]

YEPIKHODOV. Thirty degrees, morning frost, and the cherry trees in full bloom. Can't say I think much of our climate, sir. [*Sighs.*] Our climate isn't particularly accommodating, is it, sir? Not when you want it to be, anyway. And another thing. The other day I bought myself this pair of boots, and believe me, sir, they squeak so terribly that it's more than a man can endure. Do you happen to know of something I could grease them with?

LOPAKHIN. Go away. You make me tired.

YEPIKHODOV. Every day, sir, I'm overtaken by some calamity. Not that I mind. I'm used to it. I just smile. [DUNYASHA *comes in and hands* LOPAKHIN *the kvass.*] I'll be off. [*Bumps into a chair and knocks it over.*] There you are, sir. [*Triumphantly.*] You see, sir, pardon the expression, this sort of circumstance . . . I mean to say . . . Remarkable! Quite remarkable! [*Goes out.*]

DUNYASHA. I simply must tell you, sir: Yepikhodov has proposed to me.

LOPAKHIN. Oh?

DUNYASHA. I really don't know what to do, sir. He's ever such a quiet fellow, except that sometimes he starts talking and you can't understand a word he says. It sounds all right and it's ever so moving, only you can't make head or tail of it. I like him a little, I think. I'm not sure though. He's madly in love with me. He's such an unlucky fellow, sir. Every day something happens to him. Everyone teases him about it. They've nicknamed him Twenty-two Calamities.

LOPAKHIN [*listens*]. I think I can hear them coming.

DUNYASHA. They're coming! Goodness, I don't know what's the matter with me. I've gone cold all over.

LOPAKHIN. Yes, they are coming all right. Let's go and meet them. Will she recognize me? We haven't seen each other for five years.

DUNYASHA [*agitated*]. I'm going to faint. Oh dear, I'm going to faint!

Two carriages can be heard driving up to the house. LOPAKHIN *and* DUNYASHA *go out quickly. The stage is empty. People can be heard making a noise in the adjoining rooms.* FIRS, *who has been to meet* MRS. RANEVSKY *at the station, walks across the stage hurriedly, leaning on a stick. He wears an old-fashioned livery coat and a top hat; he keeps muttering to himself, but it is impossible to make out a single word. The noise offstage becomes louder. A voice is heard: "Let's go through here."* MRS. RANEVSKY, ANYA, *and* CHARLOTTE, *with a lap dog on a little chain, all wearing traveling clothes,* VARYA, *wearing an overcoat and a head scarf,* GAYEV, SIMEONOV-PISHCHIK, LOPAKHIN, DUNYASHA, *carrying a bundle and an umbrella, and other* SERVANTS *with luggage walk across the stage.*

ANYA. Let's go through here. Remember this room, Mother?

MRS. RANEVSKY [*joyfully, through tears*]. The nursery!

VARYA. It's so cold. My hands are quite numb. [*To* MRS. RANEVSKY.] Your rooms, the white one and the mauve one, are just as you left them, Mother dear.

MRS. RANEVSKY. The nursery! My dear, my beautiful room! I used to sleep here when I was a little girl. [*Cries.*] I feel like a little girl again now. [*Kisses her brother and* VARYA, *and then her brother again.*] Varya is the same as ever. Looks like a nun. And I also recognized Dunyasha. [*Kisses* DUNYASHA.]

GAYEV. The train was two hours late. How do you like that? What a way to run a railway!

CHARLOTTE [*to* PISHCHIK]. My dog also eats nuts.

PISHCHIK [*surprised*]. Good Lord!

All, except ANYA *and* DUNYASHA, *go out.*

DUNYASHA. We thought you'd never come. [*Helps* ANYA *off with her coat and hat.*]

ANYA. I haven't slept for four nights on our journey. Now I'm chilled right through.

DUNYASHA. You left before Easter. It was snowing and freezing then. It's different now, isn't it? Darling Anya! [*Laughs and kisses her.*] I've missed you so much, my darling, my precious! Oh, I must tell you at once! I can't keep it to myself a minute longer. . . .

ANYA [*apathetically*]. What is it this time?

DUNYASHA. Our clerk, Yepikhodov, proposed to me after Easter.

ANYA. Always the same. [*Tidying her hair.*] I've lost all my hairpins. [*She is so tired, she can hardly stand.*]

DUNYASHA. I don't know what to think. He loves me so much, so much!

ANYA [*tenderly, looking through the door into her room*]. My own room, my own windows, just as if I'd never been away! I'm home again! As soon as I get up in the morning, I'll run out into the orchard. . . . Oh, if only I could sleep. I didn't sleep all the way back, I was so worried.

DUNYASHA. Mr. Trofimov arrived the day before yesterday.

ANYA [*joyfully*]. Peter!

DUNYASHA. He's asleep in the bathhouse. He's been living there. Afraid of being a nuisance, he says. [*Glancing at her watch.*] I really ought to wake him, except that Miss Varya told me not to. "Don't you dare wake him!" she said.

VARYA *comes in with a bunch of keys at her waist.*

VARYA. Dunyasha, coffee quick! Mother's asking for some.

DUNYASHA. I won't be a minute! [*Goes out.*]

VARYA. Well, thank goodness you're all back. You're home again, my darling. [*Caressing her.*] My darling is home again! My sweet child is home again.

ANYA. I've had such an awful time!

VARYA. I can imagine it.

ANYA. I left before Easter. It was terribly cold then. All the way Charlotte kept talking and doing her conjuring tricks. Why did you force Charlotte on me?

VARYA. But you couldn't have gone alone, darling, could you? You're only seventeen!

ANYA. In Paris it was also cold and snowing. My French is awful. I found Mother living on the fourth floor. When I got there, she had some French visitors, a few ladies and an old Catholic priest with a book. The place was full of tobacco smoke and terribly uncomfortable. Suddenly I felt sorry for Mother, so sorry that I took her head in my arms, held it tightly, and couldn't let go. Afterwards Mother was very sweet to me. She was crying all the time.

VARYA [*through tears*]. Don't go on, Anya. Please don't.

ANYA. She'd already sold her villa near Mentone. She had nothing left. Nothing! I hadn't any money, either. There was hardly enough for the journey. Mother just won't understand! We had dinner at the station and she would order the most expensive things and tip the waiters a ruble each. Charlotte was just the same. Yasha, too, demanded to be given the same kind of food. It was simply awful! You see, Yasha is Mother's manservant. We've brought him back with us.

VARYA. Yes, I've seen the scoundrel.

ANYA. Well, what's been happening? Have you paid the interest on the mortgage?

VARYA. Heavens, no!

ANYA. Dear, oh dear . . .

VARYA. The estate will be up for sale in August.

ANYA. Oh dear!

LOPAKHIN [*puts his head through the door and bleats*]. Bah-h-h! [*Goes out.*]

VARYA [*through tears*]. Oh, I'd like to hit him! [*Shakes her fist.*]

ANYA [*gently embracing* VARYA]. Varya, has he proposed

to you? [VARYA *shakes her head.*] But he loves you. Why don't you two come to an understanding? What are you waiting for?

VARYA. I don't think anything will come of it. He's so busy. He can't be bothered with me. Why, he doesn't even notice me. I wish I'd never known him. I can't stand the sight of him. Everyone's talking about our wedding, everyone's congratulating me, while there's really nothing in it. It's all so unreal. Like a dream. [*In a different tone of voice.*] You've got a new brooch. Like a bee, isn't it?

ANYA [*sadly*]. Yes, Mother bought it. [*Goes to her room, talking quite happily, like a child.*] You know, I went up in a balloon in Paris!

VARYA. My darling's home again! My dearest one's home again! [DUNYASHA *has come back with a coffeepot and is making coffee;* VARYA *is standing at the door of* ANYA'*s room.*] All day long, darling, I'm busy about the house, and all the time I'm dreaming, dreaming. If only we could find a rich husband for you! My mind would be at rest then. I'd go into a convent and later on a pilgrimage to Kiev . . . to Moscow. Just keep going from one holy place to another. On and on. . . . Wonderful!

ANYA. The birds are singing in the orchard. What's the time?

VARYA. It's past two. It's time you were asleep, darling. [*Goes into* ANYA'*s room.*] Wonderful!

Enter YASHA *with a traveling rug and a small bag.*

YASHA [*crossing the stage, in an affected genteel voice*]. May I be permitted to go through here?

DUNYASHA. I can hardly recognize you, Yasha. You've changed so much abroad.

YASHA. Hmmm . . . And who are you, may I ask?

DUNYASHA. When you left, I was no bigger than this. [*Shows her height from the floor with her hand.*] I'm Dunyasha, Fyodor Kozoedov's daughter. Don't you remember me?

YASHA. Mmmm . . . Juicy little cucumber! [*Looks round, then puts his arms around her; she utters a little scream and drops a saucer.* YASHA *goes out hurriedly.*]

VARYA [*in the doorway, crossly*]. What's going on there?

DUNYASHA [*in tears*]. I've broken a saucer.

VARYA. That's lucky.

ANYA [*coming out of her room*]. Mother must be told Peter's here.

VARYA. I gave orders not to wake him.

ANYA [*pensively*]. Father died six years ago. A month after our brother, Grisha, was drowned in the river. Such a pretty little boy. He was only seven. Mother took it badly. She went away, went away never to come back. [*Shudders.*] Peter Trofimov was Grisha's tutor. He might remind her . . .

FIRS *comes in, wearing a jacket and a white waistcoat.*

FIRS [*walks up to the coffeepot anxiously*]. Madam will have her coffee here. [*Puts on white gloves.*] Is the coffee ready? [*Sternly, to* DUNYASHA.] You there! Where's the cream?

DUNYASHA. Oh dear! [*Goes out quickly.*]

FIRS [*fussing round the coffeepot*]. The nincompoop! [*Muttering to himself.*] She's come from Paris. . . . Master used to go to Paris. . . . Aye, by coach. . . . [*Laughs.*]

VARYA. What are you talking about, Firs?

FIRS. Sorry, what did you say? [*Joyfully.*] Madam is home again! Home at last! I can die happy now. [*Weeps with joy.*]

Enter MRS. RANEVSKY, GAYEV, *and* SIMEONOV-PISHCHIK, *the last one wearing a Russian long-waisted coat of expensive cloth and wide trousers. As he enters,* GAYEV *moves his arms and body as if he were playing billiards.*

MRS. RANEVSKY. How does it go now? Let me think. Pot the red in the corner. Double into the middle pocket.

GAYEV. And straight into the corner! A long time ago, Lyuba, you and I slept in this room. Now I'm fifty-one. . . . Funny, isn't it!

LOPAKHIN. Aye, time flies.

GAYEV. I beg your pardon?

LOPAKHIN. "Time flies," I said.

GAYEV. The place reeks of patchouli.

ANYA. I'm off to bed. Good night, Mother. [*Kisses her mother.*]

MRS. RANEVSKY. My sweet little darling! [*Kisses her hands.*] You're glad to be home, aren't you? I still can't believe it.

ANYA. Good night, Uncle.

GAYEV [*kissing her face and hands*]. God bless you. You're so like your mother! [*To his sister.*] You were just like her at that age, Lyuba.

ANYA *shakes hands with* LOPAKHIN *and* PISHCHIK. *Goes out and shuts the door behind her.*

MRS. RANEVSKY. She's terribly tired.

PISHCHIK. It was a long journey.

VARYA [*to* LOPAKHIN *and* PISHCHIK]. Well, gentlemen, it's past two o'clock. You mustn't outstay your welcome, must you?

MRS. RANEVSKY [*laughs*]. You're just the same, Varya. [*Draws* VARYA *to her and kisses her.*] Let me have my coffee first and then we'll all go. [FIRS *puts a little cushion under her feet.*] Thank you, Firs dear. I've got used to having coffee. I drink it day and night. Thank you, Firs, thank you, my dear old man. [*Kisses* FIRS.]

VARYA. I'd better make sure they've brought all the things in. [*Goes out.*]

MRS. RANEVSKY. Is it really me sitting here? [*Laughs.*] I feel like jumping about, waving my arms. [*Covers her face with her hands.*] And what if it's all a dream? God knows, I love my country. I love it dearly. I couldn't look out of the train for crying. [*Through tears.*] But, I suppose I'd better have my coffee. Thank you, Firs, thank you, dear old man. I'm so glad you're still alive.

FIRS. The day before yesterday . . .

GAYEV. He's a little deaf.

LOPAKHIN. At five o'clock I've got to leave for Kharkov. What a nuisance! I wish I could have had a good look at you, a good talk with you. You're still as magnificent as ever. . . .

PISHCHIK [*breathing heavily*]. Lovelier, I'd say. Dressed in the latest Paris fashion. If only I were twenty years younger—ho-ho-ho!

LOPAKHIN. This brother of yours says that I'm an ignorant oaf, a tightfisted peasant, but I don't mind. Let him talk. All I want is that you should believe in me as you used to, that you should look at me as you used to with those wonderful eyes of yours. Merciful heavens! My father was a serf of your father and your grandfather, but you, you alone, did so much for me in the past that I forgot everything, and I love you just as if you were my own flesh and blood, more than my own flesh and blood.

MRS. RANEVSKY. I can't sit still, I can't. . . . [*Jumps up and walks about the room in great agitation.*] This happiness is more than I can bear. Laugh at me if you like. I'm making such a fool of myself. Oh, my darling little bookcase . . . [*Kisses the bookcase.*] My sweet little table . . .

GAYEV. You know, of course, that Nanny died here while you were away.

MRS. RANEVSKY [*sits down and drinks her coffee*]. Yes, God rest her soul. They wrote to tell me about it.

GAYEV. Anastasy, too, is dead. Boss-eyed Peter left me for another job. He's with the Police Superintendent in town now. [*Takes a box of fruit drops out of his pocket and sucks one.*]

PISHCHIK. My daughter Dashenka—er—wishes to be remembered to you.

LOPAKHIN. I'd like to say something very nice and cheerful to you. [*Glances at his watch.*] I shall have to be going in a moment and there isn't much time to talk. As you know, your cherry orchard's being sold to pay your debts. The auction is on the twenty-second of August. But there's no need to worry, my dear. You can sleep soundly. There's a way out. Here's my plan. Listen carefully, please. Your estate is only about twelve miles from town, and the railway is not very far away. Now, all you have to do is break up your cherry orchard and the land along the river into building plots and lease them out for country cottages. You'll then have an income of at least twenty-five thousand a year.

GAYEV. I'm sorry, but what utter nonsense!

MRS. RANEVSKY. I don't quite follow you, Lopakhin.

LOPAKHIN. You'll be able to charge your tenants at least twenty-five rubles a year for a plot of about three acres. I bet you anything that if you advertise now, there won't be a single plot left by the autumn. They will all be snapped up. In fact, I congratulate you. You are saved. The site is magnificent and the river is deep enough for bathing. Of course, the place will have to be cleared, tidied up. . . . I mean, all the old buildings will have to be pulled down, including, I'm sorry to say, this house, but it isn't any use to anybody any more, is it? The old cherry orchard will have to be cut down.

MRS. RANEVSKY. Cut down? My dear man, I'm very sorry but I don't think you know what you're talking about. If there's anything of interest, anything quite remarkable, in fact, in the whole county, it's our cherry orchard.

LOPAKHIN. The only remarkable thing about this orchard is that it's very large. It only produces a crop every other year, and even then you don't know what to do with the cherries. Nobody wants to buy them.

GAYEV. Why, you'll find our orchard mentioned in the encyclopedia.

LOPAKHIN [*glancing at his watch*]. If we can't think of anything and if we can't come to any decision, it won't be only your cherry orchard but your whole estate that will be sold at auction on the twenty-second of August. Make up your mind. I tell you, there is no other way. Take my word for it. There isn't.

FIRS. In the old days, forty or fifty years ago, the cherries used to be dried, preserved, made into jam, and sometimes——

GAYEV. Do shut up, Firs.

FIRS. ——and sometimes cartloads of dried cherries were sent to Moscow and Kharkov. Fetched a lot of money, they did. Soft and juicy, those cherries were. Sweet and such a lovely smell . . . They knew the recipe then. . . .

MRS. RANEVSKY. And where's the recipe now?

FIRS. Forgotten. No one remembers it.

PISHCHIK [*to* MRS. RANEVSKY]. What was it like in Paris? Eh? Eat any frogs?

MRS. RANEVSKY. I ate crocodiles.

PISHCHIK. Good Lord!

LOPAKHIN. Till recently there were only the gentry and the peasants in the country. Now we have holiday-makers. All our towns, even the smallest, are surrounded by country cottages. I shouldn't be surprised if in twenty years the holiday-maker multiplies enormously. All your holiday-maker does now is drink tea on the veranda, but it's quite in the cards that if he becomes the owner of three acres of land, he'll do a bit of farming on the side, and then your cherry orchard will become a happy, prosperous, thriving place.

GAYEV [*indignantly*]. What nonsense!

Enter VARYA *and* YASHA.

VARYA. I've got two telegrams in here for you, Mother dear. [*Picks out a key and unlocks the old-fashioned bookcase with a jingling noise.*] Here they are.

MRS. RANEVSKY. They're from Paris. [*Tears the telegrams up without reading them.*] I've finished with Paris.

GAYEV. Do you know how old this bookcase is, Lyuba? Last week I pulled out the bottom drawer and saw some figures burned into it. This bookcase was made exactly a hundred years ago. What do you think of that? Eh? We ought really to celebrate its centenary. An inanimate object, but say what you like, it's a bookcase after all.

PISHCHIK [*amazed*]. A hundred years! Good Lord!

GAYEV. Yes, indeed. It's quite something. [*Feeling round the bookcase with his hands.*] Dear, highly esteemed bookcase, I salute you. For over a hundred years you have devoted yourself to the glorious ideals of goodness and justice. Throughout the hundred years your silent appeal to fruitful work has never faltered. It sustained [*through tears*] in several generations of our family, their courage and faith in a better future and fostered in us the ideals of goodness and social consciousness.

Pause.

LOPAKHIN. Aye. . . .

MRS. RANEVSKY. You haven't changed a bit, have you, darling Leonid?

GAYEV [*slightly embarrassed*]. Off the right into a corner! Pot into the middle pocket!

LOPAKHIN [*glancing at his watch*]. Well, afraid it's time I was off.

YASHA [*handing* MRS. RANEVSKY *her medicine*]. Your pills, ma'am.

PISHCHIK. Never take any medicines, dear lady. I don't

suppose they'll do you much harm, but they won't do you any good either. Here, let me have 'em, my dear lady. [*Takes the box of pills from her, pours the pills into the palm of his hand, blows on them, puts them all into his mouth, and washes them down with kvass.*] There!

MRS. RANEVSKY [*alarmed*]. You're mad!

PISHCHIK. Swallowed the lot.

LOPAKHIN. The glutton!

All laugh.

FIRS. He was here at Easter, the gentleman was. Ate half a bucketful of pickled cucumbers, he did. . . . [*Mutters.*]

MRS. RANEVSKY. What is he saying?

VARYA. He's been muttering like that for the last three years. We've got used to it.

YASHA. Old age!

CHARLOTTE, *in a white dress, very thin and tightly laced, a lorgnette dangling from her belt, crosses the stage.*

LOPAKHIN. I'm sorry, Miss Charlotte, I haven't had the chance of saying how-do-you-do to you. [*Tries to kiss her hand.*]

CHARLOTTE [*snatching her hand away*]. If I let you kiss my hand, you'll want to kiss my elbow, then my shoulder . . .

LOPAKHIN. It's not my lucky day. [*They all laugh.*] My dear Charlotte, show us a trick, please.

MRS. RANEVSKY. Yes, do show us a trick, Charlotte.

CHARLOTTE. I won't. I'm off to bed. [*Goes out.*]

LOPAKHIN. We'll meet again in three weeks. [*Kisses* MRS. RANEVSKY'*s hand.*] Good-bye for now. I must go. [*To* GAYEV.] So long. [*Embraces* PISHCHIK.] So long. [*Shakes hands with* VARYA *and then with* FIRS *and* YASHA.] I wish I didn't have to go. [*To* MRS. RANEVSKY.] Let me know if you make up your mind about the country cottages. If you decide to go ahead, I'll get you a loan of fifty thousand or more. Think it over seriously.

VARYA [*angrily*]. For goodness' sake, go!

LOPAKHIN. I'm going, I'm going. . . . [*Goes out.*]

GAYEV. The oaf! However, I'm sorry. Varya's going to marry him, isn't she? He's Varya's intended.

VARYA. Don't say things you'll be sorry for, Uncle.

MRS. RANEVSKY. But why not, Varya? I should be only too glad. He's a good man.

PISHCHIK. A most admirable fellow, to tell the truth. My Dashenka—er—also says that—er—says all sorts of things. [*Drops off and snores, but wakes up immediately.*] By the way, my dear lady, you will lend me two hundred and forty rubles, won't you? Must pay the interest on the mortgage tomorrow.

VARYA [*terrified*]. We have no money; we haven't!

MRS. RANEVSKY. We really haven't any, you know.

PISHCHIK. Have a good look around—you're sure to find it. [*Laughs.*] I never lose hope. Sometimes I think it's all over with me, I'm done for, then—hey presto—they build a railway over my land and pay me for it. Something's bound to turn up, if not today, then tomorrow. I'm certain of it. Dashenka might win two hundred thousand. She's got a ticket in the lottery, you know.

MRS. RANEVSKY. Well, I've finished my coffee. Now to bed.

FIRS [*brushing* GAYEV'*s clothes admonishingly*]. Put the wrong trousers on again, sir. What am I to do with you?

VARYA [*in a low voice*]. Anya's asleep. [*Opens a window quietly.*] The sun has risen. It's no longer cold. Look, Mother dear. What lovely trees! Heavens, what wonderful air! The starlings are singing.

GAYEV [*opens another window*]. The orchard's all white. Lyuba, you haven't forgotten, have you? The long avenue there—it runs on and on, straight as an arrow. It gleams on moonlit nights. Remember? You haven't forgotten, have you?

MRS. RANEVSKY [*looking through the window at the orchard*]. Oh, my childhood, oh, my innocence! I slept in this nursery. I used to look out at the orchard from here. Every morning happiness used to wake with me. The orchard was just the same in those days. Nothing has changed. [*Laughs happily.*] White, all white! Oh, my orchard! After the dark, rainy autumn and the cold winter, you're young again, full of happiness; the heavenly angels haven't forsaken you. If only this heavy load could be lifted from my heart; if only I could forget my past!

GAYEV. Well, and now they're going to sell the orchard to pay our debts. Funny, isn't it?

MRS. RANEVSKY. Look! Mother's walking in the orchard in . . . a white dress! [*Laughs happily.*] It *is* Mother!

GAYEV. Where?

VARYA. Really, Mother dear, what are you saying?

MRS. RANEVSKY. There's no one there. I just imagined it. Over there, on the right, near the turning to the summer house, a little white tree's leaning over. It looks like a woman. [*Enter* TROFIMOV. *He is dressed in a shabby student's uniform and wears glasses.*] What an amazing orchard! Masses of white blossom. A blue sky . . .

TROFIMOV. I say, Mrs. Ranevsky . . . [*She looks round at him.*] I've just come to say hello. I'll go at once. [*Kisses her hand warmly.*] I was told to wait till morning, but I —I couldn't, I couldn't.

MRS. RANEVSKY *gazes at him in bewilderment.*

VARYA [*through tears*]. This is Peter Trofimov.

TROFIMOV. Peter Trofimov. Your son Grisha's old tutor. I haven't changed so much, have I?

MRS. RANEVSKY *embraces him and weeps quietly.*

GAYEV [*embarrassed*]. There, there, Lyuba.

VARYA [*cries*]. I did tell you to wait till tomorrow, didn't I, Peter?

MRS. RANEVSKY. Grisha, my . . . little boy. Grisha . . . my son.

VARYA. It can't be helped, Mother. It was God's will.

TROFIMOV [*gently, through tears*]. Now, now . . .

MRS. RANEVSKY [*weeping quietly*]. My little boy died, drowned. Why? Why, my friend? [*More quietly.*] Anya's asleep in there and here I am shouting, making a noise. . . . Well, Peter? You're not as good-looking as you were, are you? Why not? Why have you aged so much?

TROFIMOV. A peasant woman in a railway carriage called me "a moth-eaten gentleman."

MRS. RANEVSKY. You were only a boy then. A charming young student. Now you're growing thin on top, you wear glasses. . . . You're not still a student, are you? [*Walks toward the door.*]

TROFIMOV. I expect I shall be an eternal student.

MRS. RANEVSKY [*kisses her brother and then* VARYA]. Well, go to bed now. You, Leonid, have aged too.

PISHCHIK [*following her*]. So, we're off to bed now, are we? Oh dear, my gout! I think I'd better stay the night here. Now, what about letting me have the—er—two hundred and forty rubles tomorrow morning, dear lady? Early tomorrow morning. . . .

GAYEV. He does keep on, doesn't he?

PISHCHIK. Two hundred and forty rubles—to pay the interest on the mortgage.

MRS. RANEVSKY. But I haven't any money, my dear man.

PISHCHIK. I'll pay you back, dear lady. Such a trifling sum.

MRS. RANEVSKY. Oh, all right. Leonid will let you have it. Let him have it, Leonid.

GAYEV. Let him have it? The hell I will.

MRS. RANEVSKY. What else can we do? Let him have it, please. He needs it. He'll pay it back.

MRS. RANEVSKY, TROFIMOV, PISHCHIK, *and* FIRS *go out.* GAYEV, VARYA, *and* YASHA *remain.*

GAYEV. My sister hasn't got out of the habit of throwing money about. [*To* YASHA.] Out of my way, fellow. You reek of the hen house.

YASHA [*grins*]. And you, sir, are the same as ever.

GAYEV. I beg your pardon? [*To* VARYA.] What did he say?

VARYA [*to* YASHA]. Your mother's come from the village. She's been sitting in the servants' quarters since yesterday. She wants to see you.

YASHA. Oh, bother her!

VARYA. You shameless bounder!

YASHA. I don't care. She could have come tomorrow, couldn't she? [*Goes out.*]

VARYA. Dear Mother is just the same as ever. Hasn't changed a bit. If you let her, she'd give away everything.

GAYEV. I suppose so. [*Pause.*] When a lot of remedies are suggested for an illness, it means that the illness is incurable. I've been thinking, racking my brains; I've got all sorts of remedies, lots of them, which, of course, means that I haven't got one. It would be marvelous if somebody left us some money. It would be marvelous if we found a very rich husband for Anya. It would be marvelous if one of us went to Yaroslavl to try our luck with our great-aunt, the Countess. She's very rich, you know. Very rich.

VARYA [*crying*]. If only God would help us.

GAYEV. Don't howl! Our aunt is very rich, but she doesn't like us. First, because my sister married a lawyer and not a nobleman. . . . [ANYA *appears in the doorway.*] She did not marry a nobleman, and she has not been leading an exactly blameless life, has she? She's a good, kind, nice person. I love her very much. But, however much you try to make allowances for her, you have to admit that she is an immoral woman. You can sense it in every movement she makes.

VARYA [*in a whisper*]. Anya's standing in the doorway.

GAYEV. I beg your pardon? [*Pause.*] Funny thing, there's something in my right eye. Can't see properly. On Thursday, too, in the district court . . .

ANYA *comes in.*

VARYA. Why aren't you asleep, Anya?

ANYA. I can't sleep, I can't.

GAYEV. My little darling! [*Kisses* ANYA'*s face and hands.*] My dear child! [*Through tears.*] You're not my niece, you're my angel. You're everything to me. Believe me. Do believe me.

ANYA. I believe you, Uncle. Everyone loves you, everyone respects you, but, dear Uncle, you shouldn't talk so much. What were you saying just now about Mother, about your own sister? What did you say it for?

GAYEV. Well, yes, yes. [*He takes her hand and covers his face with it.*] You're quite right. It was dreadful. Dear God, dear God, help me! That speech I made to the bookcase today—it was so silly. The moment I finished it, I realized how silly it was.

VARYA. It's quite true, Uncle dear. You oughtn't to talk so much. Just don't talk, that's all.

ANYA. If you stopped talking, you'd feel much happier yourself.

GAYEV. Not another word. [*Kisses* ANYA'*s and* VARYA'*s hands.*] Not another word. Now to business. Last Thursday I was at the county court, and, well—er—I met a lot of people there, and we started talking about this and that, and—er—it would seem that we might manage to raise some money on a promissory note and pay the interest to the bank.

VARYA. Oh, if only God would help us!

GAYEV. I shall be there again on Tuesday, and I'll have another talk. [*To* VARYA.] For goodness' sake, don't howl! [*To* ANYA.] Your mother will have a talk with Lopakhin. I'm sure he won't refuse her. After you've had your rest, you'll go to Yaroslavl to see your great-aunt, the Countess. That's how we shall tackle the problem from three different sides, and I'm sure we'll get it settled. The interest we shall pay. Of that I'm quite sure. [*Puts a fruit drop in his mouth.*] I give you my word of honor, I swear by anything you like, the estate will not be sold! [*Excitedly.*] Why, I'll stake my life on it! Here's my hand; call me a rotten scoundrel if I allow the auction to take place. I stake my life on it!

ANYA [*has regained her composure; she looks happy*]. You're so good, Uncle dear! So clever! [*Embraces him.*] I'm no longer worried now. Not a bit worried. I'm happy.

Enter FIRS.

FIRS [*reproachfully*]. Have you no fear of God, sir? When are you going to bed?

GAYEV. Presently, presently. Go away, Firs. Never mind, I'll undress myself this time. Well, children, bye-bye now. More about it tomorrow. Now you must go to bed. [*Kisses* ANYA *and* VARYA.] I'm a man of the eighties. People don't think much of that time, but let me tell you, I've suffered a great deal for my convictions during my life. It's not for nothing that the peasants love me. You have to know your peasant, you have to know how to——

ANYA. There you go again, Uncle.

VARYA. Please, Uncle dear, don't talk so much.

FIRS [*angrily*]. Sir!

GAYEV. I'm coming, I'm coming. You two go to bed. Off two cushions into the middle. Pot the white!

GAYEV *goes out*, FIRS *shuffling off after him.*

ANYA. I'm not worried any longer now. I don't feel like going to Yaroslavl. I don't like my great-aunt, but I'm no longer worried. I ought to thank Uncle for that. [*Sits down.*]

VARYA. I ought to go to bed, and I shall be going in a moment. I must tell you first that something unpleasant happened here while you were away. You know, of course, that only a few old servants live in the old servants' quarters: Yefimushka, Polia, Evstigney, and, well, also Karp. They had been letting some tramps sleep there, but I didn't say anything about it. Then I heard that they were telling everybody that I'd given orders for them to be fed on nothing but dried peas. I'm supposed to be a miser, you see. It was all that Evstigney's doing. Well, I said to myself, if that's how it is, you just wait! So I sent for Evstigney. [*Yawns.*] He comes. "What do you mean," I said, "Evstigney, you silly old fool?" [*Looks at* ANYA.] Darling! [*Pause.*] Asleep . . . [*Takes* ANYA *by the arm.*] Come to bed, dear. . . . Come on! [*Leads her by the arm.*] My darling's fallen asleep. Come along. [*They go out. A shepherd's pipe is heard playing from far away on the other side of the orchard.* TROFIMOV *walks across the stage and, catching sight of* VARYA *and* ANYA, *stops.*] Shh! She's asleep, asleep. Come along, my sweet.

ANYA [*softly, half asleep*]. I'm so tired. . . . I keep hearing harness bells. Uncle . . . dear . . . Mother and Uncle . . .

VARYA. Come on, my sweet, come on. . . .

They go into ANYA'*s room.*

TROFIMOV [*deeply moved*]. My sun! My spring!

Curtain.

ACT TWO

Open country. A small tumbledown wayside chapel. Near it, a well, some large stones, which look like old gravestones, and an old bench. A road can be seen leading to GAYEV'S *estate. On one side, a row of tall dark poplars; it is there that the cherry orchard begins. In the distance, some telegraph poles, and far, far away on the horizon, the outlines of a large town that is visible only in very fine, clear weather. The sun is about to set.* CHARLOTTE, YASHA, *and* DUNYASHA *are sitting on the bench;* YEPIKHODOV *is standing nearby and is playing a guitar; they all sit sunk in thought.* CHARLOTTE *wears a man's old peaked hat; she has taken a shotgun from her shoulder and is adjusting the buckle on the strap.*

CHARLOTTE [*pensively*]. I haven't a proper passport, I don't know how old I am, and I can't help thinking that I'm still a young girl. When I was a little girl, my father and mother used to travel the fairs and give performances—very good ones. I used to do the *salto mortale* and all sorts of other tricks. When Father and Mother died, a German lady adopted me and began educating me. Very well. I grew up and became a governess, but where I came from and who I am, I do not know. Who my parents were, I do not know either. They may not even have been married. I don't know. [*Takes a cucumber out of her pocket and starts eating it.*] I don't know anything. [*Pause.*] I'm longing to talk to someone, but there is no one to talk to. I haven't anyone. . . .

YEPIKHODOV [*plays his guitar and sings*]. "What care I for the world and its bustle? What care I for my friends and my foes?" . . . Nice to play a mandolin.

DUNYASHA. It's a guitar, not a mandolin. [*She looks at herself in a hand mirror and powders her face.*]

YEPIKHODOV. To a madman in love, it's a mandolin. [*Sings softly.*] "If only my heart was warmed by the fire of love requited."

YASHA *joins in.*

CHARLOTTE. How terribly these people sing! Ugh! Like hyenas.

DUNYASHA [*to* YASHA]. All the same, you're ever so lucky to have been abroad.

YASHA. Why, of course. Can't help agreeing with you there. [*Yawns, then lights a cigar.*]

YEPIKHODOV. Stands to reason. Abroad, everything's in excellent complexion. Been like that for ages.

YASHA. Naturally.

YEPIKHODOV. I'm a man of some education, I read all sorts of remarkable books, but what I simply can't understand is where it's all leading to. I mean, what do I really want—to live or to shoot myself? In any case, I always carry a revolver. Here it is. [*Shows them his revolver.*]

CHARLOTTE. That's done. Now I can go. [*Puts the shotgun over her shoulder.*] You're a very clever man, Yepikhodov. You frighten me to death. Women must be madly in love with you. Brrr! [*Walking away.*] These clever people are all so stupid. I've no one to talk to. Always alone, alone. I've no one, and who I am and what I am for is a mystery. [*Walks off slowly.*]

YEPIKHODOV. Strictly speaking, and apart from all other considerations, what I ought to say about myself, among other things, is that Fate treats me without mercy, like a storm a small boat. Even supposing I'm mistaken, why in that case should I wake up this morning and suddenly find a spider of quite enormous dimensions on my chest? As big as that. [*Uses both hands to show the spider's size.*] Or again, I pick up a jug of kvass and there's something quite outrageously indecent in it, like a cockroach. [*Pause.*] Have you ever read Buckle's *History of Civilization*? [*Pause.*] May I have a word or two with you, Dunyasha?

DUNYASHA. Oh, all right. What is it?

YEPIKHODOV. I'd be very much obliged if you'd let me speak to you in private. [*Sighs.*]

DUNYASHA [*embarrassed*]. All right, only first bring me my cape, please. It's hanging near the wardrobe. It's so damp here.

YEPIKHODOV. Very well, I'll fetch it. . . . Now I know

what to do with my revolver. [*Picks up his guitar and goes out strumming it.*]

YASHA. Twenty-two Calamities! A stupid fellow, between you and me. [*Yawns.*]

DUNYASHA. I hope to goodness he won't shoot himself. [*Pause.*] I'm ever so nervous. I can't help being worried all the time. I was taken into service when I was a little girl, and now I can't live like a peasant any more. See my hands? They're ever so white, as white as a young lady's. I've become so nervous, so sensitive, so like a lady. I'm afraid of everything. I'm simply terrified. So if you deceived me, Yasha, I don't know what would happen to my nerves.

YASHA [*kisses her*]. Little cucumber! Mind you, I expect every girl to be respectable. What I dislike most is for a girl to misbehave herself.

DUNYASHA. I've fallen passionately in love with you, Yasha. You're so educated. You can talk about anything.

Pause.

YASHA [*yawning*]. You see, in my opinion, if a girl is in love with somebody, it means she's immoral. [*Pause.*] It is so pleasant to smoke a cigar in the open air. [*Listens.*] Someone's coming. It's them. . . . [DUNYASHA *embraces him impulsively.*] Please go home and look as if you've been down to the river for a swim. Take that path or they'll think I had arranged to meet you here. Can't stand that sort of thing.

DUNYASHA [*coughing quietly*]. Your cigar has given me an awful headache. [*Goes out.*]

YASHA *remains sitting near the chapel. Enter* MRS. RANEVSKY, GAYEV, *and* LOPAKHIN.

LOPAKHIN. You must make up your minds once and for all. There's not much time left. After all, it's quite a simple matter. Do you agree to lease your land for country cottages or don't you? Answer me in one word: yes or no. Just one word.

MRS. RANEVSKY. Who's been smoking such horrible cigars here? [*Sits down.*]

GAYEV. Now that they've built the railway, things are much more convenient. [*Sits down.*] We've been to town for lunch—pot the red in the middle! I really should have gone in to have a game first.

MRS. RANEVSKY. There's plenty of time.

LOPAKHIN. Just one word. [*Imploringly.*] Please give me your answer!

GAYEV [*yawns*]. I beg your pardon?

MRS. RANEVSKY [*looking in her purse*]. Yesterday I had a lot of money, but I've hardly any left today. My poor Varya! Tries to economize by feeding everybody on milk soup and the old servants in the kitchen on peas, and I'm just throwing money about stupidly. [*Drops her purse, scattering some gold coins.*] Goodness gracious, all over the place! [*She looks annoyed.*]

YASHA. Allow me to pick 'em up, madam. It won't take a minute. [*Starts picking up the coins.*]

MRS. RANEVSKY. Thank you, Yasha. Why on earth did I go out to lunch? That disgusting restaurant of yours with its stupid band, and those tablecloths smelling of soap. Why did you have to drink so much, Leonid? Or eat so much? Or talk so much? You did talk a lot again in the restaurant today and all to no purpose. About the seventies and the decadents . . . And who to? Talking about the decadents to waiters!

LOPAKHIN. Aye. . . .

GAYEV [*waving his arm*]. I'm incorrigible, that's clear. [*Irritably to* YASHA.] What are you hanging around here for?

YASHA [*laughs*]. I can't hear your voice without laughing, sir.

GAYEV [*to his sister*]. Either he or I.

MRS. RANEVSKY. Go away, Yasha. Run along.

YASHA [*returning the purse to* MRS. RANEVSKY]. At once, madam. [*Is hardly able to suppress his laughter.*] This very minute. [*Goes out.*]

LOPAKHIN. The rich merchant Deriganov is thinking of buying your estate. I'm told he's coming to the auction himself.

MRS. RANEVSKY. Where did you hear that?

LOPAKHIN. That's what they're saying in town.

GAYEV. Our Yaroslavl great-aunt has promised to send us money, but when and how much we do not know.

LOPAKHIN. How much will she send? A hundred thousand? Two hundred?

MRS. RANEVSKY. Well, I hardly think so. Ten or fifteen thousand at most. We must be thankful for that.

LOPAKHIN. I'm sorry, but such improvident people as you, such peculiar, unbusinesslike people, I've never met in my life! You're told in plain language that your estate's going to be sold, and you don't seem to understand.

MRS. RANEVSKY. But what are we to do? Tell us, please.

LOPAKHIN. I tell you every day. Every day I go on repeating the same thing over and over again. You must let out the cherry orchard and the land for country cottages, and you must do it now, as quickly as possible. The auction is on top of you! Try to understand! The moment you decide to let your land, you'll be able to raise as much money as you like, and you'll be saved.

MRS. RANEVSKY. Country cottages, holiday-makers—I'm sorry, but it's so vulgar.

GAYEV. I'm of your opinion entirely.

LOPAKHIN. I shall burst into tears or scream or have a fit. I can't stand it. You've worn me out! [*To* GAYEV.] You're a silly old woman!

GAYEV. I beg your pardon?

LOPAKHIN. A silly old woman! [*He gets up to go.*]

MRS. RANEVSKY [*in dismay*]. No, don't go. Please stay. I beg you. Perhaps we'll think of something.

LOPAKHIN. What is there to think of?

MRS. RANEVSKY. Please don't go. I beg you. Somehow I feel so much more cheerful with you here. [*Pause.*] I keep expecting something to happen, as though the house was going to collapse on top of us.

GAYEV [*deep in thought*]. Cannon off the cushion. Pot into the middle pocket. . . .

MRS. RANEVSKY. I'm afraid we've sinned too much——

LOPAKHIN. You sinned!

GAYEV [*putting a fruit drop into his mouth*]. They say I squandered my entire fortune on fruit drops. [*Laughs.*]

MRS. RANEVSKY. Oh, my sins! . . . I've always thrown money about aimlessly, like a madwoman. Why, I even married a man who did nothing but pile up debts. My husband died of champagne. He drank like a fish. Then, worse luck, I fell in love with someone, had an affair with him, and it was just at that time—it was my first punishment, a blow that nearly killed me—that my boy was drowned in the river here. I went abroad, never to come back, never to see that river again. I shut my eyes and ran, beside myself, and *he* followed me—pitilessly, brutally. I bought a villa near Mentone because *he* had fallen ill. For the next three years I knew no rest, nursing him day and night. He wore me out. Everything inside me went dead. Then, last year, I had to sell the villa to pay my debts. I left for Paris, where he robbed me, deserted me, and went to live with another woman. I tried to poison myself. Oh, it was all so stupid, so shaming. . . . It was then that I suddenly felt an urge to go back to Russia, to my homeland, to my daughter. [*Dries her eyes.*] Lord, O Lord, be merciful! Forgive me my sins! Don't punish me any more! [*Takes a telegram from her pocket.*] I received this telegram from Paris today. He asks me to forgive him. He implores me to go back. [*Tears up the telegram.*] What's that? Music? [*Listens intently.*]

GAYEV. That's our famous Jewish band. Remember? Four fiddles, a flute, and a double bass.

MRS. RANEVSKY. Does it still exist? We ought to arrange a party and have them over to the house.

LOPAKHIN [*listening*]. I don't hear anything. [*Sings quietly.*] "And the Germans, if you pay 'em, will turn a Russian into a Frenchman." [*Laughs.*] I saw an excellent play at the theatre last night. It was very amusing.

MRS. RANEVSKY. I don't suppose it was amusing at all. You shouldn't be watching plays, but should be watching yourselves more often. What dull lives you live. What nonsense you talk.

LOPAKHIN. Perfectly true. Let's admit quite frankly that the life we lead is utterly stupid. [*Pause.*] My father was a peasant, an idiot. He understood nothing. He taught me nothing. He just beat me when he was drunk and always with a stick. As a matter of fact, I'm just as big a blockhead and an idiot myself. I never learnt anything, and my handwriting is so abominable that I'm ashamed to let people see it.

MRS. RANEVSKY. You ought to get married, my friend.

LOPAKHIN. Yes. That's true.

MRS. RANEVSKY. Married to our Varya. She's a nice girl.

LOPAKHIN. Aye. . . .

MRS. RANEVSKY. Her father was a peasant too. She's a hard-working girl, and she loves you. That's the important thing. Why, you've been fond of her for a long time yourself.

LOPAKHIN. Very well. I've no objection. She's a good girl.

Pause.

GAYEV. I've been offered a job in a bank. Six thousand a year. Have you heard, Lyuba?

MRS. RANEVSKY. You in a bank! You'd better stay where you are.

FIRS *comes in carrying an overcoat.*

FIRS [*to* GAYEV]. Please put it on, sir. It's damp out here.

GAYEV [*putting on the overcoat*]. You're a damned nuisance, my dear fellow.

FIRS. Come along, sir. Don't be difficult. . . . This morning, too, you went off without saying a word. [*Looks him over.*]

MRS. RANEVSKY. How you've aged, Firs!

FIRS. What's that, ma'am?

LOPAKHIN. Your mistress says you've aged a lot.

FIRS. I've been alive a long time. They were trying to marry me off before your dad was born. . . . [*Laughs.*] When freedom came, I was already chief valet. I refused to accept freedom and stayed on with my master. [*Pause.*] I well remember how glad everyone was, but what they were glad about, they did not know themselves.

LOPAKHIN. It wasn't such a bad life before, was it? At least, they flogged you.

FIRS [*not hearing him*]. I should say so. The peasants stuck to their masters and the masters to their peasants. Now everybody does what he likes. You can't understand nothing.

GAYEV. Shut up, Firs. I have to go to town tomorrow. I've been promised an introduction to a general who might lend us some money on a promissory note.

LOPAKHIN. Nothing will come of it. You won't pay the interest, either. You may be sure of that.

MRS. RANEVSKY. Oh, he's just imagining things. There aren't any generals.

Enter TROFIMOV, ANYA, *and* VARYA.

GAYEV. Here they are at last.

ANYA. There's Mother.

MRS. RANEVSKY [*affectionately*]. Come here, come here, my dears. [*Embracing* ANYA *and* VARYA.] If only you knew how much I love you both. Sit down beside me. That's right.

All sit down.

LOPAKHIN. Our eternal student is always walking about with the young ladies.

TROFIMOV. Mind your own business.

LOPAKHIN. He's nearly fifty and he's still a student.

TROFIMOV. Do drop your idiotic jokes.

LOPAKHIN. Why are you so angry, you funny fellow?

TROFIMOV. Well, stop pestering me.

LOPAKHIN [*laughs*]. Tell me, what do you think of me?

TROFIMOV. Simply this: You're a rich man and you'll soon be a millionaire. Now, just as a beast of prey devours everything in its path and so helps to preserve the balance of nature, so you, too, perform a similar function.

They all laugh.

VARYA. You'd better tell us about the planets, Peter.

MRS. RANEVSKY. No, let's carry on with what we were talking about yesterday.

TROFIMOV. What was that?

GAYEV. Pride.

TROFIMOV. We talked a lot yesterday, but we didn't arrive at any conclusion. As you see it, there's something mystical about the proud man. You may be right for all I know. But try to look at it simply, without being too clever. What sort of pride is it, is there any sense in it if, physiologically, man is far from perfect? If, in fact, he is, in the vast majority of cases, coarse, stupid, and profoundly unhappy? It's time we stopped admiring ourselves. All we must do is—work!

GAYEV. We're going to die all the same.

TROFIMOV. Who knows? And what do you mean by "we're going to die"? A man may possess a hundred senses. When he dies, he loses only the five we know. The other ninety-five live on.

MRS. RANEVSKY. How clever you are, Peter!

LOPAKHIN [*ironically*]. Oh, frightfully!

TROFIMOV. Mankind marches on, perfecting its powers. Everything that is incomprehensible to us now, will one day become familiar and comprehensible. All we have to do is to work and do our best to assist those who are looking for the truth. Here in Russia only a few people are working so far. The vast majority of the educated people I know, do nothing. They aren't looking for anything. They are quite incapable of doing any work. They call themselves intellectuals, but speak to their servants as inferiors and treat the peasants like animals. They're not particularly keen on their studies, they don't do any serious reading, they are bone idle, they merely talk about science, and they understand very little about art. They are all so solemn, they look so very grave, they talk only of important matters, they philosophize. Yet anyone can see that our workers are abominably fed, sleep on bare boards, thirty and forty to a room—bedbugs everywhere, stench, damp, moral turpitude. It's therefore obvious that all our fine phrases are merely a way of deluding ourselves and others. Tell me, where are all those children's crèches people are talking so much about? Where are the reading rooms? You find them only in novels. Actually, we haven't any. All we have is dirt, vulgarity, brutality. I dislike and I'm frightened of all these solemn countenances, just as I'm frightened of all serious conversations. Why not shut up for once?

LOPAKHIN. Well, I get up at five o'clock in the morning, I work from morning till night, and I've always lots of money on me—mine and other people's—and I can see what the people around me are like. One has only to start doing something to realize how few honest, decent people there are about. Sometimes when I lie awake, I keep thinking: Lord, you've given us vast forests, boundless plains, immense horizons, and living here, we ourselves ought really to be giants——

MRS. RANEVSKY. You want giants, do you? They're all right only in fairy tales. Elsewhere they frighten me. [YEPIKHODOV *crosses the stage in the background, playing his guitar. Pensively.*] There goes Yepikhodov.

ANYA [*pensively*]. There goes Yepikhodov.

GAYEV. The sun's set, ladies and gentlemen.

TROFIMOV. Yes.

GAYEV [*softly, as though declaiming*]. Oh, nature, glorious nature! Glowing with eternal radiance, beautiful and indifferent, you, whom we call Mother, uniting in yourself both life and death, you—life-giver and destroyer . . .

VARYA [*imploringly*]. Darling Uncle!

ANYA. Uncle, again!

TROFIMOV. You'd far better pot the red in the middle.

GAYEV. Not another word! Not another word!

They all sit deep in thought. Everything is still. The silence is broken only by the subdued muttering of FIRS. *Suddenly a distant sound is heard. It seems to come from the sky, the sound of a breaking string, slowly dying away, melancholy.*

MRS. RANEVSKY. What's that?

LOPAKHIN. I don't know. I expect a bucket must have broken somewhere far away in a coal mine, but somewhere a very long distance away.

GAYEV. Perhaps it was a bird, a heron or something.

TROFIMOV. Or an eagle-owl.

MRS. RANEVSKY [*shudders*]. It makes me feel dreadful for some reason.

Pause.

FIRS. Same thing happened before the misfortune: the owl hooted and the samovar kept hissing.

GAYEV. Before what misfortune?

FIRS. Before they gave us our freedom.

Pause.

MRS. RANEVSKY. Come, let's go in, my friends. It's getting

dark. [*To* ANYA.] There are tears in your eyes. What's the matter, darling? [*Embraces her.*]

ANYA. It's nothing, Mother. Nothing.

TROFIMOV. Someone's coming.

A HIKER *appears. He wears a shabby white peaked cap and an overcoat; he is slightly drunk.*

HIKER. Excuse me, is this the way to the station?

GAYEV. Yes, follow that road.

HIKER. I'm greatly obliged to you, sir. [*Coughs.*] Glorious weather . . . [*Declaiming.*] Brother, my suffering brother, come to the Volga, you whose groans . . . [*To* VARYA.] Mademoiselle, won't you give thirty kopecks to a starving Russian citizen?

VARYA, *frightened, utters a little scream.*

LOPAKHIN [*angrily*]. There's a limit to the most disgraceful behavior.

MRS. RANEVSKY [*at a loss*]. Here, take this. [*Looks for some money in her purse.*] No silver. Never mind, have this gold one.

HIKER. Profoundly grateful to you, ma'am. [*Goes out.*]

Laughter.

VARYA [*frightened*]. I'm going away. I'm going away. Good heavens, Mother dear, there's no food for the servants in the house, and you gave him a gold sovereign!

MRS. RANEVSKY. What's to be done with a fool like me? I'll give you all I have when we get home. You'll lend me some more money, Lopakhin, won't you?

LOPAKHIN. With pleasure.

MRS. RANEVSKY. Let's go in. It's time. By the way, Varya, we've found you a husband here. Congratulations.

VARYA [*through tears*]. This isn't a joking matter, Mother.

LOPAKHIN. Okhmelia, go to a nunnery!

GAYEV. Look at my hands. They're shaking. It's a long time since I had a game of billiards.

LOPAKHIN. Okhmelia, O nymph, remember me in your prayers!

MRS. RANEVSKY. Come along, come along, it's almost supper time.

VARYA. That man frightened me. My heart's still pounding.

LOPAKHIN. Let me remind you, ladies and gentlemen: The cherry orchard is up for sale on the twenty-second of August. Think about it! Think!

They all go out except TROFIMOV *and* ANYA.

ANYA [*laughing*]. I'm so glad the hiker frightened Varya. Now we are alone.

TROFIMOV. Varya's afraid we might fall in love. That's why she follows us around for days on end. With her narrow mind she cannot grasp that we are above love. The whole aim and meaning of our life is to bypass everything that is petty and illusory, that prevents us from being free and happy. Forward! Let us march on irresistibly toward the bright star shining there in the distance! Forward! Don't lag behind, friends!

ANYA [*clapping her hands excitedly*]. You talk so splendidly! [*Pause.*] It's so heavenly here today!

TROFIMOV. Yes, the weather is wonderful.

ANYA. What have you done to me, Peter? Why am I no longer as fond of the cherry orchard as before? I loved it so dearly. I used to think there was no lovelier place on earth than our orchard.

TROFIMOV. The whole of Russia is our orchard. The earth is great and beautiful. There are lots of lovely places on it. [*Pause.*] Think, Anya: your grandfather, your great-grandfather, and all your ancestors owned serfs. They owned living souls. Can't you see human beings looking at you from every cherry tree in your orchard, from every leaf and every tree trunk? Don't you hear their voices? To own living souls—that's what has changed you all so much, you who are living now and those who lived before you. That's why your mother, you yourself, and your uncle no longer realize that you are living on borrowed capital, at other people's expense, at the expense of those whom you don't admit farther than your entrance hall. We are at least two hundred years behind the times. We haven't got anything at all. We have no definite attitude toward our past. We just philosophize, complain of depression, or drink vodka. Isn't it abundantly clear that before we start living in the present, we must atone for our past, make an end of it? And atone for it we can only by suffering, by extraordinary, unceasing labor. Understand that, Anya.

ANYA. The house we live in hasn't really been ours for a long time. I'm going to leave it. I give you my word.

TROFIMOV. If you have the keys of the house, throw them into the well and go away. Be free as the wind.

ANYA [*rapturously*]. How well you said it!

TROFIMOV. Believe me, Anya, believe me! I'm not yet thirty, I'm young, I'm still a student, but I've been through hell more than once. I'm driven from pillar to post. In winter I'm half-starved, I'm ill, worried, poor as a beggar. You can't imagine the terrible places I've been to! And yet, always, every moment of the day and night, my heart was full of ineffable visions of the future. I feel, I'm quite sure, that happiness is coming, Anya. I can see it coming already.

ANYA [*pensively*]. The moon is rising.

YEPIKHODOV *can be heard playing the same sad tune as before on his guitar. The moon rises. Somewhere near the poplars* VARYA *is looking for* ANYA *and calling, "Anya, where are you?"*

TROFIMOV. Yes, the moon is rising. [*Pause.*] There it is—happiness! It's coming nearer and nearer. Already I can hear its footsteps, and if we never see it, if we never know it, what does that matter? Others will see it.

VARYA [*offstage*]. Anya, where are you?

TROFIMOV. That Varya again! [*Angrily.*] Disgusting!

ANYA. Never mind, let's go to the river. It's lovely there.

TROFIMOV. Yes, let's.

They go out.

VARYA [*offstage*]. Anya! Anya!

Curtain.

ACT THREE

The drawing room, separated by an archway from the ballroom. A candelabra is alight. The Jewish band can be heard playing in the entrance hall. It is the same band that is mentioned in Act Two. Evening. In the ballroom people are dancing the Grande Ronde. SIMEONOV-PISHCHIK'S *voice can be heard crying out, "Promenade à une paire!" They all come out into the drawing room:* PISHCHIK *and* CHARLOTTE *the first couple,* TROFIMOV *and* MRS. RANEVSKY *the second,* ANYA *and a* POST OFFICE CLERK *the third,* VARYA *and the* STATIONMASTER *the fourth, and so on.* VARYA *is quietly crying and dries her eyes as she dances. The last couple consists of* DUNYASHA *and a partner. They walk across the drawing room.* PISHCHIK *shouts, "Grande Ronde balancez!" and "Les cavaliers à genoux et remerciez vos dames!"*

FIRS, *wearing a tailcoat, brings in soda water on a tray.* PISHCHIK *and* TROFIMOV *come into the drawing room.*

PISHCHIK. I've got high blood-pressure. I've had two strokes already, and I find dancing hard work. But, as the saying goes, if you're one of a pack, wag your tail, whether you bark or not. As a matter of fact, I'm as strong as a horse. My father, may he rest in peace, liked his little joke, and speaking about our family pedigree, he used to say that the ancient line of the Simeonov-Pishchiks came from the horse that Caligula had made a senator. [*Sits down.*] But you see, the trouble is that I have no money. A hungry dog believes only in meat. [*Snores, but wakes up again at once.*] I'm just the same. All I can think of is money.

TROFIMOV. There really is something horsy about you.

PISHCHIK. Well, a horse is a good beast. You can sell a horse.

From an adjoining room comes the sound of people playing billiards. VARYA *appears in the ballroom under the archway.*

TROFIMOV [*teasing her*]. Mrs. Lopakhin! Mrs. Lopakhin!

VARYA [*angrily*]. Moth-eaten gentleman!

TROFIMOV. Well, I am a moth-eaten gentleman and proud of it.

VARYA [*brooding bitterly*]. We've hired a band, but how we are going to pay for it, I don't know. [*Goes out.*]

TROFIMOV [*to* PISHCHIK]. If the energy you have wasted throughout your life looking for money to pay the interest on your debts had been spent on something else, you'd most probably have succeeded in turning the world upside down.

PISHCHIK. Nietzsche, the famous philosopher—a great man, a man of great intellect—says in his works that there's nothing wrong about forging bank notes.

TROFIMOV. Have you read Nietzsche?

PISHCHIK. Well, actually, Dashenka told me about it. I don't mind telling you, though, that in my present position I might even forge bank notes. The day after tomorrow I've got to pay three hundred and ten rubles. I've already got one hundred and thirty. [*Feels his pockets, in alarm.*] My money's gone, I've lost my money! [*Through tears.*] Where is it? [*Happily.*] Ah, here it is, in the lining. Lord, the shock brought me out in a cold sweat!

Enter MRS. RANEVSKY *and* CHARLOTTE.

MRS. RANEVSKY [*hums a popular Georgian dance tune*]. Why is Leonid so late? What's he doing in town? [*To* DUNYASHA.] Offer the band tea, please.

TROFIMOV. I don't suppose the auction has taken place.

MRS. RANEVSKY. What a time to have a band! What a time to give a party! Oh well, never mind. [*Sits down and hums quietly.*]

CHARLOTTE [*hands* PISHCHIK *a pack of cards*]. Here's a pack of cards. Think of a card.

PISHCHIK. All right.

CHARLOTTE. Now shuffle the pack. That's right. Now give it to me. Now, then, my dear Mr. Pishchik, *eins, zwei, drei!* Look in your breast pocket. Is it there?

PISHCHIK [*takes the card out of his breast pocket*]. The eight of spades! Absolutely right! [*Surprised.*] Good Lord!

CHARLOTTE [*holding a pack of cards on the palm of her hand, to* TROFIMOV]. Tell me, quick, what's the top card?

TROFIMOV. Well, let's say the queen of spades.

CHARLOTTE. Here it is. [*To* PISHCHIK.] What's the top card now?

PISHCHIK. The ace of hearts.

CHARLOTTE. Here you are! [*Claps her hands and the pack of cards disappears.*] What lovely weather we're having today. [*A mysterious female voice, which seems to come from under the floor, answers: "Oh yes, glorious weather, madam!"*] You're my ideal, you're so nice! [*The voice: "I like you very much too, madam."*]

STATIONMASTER [*clapping his hands*]. Bravo, Madame Ventriloquist!

PISHCHIK [*looking surprised*]. Good Lord! Enchanting, Miss Charlotte, I'm simply in love with you.

CHARLOTTE. In love! Are you sure you can love? *Guter Mensch, aber schlechter Musikant.*

TROFIMOV [*claps* PISHCHIK *on the shoulder*]. Good old horse!

CHARLOTTE. Attention, please. One more trick. [*She takes a rug from a chair.*] Here's a very good rug. I'd like to sell it. [*Shaking it.*] Who wants to buy it?

PISHCHIK [*surprised*]. Good Lord!

CHARLOTTE. *Eins, zwei, drei!* [*Quickly snatching up the rug, which she had let fall, she reveals* ANYA *standing behind it.* ANYA *curtseys, runs to her mother, embraces her, and runs back to the ballroom amid general enthusiasm.*]

MRS. RANEVSKY [*applauding*]. Bravo, bravo!

CHARLOTTE. Now, once more. *Eins, zwei, drei!* [*Lifts the rug; behind it stands* VARYA, *who bows.*]

PISHCHIK [*surprised*]. Good Lord!

CHARLOTTE. The end! [*Throws the rug over* PISHCHIK, *curtseys, and runs off to the ballroom.*]

PISHCHIK [*running after her*]. The hussy! What a woman, eh? What a woman! [*Goes out.*]

MRS. RANEVSKY. Still no Leonid. I can't understand what he can be doing in town all this time. It must be over now. Either the estate has been sold or the auction didn't take place. Why keep us in suspense so long?

VARYA [*trying to comfort her*]. I'm certain Uncle must have bought it.

TROFIMOV [*sarcastically*]. Oh, to be sure!

VARYA. Our great-aunt sent him power of attorney to buy the estate in her name and transfer the mortgage to her. She's done it for Anya's sake. God will help us and Uncle will buy it. I'm sure of it.

MRS. RANEVSKY. Your great-aunt sent fifteen thousand to buy the estate in her name. She doesn't trust us—but the money wouldn't even pay the interest. [*She covers her face with her hands.*] My whole future is being decided today, my future. . . .

TROFIMOV [*teasing* VARYA]. Mrs. Lopakhin!

VARYA [*crossly*]. Eternal student! Expelled twice from the university, weren't you?

MRS. RANEVSKY. Why are you so cross, Varya? He's teasing you about Lopakhin. Well, what of it? Marry Lopakhin if you want to. He is a nice, interesting man. If you don't want to, don't marry him. Nobody's forcing you, darling.

VARYA. I regard such a step seriously, Mother dear. I don't mind being frank about it: He is a nice man, and I like him.

MRS. RANEVSKY. Well, marry him. What are you waiting for? That's what I can't understand.

VARYA. But, Mother dear, I can't very well propose to him myself, can I? Everyone's been talking to me about him for the last two years. Everyone! But he either says nothing or makes jokes. I quite understand. He's making money. He has his business to think of, and he hasn't time for me. If I had any money, just a little, a hundred rubles, I'd give up everything and go right away as far as possible. I'd have gone into a convent.

TROFIMOV. Wonderful!

VARYA [*to* TROFIMOV]. A student ought to be intelligent! [*In a gentle voice, through tears.*] How plain you've grown, Peter! How you've aged! [*To* MRS. RANEVSKY, *no longer crying.*] I can't live without having something to do, Mother! I must be doing something all the time.

Enter YASHA.

YASHA [*hardly able to restrain his laughter*]. Yepikhodov's broken a billiard cue! [*Goes out.*]

VARYA. What's Yepikhodov doing here? Who gave him

permission to play billiards? Can't understand these people! [*Goes out.*]

MRS. RANEVSKY. Don't tease her, Peter. Don't you see she is unhappy enough already?

TROFIMOV. She's a bit too conscientious. Pokes her nose into other people's affairs. Wouldn't leave me and Anya alone all summer. Afraid we might have an affair. What business is it of hers? Besides, the idea never entered my head. Such vulgarity is beneath me. We are above love.

MRS. RANEVSKY. So, I suppose I must be beneath love. [*In great agitation.*] Why isn't Leonid back? All I want to know is: Has the estate been sold or not? Such a calamity seems so incredible to me that I don't know what to think. I'm completely at a loss. I feel like screaming, like doing something silly. Help me, Peter. Say something. For God's sake, say something!

TROFIMOV. What does it matter whether the estate's been sold today or not? The estate's been finished and done with long ago. There's no turning back. The road to it is closed. Stop worrying, my dear. You mustn't deceive yourself. Look the truth straight in the face for once in your life.

MRS. RANEVSKY. What truth? You can see where truth is and where it isn't, but I seem to have gone blind. I see nothing. You boldly solve all important problems, but tell me, dear boy, isn't it because you're young, isn't it because you haven't had the time to live through the consequences of any of your problems? You look ahead boldly, but isn't it because you neither see nor expect anything terrible to happen to you, because life is still hidden from your young eyes? You're bolder, more honest, you see much deeper than any of us, but think carefully, try to understand our position, be generous even a little, spare me. I was born here, you know. My father and mother lived here, and my grandfather also. I love this house. Life has no meaning for me without the cherry orchard, and if it has to be sold, then let me be sold with it. [*Embraces* TROFIMOV *and kisses him on the forehead.*] Don't you see, my son was drowned here. [*Weeps.*] Have pity on me, my good, kind friend.

TROFIMOV. You know I sympathize with you with all my heart.

MRS. RANEVSKY. You should have put it differently. [*Takes out her handkerchief. A telegram falls on the floor.*] My heart is so heavy today. You can't imagine how heavy. I can't bear this noise. The slightest sound makes me shudder. I'm trembling all over. I'm afraid to go to my room. I'm terrified to be alone. . . . Don't condemn me, Peter. I love you as my own son. I'd gladly let Anya marry you, I swear I would. Only, my dear boy, you must study, you must finish your course at the university. You never do anything. You just drift from one place to another. That's what's so strange. Isn't that so? Isn't it? And you should do something about your beard. Make it grow, somehow. [*Laughs.*] You are funny!

TROFIMOV [*picking up the telegram*]. I have no wish to be handsome.

MRS. RANEVSKY. That telegram's from Paris. I get one every day. Yesterday and today. That wild man is ill again, in trouble again. He asks me to forgive him. He begs me to come back to him, and I really think I ought to be going back to Paris to be near him for a bit. You're looking very stern, Peter. But what's to be done, my dear boy? What am I to do? He's ill. He's lonely. He's unhappy. Who'll look after him there? Who'll stop him from doing something silly? Who'll give him his medicine at the right time? And, why hide it? Why be silent about it? I love him. That's obvious. I love him. I love him. He's a millstone round my neck and he's dragging me down to the bottom with him, but I love the millstone, and I can't live without it. [*Presses* TROFIMOV*'s hand.*] Don't think badly of me, Peter. Don't say anything. Don't speak.

TROFIMOV [*through tears*]. For God's sake—forgive my being so frank, but he left you penniless!

MRS. RANEVSKY. No, no, no! You mustn't say that. [*Puts her hands over her ears.*]

TROFIMOV. Why, he's a scoundrel, and you're the only one who doesn't seem to know it. He's a petty scoundrel, a nonentity.

MRS. RANEVSKY [*angry but restraining herself*]. You're twenty-six or twenty-seven, but you're still a schoolboy —a sixth-grade schoolboy!

TROFIMOV. What does that matter?

MRS. RANEVSKY. You ought to be a man. A person of your age ought to understand people who are in love. You ought to be in love yourself. You ought to fall in love. [*Angrily.*] Yes! Yes! And you're not so pure either. You're just a prude, a ridiculous crank, a freak!

TROFIMOV [*horrified*]. What is she saying?

MRS. RANEVSKY. "I'm above love!" You're not above love, you're simply what Firs calls a nincompoop. Not have a mistress at your age!

TROFIMOV [*horrified*]. This is terrible! What is she saying? [*Walks quickly into the ballroom, clutching his head.*] It's dreadful! I can't! I'll go away! [*Goes out but immediately comes back.*] All is at an end between us! [*Goes out into the hall.*]

MRS. RANEVSKY [*shouting after him*]. Peter, wait! You funny boy, I was only joking. Peter!

Someone can be heard running rapidly up the stairs and then suddenly falling downstairs with a crash. ANYA *and* VARYA *scream, followed immediately by laughter.*

MRS. RANEVSKY. What's happened?

ANYA [*laughing, runs in*]. Peter's fallen down the stairs! [*Runs out.*]

MRS. RANEVSKY. What an eccentric! [*The* STATIONMASTER *stands in the middle of the ballroom and recites "The Fallen Woman" by Alexey Tolstoy. The others listen. But he has hardly time to recite a few lines when the sound of a waltz comes from the entrance hall, and the recitation breaks off. Everyone dances.* TROFIMOV, ANYA, VARYA, *and* MRS. RANEVSKY *enter from the hall.*] Well, Peter dear, you pure soul, I'm sorry. . . . Come, let's dance. [*Dances with* TROFIMOV.]

ANYA *and* VARYA *dance together.* FIRS *comes in and stands his walking stick near the side door.* YASHA *has also come in from the drawing room and is watching the dancing.*

YASHA. Well, Granpa!

FIRS. I'm not feeling too well. We used to have generals, barons, and admirals at our dances before, but now we send for the post office clerk and the stationmaster. Even they are not too keen to come. Afraid I'm getting weak. The old master, the mistress's grandfather, that is, used to give us powdered sealing wax for medicine. It was his prescription for all illnesses. I've been taking sealing wax every day for the last twenty years or more. That's perhaps why I'm still alive.

YASHA. You make me sick, Grandpa. [*Yawns.*] I wish you was dead.

FIRS. Ugh, you nincompoop! [*Mutters.*]

TROFIMOV *and* MRS. RANEVSKY *dance in the ballroom and then in the drawing room.*

MRS. RANEVSKY. *Merci.* I think I'll sit down a bit. [*Sits down.*] I'm tired.

Enter ANYA.

ANYA [*agitated*]. A man in the kitchen said just now that the cherry orchard has been sold today.

MRS. RANEVSKY. Sold? Who to?

ANYA. He didn't say. He's gone away now.

ANYA *dances with* TROFIMOV; *both go off to the ballroom.*

YASHA. Some old man gossiping, madam. A stranger.

FIRS. Master Leonid isn't here yet. Hasn't returned. Wearing his light autumn overcoat. He might catch cold. Oh, these youngsters!

MRS. RANEVSKY. I shall die! Yasha, go and find out who bought it.

YASHA. But he's gone, the old man has. [*Laughs.*]

MRS. RANEVSKY [*a little annoyed*]. Well, what are you laughing at? What are you so pleased about?

YASHA. Yepikhodov's a real scream. Such a fool! Twenty-two Calamities!

MRS. RANEVSKY. Firs, where will you go if the estate's sold?

FIRS. I'll go wherever you tell me, ma'am.

MRS. RANEVSKY. You look awful! Are you ill? You'd better go to bed.

FIRS. Me to bed, ma'am? [*Ironically.*] If I goes to bed, who's going to do the waiting? Who's going to look after everything? I'm the only one in the whole house.

YASHA [*to* MRS. RANEVSKY]. I'd like to ask you a favor, madam. If you go back to Paris, will you take me with you? It's quite impossible for me to stay here. [*Looking *round, in an undertone.*] You know perfectly well yourself what an uncivilized country this is—the common people are so immoral—and besides, it's so boring here, the food in the kitchen is disgusting, and on top of it, there's that old Firs wandering about, muttering all sorts of inappropriate words. Take me with you, madam, please!

Enter PISHCHIK.

PISHCHIK. May I have the pleasure of a little dance, fair lady? [MRS. RANEVSKY *goes with him.*] I'll have one hundred and eighty rubles off you all the same, my dear, charming lady. . . . I will, indeed. [*They dance.*] One hundred and eighty rubles. . . .

They go into the ballroom.

YASHA [*singing softly*]. "Could you but feel the agitated beating of my heart."

In the ballroom a woman in a gray top hat and check trousers can be seen jumping about and waving her arms. Shouts of "Bravo, Charlotte! Bravo!"

DUNYASHA [*stops to powder her face*]. Miss Anya told me to join the dancers because there are lots of gentlemen and very few ladies. But dancing makes me dizzy and my heart begins beating so fast. I say, Firs, the post office clerk said something to me just now that quite took my breath away.

The music becomes quieter.

FIRS. What did he say to you?

DUNYASHA. "You're like a flower," he said.

YASHA [*yawning*]. What ignorance! [*Goes out.*]

DUNYASHA. Like a flower! I'm ever so delicate, and I love people saying nice things to me!

FIRS. You'll come to a bad end, my girl. Mark my words.

Enter YEPIKHODOV.

YEPIKHODOV. You seem to avoid me, Dunyasha. Just as if I was some insect. [*Sighs.*] Oh, life!

DUNYASHA. What do you want?

YEPIKHODOV. No doubt you may be right. [*Sighs.*] But, of course, if one looks at things from a certain point of view, then, if I may say so and if you'll forgive my frankness, you have reduced me absolutely to a state of mind. I know what Fate has in store for me. Every day some calamity overtakes me, but I got used to it so long ago that I just look at my Fate and smile. You gave me your word, and though I——

DUNYASHA. Let's talk about it some other time. Leave me alone now. Now, I am dreaming. [*Plays with her fan.*]

YEPIKHODOV. Every day some calamity overtakes me, and I—let me say it quite frankly—why, I just smile, laugh even.

Enter VARYA *from the ballroom.*

VARYA. Are you still here, Simon! What an ill-mannered fellow you are, to be sure! [*To* DUNYASHA.] Be off with you, Dunyasha. [*To* YEPIKHODOV.] First you go and play billiards and break a cue, and now you wander about the drawing room as if you were a guest.

YEPIKHODOV. It's not your place to reprimand me, if you don't mind my saying so.

VARYA. I'm not reprimanding you. I'm telling you. All you do is drift about from one place to another without ever doing a stroke of work. We're employing an office clerk, but goodness knows why.

YEPIKHODOV [*offended*]. Whether I work or drift about, whether I eat or play billiards, is something which only people older than you, people who know what they're talking about, should decide.

VARYA. How dare you talk to me like that? [*Flaring up.*] How dare you? I don't know what I'm talking about, don't I? Get out of here! This instant!

YEPIKHODOV [*cowed*]. Express yourself with more delicacy, please.

VARYA [*beside herself*]. Get out of here this minute! Out! [*He goes toward the door, and she follows him.*] Twenty-two Calamities! Don't let me see you here again! Never set foot here again! [YEPIKHODOV *goes out. He can be heard saying behind the door: "I'll lodge a complaint."*] Oh, so you're coming back, are you? [*Picks up the stick which* FIRS *has left near the door.*] Come on, come on, I'll show you! Coming, are you? Well, take that! [*Swings the stick as* LOPAKHIN *comes in.*]

LOPAKHIN. Thank you very much!

VARYA [*angrily and derisively*]. I'm so sorry!

LOPAKHIN. It's quite all right. Greatly obliged to you for the kind reception.

VARYA. Don't mention it. [*Walks away, then looks round and inquires gently.*] I didn't hurt you, did I?

LOPAKHIN. Oh no, not at all. There's going to be an enormous bump on my head for all that.

Voices in the ballroom: "Lopakhin's arrived. Lopakhin!"

PISHCHIK. Haven't heard from you or seen you for ages, my dear fellow! [*Embraces* LOPAKHIN.] Do I detect a smell of brandy, dear boy? We're doing very well here, too.

Enter MRS. RANEVSKY.

MRS. RANEVSKY. Is it you, Lopakhin? Why have you been so long? Where's Leonid?

LOPAKHIN. He came back with me. He'll be here in a moment.

MRS. RANEVSKY [*agitated*]. Well, what happened? Did the auction take place? Speak, for heaven's sake!

LOPAKHIN [*embarrassed, fearing to betray his joy*]. The auction was over by four o'clock. We missed our train and had to wait till half past nine. [*With a deep sigh.*] Oh dear, I'm afraid I feel a little dizzy.

Enter GAYEV. *He carries some parcels in his right hand and wipes away his tears with his left.*

MRS. RANEVSKY. What's the matter, Leonid? Well? [*Impatiently, with tears.*] Quick, tell me for heaven's sake!

GAYEV [*doesn't answer, only waves his hand resignedly; to* FIRS, *weeping*]. Here, take these—anchovies, Kerch herrings . . . I've had nothing to eat all day. I've had a terrible time. [*The door of the billiard room is open; the click of billiard balls can be heard and* YASHA'*s voice: "Seven and eighteen!"* GAYEV'*s expression changes. He is no longer crying.*] I'm awfully tired. Come and help me change, Firs.

GAYEV *goes off through the ballroom to his own room, followed by* FIRS.

PISHCHIK. Well, what happened at the auction? Come, tell us!

MRS. RANEVSKY. Has the cherry orchard been sold?

LOPAKHIN. It has.

MRS. RANEVSKY. Who bought it?

LOPAKHIN. I bought it. [*Pause.* MRS. RANEVSKY *is crushed; she would have collapsed on the floor if she had not been standing near an armchair.* VARYA *takes the keys from her belt, throws them on the floor in the center of the drawing room, and goes out.*] I bought it! One moment, please, ladies and gentlemen. I feel dazed. I can't talk. . . . [*Laughs.*] Deriganov was already there when we got to the auction. Gayev had only fifteen thousand, and Deriganov began his bidding at once with thirty thousand over and above the mortgage. I realized the position at once and took up his challenge. I bid forty. He bid forty-five. He kept raising his bid by five thousand and I by adding another ten thousand. Well, it was soon over. I bid ninety thousand on top of the arrears, and the cherry orchard was knocked down to me. Now the cherry orchard is mine! Mine! [*Laughs loudly.*] Merciful heavens, the cherry orchard's mine! Come on, tell me, tell me I'm drunk. Tell me I'm out of my mind. Tell me I'm imagining it all. [*Stamps his feet.*] Don't laugh at me! If my father and my grandfather were to rise from their graves and see what's happened, see how their Yermolay, their beaten and half-literate Yermolay, Yermolay who used to run around barefoot in winter, see how that same Yermolay bought this estate, the most beautiful estate in the world! I've bought the estate where my father and grandfather were slaves, where they weren't even allowed inside the kitchen. I must be dreaming. I must be imagining it all. It can't be true. It's all a figment of your imagination, shrouded in mystery. [*Picks up the keys, smiling affectionately.*] She's thrown down the keys. Wants to show she's no longer the mistress here. [*Jingles the keys.*] Oh well, never mind. [*The band is heard tuning up.*] Hey you, musicians, play something! I want to hear you. Come, all of you! Come and watch Yermolay Lopakhin take an axe to the cherry orchard. Watch the trees come crashing down. We'll cover the place with country cottages, and our grandchildren and great-grandchildren will see a new life springing up here. Strike up the music! [*The band plays.* MRS. RANEVSKY *has sunk into a chair and is weeping bitterly. Reproachfully.*] Why did you not listen to me? You poor dear, you will never get it back now. [*With tears.*] Oh, if only all this could be over soon, if only our unhappy, disjointed life could somehow be changed soon.

PISHCHIK [*takes his arm, in an undertone*]. She's crying. Let's go into the ballroom. Let's leave her alone. Come on. [*Takes his arm and leads him away to the ballroom.*]

LOPAKHIN. What's the matter? You there in the band, play up, play up! Let's hear you properly. Let's have everything as I want it now. [*Ironically.*] Here comes the new landowner, the owner of the cherry orchard! [*Knocks against a small table accidentally and nearly knocks over the candelabra.*] I can pay for everything!

LOPAKHIN *goes out with* PISHCHIK. *There is no one left in the ballroom except* MRS. RANEVSKY, *who remains sitting in a chair, hunched up and crying bitterly. The band plays quietly.* ANYA *and* TROFIMOV *come in quickly.* ANYA *goes up to her mother and kneels in front of her.* TROFIMOV *remains standing by the entrance to the ballroom.*

ANYA. Mother, Mother, why are you crying? My dear, good, kind Mother, my darling Mother, I love you; God bless you, Mother. The cherry orchard is sold. It's gone. That's true, quite true, but don't cry, Mother. You still have your life ahead of you, and you've still got your kind and pure heart. . . . Come with me, darling. Come. Let's go away from here. We shall plant a new orchard, an orchard more splendid than this one. You will see it, you will understand, and joy, deep, serene joy, will steal into your heart, sink into it like the sun in the evening, and you will smile, Mother! Come, darling! Come!

Curtain.

ACT FOUR

The scene is the same as in the first act. There are no curtains at the windows or pictures on the walls. Only a few pieces of furniture are left. They have been stacked in one corner as if for sale. There is a feeling of emptiness. Near the front door and at the back of the stage, suitcases, traveling bags, etc., are piled up. The door on the left is open and the voices of VARYA *and* ANYA *can be heard.* LOPAKHIN *stands waiting.* YASHA *is holding a tray with glasses of champagne. In the entrance hall* YEPIKHODOV *is tying up a box. There is a constant murmur of voices off-stage, the voices of peasants who have come to say good-bye.* GAYEV'S *voice is heard: "Thank you, my dear people, thank you."*

YASHA. The peasants have come to say good-bye. In my opinion, sir, the peasants are decent enough fellows, but they don't understand a lot.

The murmur of voices dies away. MRS. RANEVSKY *and* GAYEV *come in through the entrance hall; she is not crying, but she is pale. Her face is quivering. She cannot speak.*

GAYEV. You gave them your purse, Lyuba. You shouldn't. You really shouldn't!

MRS. RANEVSKY. I—I couldn't help it. I just couldn't help it.

Both go out.

LOPAKHIN [*calling through the door after them*]. Please take a glass of champagne. I beg you. One glass each before we leave. I forgot to bring any from town, and I could find only one bottle at the station. Please! [*Pause.*] Why, don't you want any? [*Walks away from the door.*] If I'd known, I wouldn't have bought it. Oh well, I don't think I'll have any, either. [YASHA *puts the tray down carefully on a chair.*] You'd better have some, Yasha.

YASHA. Thank you, sir. To those who're going away! And

here's to you, sir, who're staying behind! [*Drinks.*] This isn't real champagne. Take it from me, sir.

LOPAKHIN. Paid eight rubles a bottle. [*Pause.*] Damn cold here.

YASHA. The stoves haven't been lit today. We're leaving, anyway. [*Laughs.*]

LOPAKHIN. What's so funny?

YASHA. Oh, nothing. Just feeling happy.

LOPAKHIN. It's October, but it might just as well be summer: it's so sunny and calm. Good building weather. [*Glances at his watch and calls through the door.*] I say, don't forget the train leaves in forty-seven minutes. In twenty minutes we must start for the station. Hurry up!

TROFIMOV *comes in from outside, wearing an overcoat.*

TROFIMOV. I think it's about time we were leaving. The carriages are at the door. Where the blazes could my galoshes have got to? Disappeared without a trace. [*Through the door.*] Anya, I can't find my galoshes! Can't find them!

LOPAKHIN. I've got to go to Kharkov. I'll leave with you on the same train. I'm spending the winter in Kharkov. I've been hanging about here too long. I'm worn out with having nothing to do. I can't live without work. Don't know what to do with my hands. They just flop about as if they belonged to someone else.

TROFIMOV. Well, we'll soon be gone and then you can resume your useful labors.

LOPAKHIN. Come on, have a glass of champagne.

TROFIMOV. No, thank you.

LOPAKHIN. So you're off to Moscow, are you?

TROFIMOV. Yes. I'll see them off to town, and I'm off to Moscow tomorrow.

LOPAKHIN. I see. I suppose the professors have stopped lecturing while you've been away. They're all waiting for you to come back.

TROFIMOV. Mind your own business.

LOPAKHIN. How many years have you been studying at the university?

TROFIMOV. Why don't you think of something new for a change? This is rather old, don't you think?—and stale. [*Looking for his galoshes.*] I don't suppose we shall ever meet again, so let me give you a word of advice as a farewell gift: Don't wave your arms about. Get rid of the habit of throwing your arms about. And another thing: To build country cottages in the hope that in the fullness of time vacationers will become landowners is the same as waving your arms about. Still, I like you in spite of everything. You've got fine sensitive fingers, like an artist's, and you have a fine sensitive soul.

LOPAKHIN [*embraces him*]. My dear fellow, thanks for everything. Won't you let me lend you some money for your journey? You may need it.

TROFIMOV. Need it? Whatever for?

LOPAKHIN. But you haven't any, have you?

TROFIMOV. Oh, but I have. I've just got some money for a translation. Got it here in my pocket. [*Anxiously.*] Where could those galoshes of mine have got to?

VARYA [*from another room*]. Oh, take your filthy things! [*Throws a pair of galoshes onto the stage.*]

TROFIMOV. Why are you so cross, Varya? Good heavens, these are not my galoshes!

LOPAKHIN. I had about three thousand acres of poppy sown last spring. Made a clear profit of forty thousand. When my poppies were in bloom, what a beautiful sight they were! Well, so you see, I made forty thousand and I'd be glad to lend you some of it because I can afford to. So why be so high and mighty? I'm a peasant. . . . I'm offering it to you without ceremony.

TROFIMOV. Your father was a peasant, my father was a pharmacist, all of which proves exactly nothing. [LOPAKHIN *takes out his wallet.*] Put it back! Put it back! If you offered me two hundred thousand, I wouldn't accept it. I'm a free man. Everything you prize so highly, everything that means so much to all of you, rich or poor, has no more power over me than a bit of fluff blown about in the air. I can manage without you. I can pass you by. I'm strong and proud. Mankind is marching toward a higher truth, toward the greatest happiness possible on earth, and I'm in the front ranks!

LOPAKHIN. Will you get there?

TROFIMOV. I will. [*Pause.*] I will get there or show others the way to get there.

The sound of an axe striking a tree can be heard in the distance.

LOPAKHIN. Well, good-bye, my dear fellow. Time to go. You and I are trying to impress one another, but life goes on regardless. When I work hard for hours on end, I can think more clearly, and then I can't help feeling that I, too, know what I live for. Have you any idea how many people in Russia exist goodness only knows why? However, no matter. It isn't they who make the world go round. I'm told Gayev has taken a job at the bank at six thousand a year. He'll never stick to it. Too damn lazy.

ANYA [*in the doorway*]. Mother asks you not to begin cutting the orchard down till she's gone.

TROFIMOV. Really, haven't you any tact at all? [*Goes out through the hall.*]

LOPAKHIN. Sorry, I'll see to it at once, at once! The damned idiots! [*Goes out after* TROFIMOV.]

ANYA. Has Firs been taken to the hospital?

YASHA. I told them to this morning. They must have taken him, I should think.

ANYA [*to* YEPIKHODOV, *who is crossing the ballroom*]. Please find out if Firs has been taken to the hospital.

YASHA [*offended*]. I told Yegor this morning. I haven't got to tell him a dozen times, have I?

YEPIKHODOV. Old man Firs, if you want my final opinion, is beyond repair, and it's high time he was gathered to his fathers. So far as I'm concerned, I can only envy him. [*Puts a suitcase on a hatbox and squashes it.*] There, you see! I knew it. [*Goes out.*]

YASHA [*sneeringly*]. Twenty-two Calamities!

VARYA [*from behind the door*]. Has Firs been taken to the hospital?

ANYA. He has.

VARYA. Why didn't they take the letter for the doctor?

ANYA. We'd better send it on after him. [*Goes out.*]

VARYA [*from the next room*]. Where's Yasha? Tell him his mother's here. She wants to say good-bye to him.

YASHA [*waves his hand impatiently*]. Oh, that's too much!

All this time DUNYASHA *has been busy with the luggage. Now that* YASHA *is alone, she goes up to him.*

DUNYASHA. You haven't even looked at me once, Yasha. You're going away, leaving me behind. [*Bursts out crying and throws her arms around his neck.*]

YASHA. Must you cry? [*Drinks champagne.*] I'll be back in Paris in a week. Tomorrow we catch the express and off we go! That's the last you'll see of us. I can hardly believe it, somehow. *Vive la France!* I hate it here. It doesn't suit me at all. It's not the kind of life I like. I'm afraid it can't be helped. I've had enough of all this ignorance. More than enough. [*Drinks champagne.*] So what's the use of crying? Behave yourself and you won't end up crying.

DUNYASHA [*powdering her face, looking in a hand mirror*]. Write to me from Paris, please. I did love you, Yasha, after all. I loved you so much. I'm such an affectionate creature, Yasha.

YASHA. They're coming here. [*Busies himself around the suitcases, humming quietly.*]

Enter MRS. RANEVSKY, GAYEV, ANYA, *and* CHARLOTTE.

GAYEV. We ought to be going. There isn't much time left. [*Looking at* YASHA.] Who's smelling of pickled herrings here?

MRS. RANEVSKY. In another ten minutes we ought to be getting into the carriages. [*Looks round the room.*] Good-bye, dear house, good-bye, old grandfather house! Winter will pass, spring will come, and you won't be here any more. They'll have pulled you down. The things these walls have seen! [*Kisses her daughter affectionately.*] My precious one, you look radiant. Your eyes are sparkling like diamonds. Happy? Very happy?

ANYA. Oh yes, very! A new life is beginning, Mother!

GAYEV [*gaily*]. It is, indeed. Everything's all right now. We were all so worried and upset before the cherry orchard was sold, but now, when everything has been finally and irrevocably settled, we have all calmed down and even cheered up. I'm a bank official now, a financier. Pot the red in the middle. As for you, Lyuba, say what you like, but you too are looking a lot better. There's no doubt about it.

MRS. RANEVSKY. Yes, my nerves are better, that's true. [*Someone helps her on with her hat and coat.*] I sleep well. Take my things out, Yasha. It's time. [*To* ANYA.] We'll soon be seeing each other again, darling. I'm going to Paris. I'll live there on the money your great-aunt sent from Varoslavl to buy the estate—three cheers for Auntie!—but the money won't last long, I'm afraid.

ANYA. You'll come home soon, Mother, very soon. I'm going to study, pass my school exams, and then I'll work and help you. We shall read all sorts of books together, won't we, Mother? [*Kisses her mother's hands.*] We shall read during the autumn evenings. We'll read lots and lots of books, and a new, wonderful world will open up to us. [*Dreamily.*] Oh, do come back, Mother!

MRS. RANEVSKY. I'll come back, my precious. [*Embraces her daughter.*]

Enter LOPAKHIN. CHARLOTTE *quietly hums a tune.*

GAYEV. Happy Charlotte! She's singing.

CHARLOTTE [*picks up a bundle that looks like a baby in swaddling clothes*]. My darling baby, go to sleep, my baby. [*A sound of a baby crying is heard.*] Hush, my sweet, my darling boy. [*The cry is heard again.*] Poor little darling, I'm so sorry for you! [*Throws the bundle down.*] So you will find me another job, won't you? I can't go on like this.

LOPAKHIN. We'll find you one, don't you worry.

GAYEV. Everybody's leaving us. Varya's going away. All of a sudden, we're no longer wanted.

CHARLOTTE. I haven't anywhere to live in town. I must go away. [*Sings quietly.*] It's all the same to me. . . .

Enter PISHCHIK.

LOPAKHIN. The nine days' wonder!

PISHCHIK [*out of breath*]. Oh dear, let me get my breath back! I'm all in. Dear friends . . . a drink of water, please.

GAYEV. Came to borrow some money, I'll be bound. Not from me this time. Better make myself scarce. [*Goes out.*]

PISHCHIK. Haven't seen you for ages, dearest lady. [*To* LOPAKHIN.] You here too? Glad to see you . . . man of immense intellect. . . . Here, that's for you, take it. [*Gives* LOPAKHIN *money.*] Four hundred rubles. That leaves eight hundred and forty I still owe you.

LOPAKHIN [*puzzled, shrugging his shoulders*]. I must be dreaming. Where did you get it?

PISHCHIK. One moment . . . Terribly hot . . . Most extraordinary thing happened. Some Englishmen came to see me. They found some kind of white clay on my land. [*To* MRS. RANEVSKY.] Here's four hundred for you too, beautiful, ravishing lady. [*Gives her the money.*] The rest later. [*Drinks some water.*] Young fellow in the train just now was telling me that some—er—great philosopher advises people to jump off roofs. "Jump!" he says, and that'll solve all your problems. [*With surprise.*] Good Lord! More water, please.

LOPAKHIN. Who were these Englishmen?

PISHCHIK. I let them a plot of land with the clay on a twenty-four years' lease. And now you must excuse me, my friends. I'm in a hurry. Must be rushing off somewhere else. To Znoykov's, to Kardamonov's . . . Owe them all money. [*Drinks.*] Good-bye. I'll look in on Thursday.

MRS. RANEVSKY. We're just leaving for town. I'm going abroad tomorrow.

PISHCHIK. What? [*In a worried voice.*] Why are you going to town? Oh! I see! The furniture, the suitcases . . . Well, no matter. [*Through tears.*] No matter. Men of immense intellect, these Englishmen. . . . No matter. . . . No matter. I wish you all the best. May God help you. . . . No matter. Everything in this world comes to an end. [*Kisses* MRS. RANEVSKY'*s hand.*] When you hear that my end has come, remember the—er—old horse and say: Once there lived a man called Simeonov-Pishchik; may he rest in peace. Remarkable weather we've been having. . . . Yes. [*Goes out in great embarrassment, but immediately comes back and says, standing in the doorway.*] My Dashenka sends her regards. [*Goes out.*]

MRS. RANEVSKY. Well, we can go now. I'm leaving with two worries on my mind. One concerns Firs. He's ill. [*With a glance at her watch.*] We still have about five minutes.

ANYA. Firs has been taken to the hospital, Mother. Yasha sent him off this morning.

MRS. RANEVSKY. My other worry concerns Varya. She's used to getting up early and working. Now that she has nothing to do, she's like a fish out of water. She's grown thin and pale, and she's always crying, poor thing. [*Pause.*] You must have noticed it, Lopakhin. As you very well know, I'd always hoped to see her married to you. Indeed, everything seemed to indicate that you two would get married. [*She whispers to* ANYA, *who nods to* CHARLOTTE, *and they both go out.*] She loves you, you like her, and I simply don't know why you two always seem to avoid each other. I don't understand it.

LOPAKHIN. To tell you the truth, neither do I. The whole thing's odd somehow. If there's still time, I'm ready even now. . . . Let's settle it at once and get it over. I don't feel I'll ever propose to her without you here.

MRS. RANEVSKY. Excellent! Why, it shouldn't take more than a minute. I'll call her at once.

LOPAKHIN. And there's champagne here too. Appropriate to the occasion. [*Looks at the glasses.*] They're empty. Someone must have drunk it. [YASHA *coughs.*] Lapped it up, I call it.

MRS. RANEVSKY [*excitedly*]. Fine! We'll go out. Yasha, *allez!* I'll call her. [*Through the door.*] Varya, leave what you're doing and come here for a moment. Come on.

MRS. RANEVSKY *goes out with* YASHA.

LOPAKHIN [*glancing at his watch*]. Aye. . . .

Pause. Behind the door suppressed laughter and whispering can be heard. Enter VARYA.

VARYA [*spends a long time examining the luggage*]. Funny, can't find it.

LOPAKHIN. What are you looking for?

VARYA. Packed it myself, and can't remember.

Pause.

LOPAKHIN. Where are you going now, Varya?

VARYA. Me? To the Ragulins'. I've agreed to look after their house—to be their housekeeper, I suppose.

LOPAKHIN. In Yashnevo, isn't it? About fifty miles from here. [*Pause.*] Aye. . . . So life's come to an end in this house.

VARYA [*examining the luggage*]. Where can it be? Must have put it in the trunk. Yes, life's come to an end in this house. It will never come back.

LOPAKHIN. I'm off to Kharkov by the same train. Lots to see to there. I'm leaving Yepikhodov here to keep an eye on things. I've given him the job.

VARYA. Have you?

LOPAKHIN. This time last year it was already snowing, you remember. Now, it's calm and sunny. A bit cold, though. Three degrees of frost.

VARYA. I haven't looked. [*Pause.*] Anyway, our thermometer's broken.

Pause. A voice from outside, through the door: "Mr. Lopakhin!"

LOPAKHIN [*as though he had long been expecting this call*]. Coming! [*Goes out quickly.*]

VARYA *sits down on the floor, lays her head on a bundle of clothes, and sobs quietly. The door opens and* MRS. RANEVSKY *comes in cautiously.*

MRS. RANEVSKY. Well? [*Pause.*] We must go.

VARYA [*no longer crying, dries her eyes*]. Yes, it's time, Mother dear. I'd like to get to the Ragulins' today. I only hope we don't miss the train.

MRS. RANEVSKY [*calling through the door*]. Anya, put your things on!

Enter ANYA, *followed by* GAYEV *and* CHARLOTTE. GAYEV *wears a warm overcoat with a hood.* SERVANTS *and* COACHMEN *come in.* YEPIKHODOV *is busy with the luggage.*

MRS. RANEVSKY. Now we can be on our way.

ANYA [*joyfully*]. On our way. Oh, yes!

GAYEV. My friends, my dear, dear friends, leaving this house for good, how can I remain silent, how can I, before parting from you, refrain from expressing the feelings which now pervade my whole being——

ANYA [*imploringly*]. Uncle!

VARYA. Uncle dear, please don't.

GAYEV [*dejectedly*]. Double the red into the middle. . . . Not another word!

Enter TROFIMOV, *followed by* LOPAKHIN.

TROFIMOV. Well, ladies and gentlemen, it's time to go.

LOPAKHIN. Yepikhodov, my coat!

MRS. RANEVSKY. Let me sit down a minute. I feel as though I've never seen the walls and ceilings of this house before. I look at them now with such eagerness, with such tender emotion. . . .

GAYEV. I remember when I was six years old sitting on this window sill on Trinity Sunday and watching Father going to church.

MRS. RANEVSKY. Have all the things been taken out?

LOPAKHIN. I think so. [*To* YEPIKHODOV *as he puts on his coat.*] Mind, everything's all right here, Yepikhodov.

YEPIKHODOV [*in a hoarse voice*]. Don't you worry, sir.

LOPAKHIN. What's the matter with your voice?

YEPIKHODOV. I've just had a drink of water and I must have swallowed something.

YASHA [*contemptuously*]. What ignorance!

MRS. RANEVSKY. There won't be a soul left in this place when we've gone.

LOPAKHIN. Not till next spring.

VARYA *pulls an umbrella out of a bundle of clothes with such force that it looks as if she were going to hit someone with it;* LOPAKHIN *pretends to be frightened.*

VARYA. Good heavens, you didn't really think that——

TROFIMOV. Come on, let's get into the carriages! It's time. The train will be in soon.

VARYA. There are your galoshes, Peter. By that suitcase. [*Tearfully.*] Oh, how dirty they are, how old. . . .

TROFIMOV [*putting on his galoshes*]. Come along, ladies and gentlemen.

Pause.

GAYEV [*greatly put out, afraid of bursting into tears*]. Train

. . . station . . . in off into the middle pocket . . . double the white into the corner.

MRS. RANEVSKY. Come along!

LOPAKHIN. Is everyone here? No one left behind? [*Locks the side door on the left.*] There are some things in there. I'd better keep it locked. Come on!

ANYA. Good-bye, old house! Good-bye, old life!

TROFIMOV. Welcome new life!

TROFIMOV *goes out with* ANYA. VARYA *casts a last look round the room and goes out unhurriedly.* YASHA *and* CHARLOTTE, *carrying her lap dog, go out.*

LOPAKHIN. So, it's till next spring. Come along, ladies and gentlemen. Till we meet again. [*Goes out.*]

MRS. RANEVSKY *and* GAYEV *are left alone. They seem to have been waiting for this moment. They fling their arms around each other, sobbing quietly, restraining themselves, as though afraid of being overheard.*

GAYEV [*in despair*]. My sister! My sister!

MRS. RANEVSKY. Oh, my dear, my sweet, my beautiful orchard! My life, my youth, my happiness, good-bye! . . .

ANYA [*offstage, happily, appealingly*]. Mo-ther!

TROFIMOV [*offstage, happily, excitedly*]. Where are you?

MRS. RANEVSKY. One last look at the walls and the windows. Mother loved to walk in this room.

GAYEV. My sister, my sister!

ANYA [*offstage*]. Mo-ther!

TROFIMOV [*offstage*]. Where are you?

MRS. RANEVSKY. We're coming.

They go out. The stage is empty. The sound of all the doors being locked is heard, then of carriages driving off. It grows quiet. The silence is broken by the muffled noise of an axe striking a tree, sounding forlorn and sad. Footsteps can be heard. FIRS *appears from the door on the right. He is dressed, as always, in a jacket and white waistcoat. He is wearing slippers. He looks ill.*

FIRS [*walks up to the door and tries the handle*]. Locked! They've gone. [*Sits down on the sofa.*] Forgot all about me. Never mind. Let me sit down here for a bit. Forgotten to put on his fur coat, the young master has. Sure of it. Gone off in his light overcoat. [*Sighs anxiously.*] I should have seen to it. . . . Oh, these youngsters! [*Mutters something which cannot be understood.*] My life's gone just as if I'd never lived. . . . [*Lies down.*] I'll lie down a bit. No strength left. Nothing's left. Nothing. Ugh, you—nincompoop! [*Lies motionless.*]

A *distant sound is heard, which seems to come from the sky, the sound of a breaking string, slowly dying away, melancholy. It is followed by silence, broken only by the sound of an axe striking a tree far away in the orchard.*

Curtain.